The Old Car Nut Book #3

"A century of road trips across America"

Created and Edited by David Dickinson

Evancourt Press
Seattle, Washington

Creator/Editor: David Dickinson
Cover Design: David Dickinson
Cover Photo: Jack Butler
Interior Design: Susan Leonard, Rose Island Bookworks

ISBN 978-0-9898065-2-7

Published in the United States by Evancourt Press

Dedication

This third book in The Old Car Nut Book series is dedicated to the Washington State Hot Rod Hall of Fame, its Board of Directors, Advisors, and Inducted Members. The generosity and caring of this organization knows no bounds.

Excerpts from
The Old Car Nut Book
Volume 3

Before arriving in the town of Wall, it was necessary for us to traverse the famous Bad Lands where many a traveler and unfortunate animal had lost their lives before the railroad was put through. This section for miles is a succession of white hills and broken ground, in many places suddenly dropping off five or six feet, and the entire soil of a chalky whiteness that dazzled our eyes as we drove across this spooky section.

Excerpt from Cross Country by Auto in 1915
by Dr. Stanley Burr Dickinson

Dusk, in the middle of nowhere, goes to completely dark in about a heartbeat. Remote is a very quiet place. There was no noise, unless you count the quiet buzzing of mosquitos and other life sucking pests. Being the sweet and tasty morsel that is me, I became a banquet fit for all creatures small and winged. Between the dead car, my concern for my lady, and the ever maddening bugs, I was quickly becoming distressed and had no plan.

Excerpt from Road Angel
by David Dickinson

In 1957, my friend, Jerry Burns, and I drove to San Francisco in his nearly new MG-A and it was really a life-changing experience. The distance wasn't great, but the trip's importance was and it came at a crucial time. Jack Kerouac's novel, On the

Road, had recently been published and it was widely read. It seemed like a manifesto for the postwar generation. Get behind the wheel and go, man, go!

Excerpt from In the Shadow of Sputnik
by Albert Drake

So, he asked me to help him park the trailer and I did. It was one of those things where you're yelling... "Stop... Stop... Wait... Hold it... Stop!" Well, he backs into this guy's car and says "You got to learn not to mumble, boy!" This was typical Ed Roth as I came to find out.

Excerpt from Meeting Big Daddy
by Dick Page

Driving across North Dakota was a real challenge. I would guess the cross winds gusted close to a million miles an hour and every inch of travel was a workout to keep the car and trailer on the road. I told Colette I was determined to outrun the storm and had to keep going. She, the know-it-all smarty aleck, impolitely informed me, the idiot behind the wheel that I was driving into the storm and not running away from it!

Excerpt from The Sheepmobile
by Gary M Hughes

As luck would have it, I have been out of style so long that I am now in style. Legendary Route 66 is now America's longest attraction. It has morphed into a living, breathing time capsule with just an overlay of Disneyland and as a result, a bit of time travel tinges our road trips since the past and present blend together seamlessly on the double six.

Excerpt from A Life on the Road
by Jim Hinckley

As we come and go to Grand Rapids, The Naniboujou is a favorite spot to have a meal on the North Shore in Minnesota. However, the last time we took the '39, we decided to take a little different way home. It was decided to take the scenic route home for a change as we never have taken it. It cuts out Duluth and angles south east towards Lake Superior. I think I had heard that it was a short cut.

Excerpt from Some Short Cut
by Ron Limbrick

When we arrived I pulled out a little bottle of spray-on detailer and we proceeded to clean the day's bugs off the nose and windshield. Then I saw it. There was a paint chip on the front of the car!

Blake could see the frown on my brow and asked what was wrong.

"Our first rock chip. Darn it!" Then something really amazing happened.

Blake put his hand on my shoulder and said, "Don't worry dad. That's not a rock chip. That's a memory mark. Every time you look at that you'll be reminded what a special day today was." I about started crying right then and there. This was an eight year old teaching his old man the meaning of life. It's the adventures, not the things that count. I'll never forget that moment.

Excerpt from The Greene Mille
by Mark Greene

We pressed on for Colorado. "Just another six hundred miles" said Mom, taking a long drag on her cigarette. Dad leaned into the steering wheel, glaring hard at the road ahead. We passed signs directing "This way to the Grand Canyon!" but Dad would not be detoured to look at some culvert lined with souvenir shacks.

Excerpt from The Great Road Trip
by Steve Walker

The car I would be taking was my well-traveled 1927 Model T roadster that I have owned for the past 10 years. I built the car in style of a late 1920's era early Hot Rod or "Gow Job" as they were called in the period. These cars are widely regarded as the "Grandfathers of the Hot Rod" and are something that is only now finally coming back to the main stream again.

Excerpt from The Road Was A Blur
by Clayton Paddison

Table of Contents

Acknowledgements

There are numerous historic roads across America. Some of them are thriving due to tourism and some are under threat of extinction due to planned and unplanned events, neglect, or poor management.

We would like to acknowledge the various associations and organizations, both public and private, which are dedicated to the preservation of our nation's historic roads and highways and the communities that are still dependent on them for their survival.

Within these organizations and community efforts, there are individuals that are the driving force or center of influence and it is these people that truly deserve our thanks for all that they do.

Additionally, there are a group of writers in both the print and digital worlds that should be recognized for their ongoing efforts of sharing history and raising awareness.

And finally, it is important to give a nod to all of the individuals and families that share the beauty of America, its history and traditions, by jumping in their cars and hitting the roads in search of adventure.

Foreword

by John D'Agostino

Travel in automobiles has become an American way of life.

In the early twentieth century, as the automobile was beginning to become a more common sight, there were still very few people that could afford to buy one. Henry Ford and others strived to make it something that most working people could afford, but the Depression came along and took a bite out of many of those manufacturers' best efforts for a time.

However, America would not be denied and the automobile grew more affordable and more popular as the preferred method of travel. Trails and rut worn paths became roads and more and more paths were cleared to make room for a different type of four wheeled beast. The days of horses and buggies were passing. The car was here to stay.

There were, of course, no freeways that crossed the country; only two lane highways, if you were lucky. Most were dirt roads and the cars of the early 1920's did not have the horsepower to travel at high speeds let alone long distances. People would get their families together on a weekend and spend hours on the road, not really travelling very far distances, just to get to their favorite destination hot spots.

In the late 1930's and into the 1940's, things started to change. The cars were bigger, more solid, and had more power. Now five or six family members could fit into a car and travel at higher speeds on better roads, going longer distances with better comfort to their favorite destination. But, it wasn't until the 1950's that the real change occurred across America.

Construction of The Dwight D. Eisenhower National System of Interstate and Defense Highways was authorized by the Federal Aid Highway Act of 1956. Today, there are over 160,000 miles of highway and over 3 trillion miles of vehicle travel is done on our interstate freeways and major arterial highways each year. It has been quite an investment to move people and goods and is a big business in keeping it all running smoothly.

With the advent of such a road system being laid out before them, Americans started travelling much more. There were more auto manufacturers to choose from and families could not wait to go farther, faster, and in greater comfort on the smooth new roads all around America. The places that Americans had only seen in books, magazines, and movies were now coming to life right before their very eyes. And it only got better.

The 1960's were even more fascinating with the stylish cars of the era featuring greater creature comforts, like air conditioning, power steering and brakes, and more. They began travelling more and taking longer trips.

By the 1970s and 1980s, car people were travelling farther distances to congregate with new friends, see a greater variety of the old iron, and to soak in the sights that our great country had to offer as each mile passed. Car clubs were gaining ground and enthusiastic young car guys started putting on bigger shows, both inside and outside.

Organizations like Kustom Kemps of America, West Coast Kustoms, and Goodguys Rod & Custom created large shows across America. Gearheads (and their families) would gather and hit the roads together. These road trips to car shows were like "cruisin' the gut" in their own towns only at higher speeds. There were stops to eat, chat, and take in the sights. Only there were new burger joints along the way and often people that you didn't get to see on a regular basis would show up. Die hard car nuts now had dozens of places that the roads would take them to see new friends and old iron.

In 1995, Hot Rod Magazine staff members wanted to take some of their project cars on a trip across the country and the Hot Rod Power Tour was born. As the tour made its way from California to Ohio, thousands joined in on the pre-planned route, but there were only seven people other than staff members that made the whole trip. They were honored with their induction into the Long Hauler Gang.

Since that first tour, this granddaddy of all road trips has continued to grow and is now one of the most anticipated car events in America each year. It has consumed the hearts and minds of thousands of car guys and gals along with lots of fuel and repair parts at each stop. The event has not only grown, but it has evolved, as well, and there are events and activities along the way that are as diverse as the people and communities it touches each year.

Planning and documenting road trips has changed travel as much as the evolution of the cars and roads themselves. Today, you can download a planning app, open a map to check directions, and take flawless high resolution pictures to share with friends back home... all with the touch of a button. You can even call back home with the same device.

Whether you're reading this on one of those devices or you are holding an old fashioned printed book, you're going to love these stories. So, dig in and enjoy... and tell your friends about the books in The Old Car Nut Book series!

Introduction

by David Dickinson

The Old Car Nut Book series began as an idea for one book to just share some of the old stories that get told around the back bumper of a car at a show or in the intimate confines of a shop or garage. It has actually become an on-going effort and more about preserving those stories for the future. The stories have continued to come in, the project has continued to grow, and the series will wind up being more than I had initially planned. The public's appetite has been whetted and now needs to be fed.

I have been absolutely amazed at the wonderful reviews from readers and the press and bolstered by a handful of invitations to do interviews on podcasts and for written articles. Receiving an Outstanding Automotive Historian Award at the Washington State Hot Rod Hall of Fame this year would have to count as my best accolade to date and if there has ever been any lingering doubt in my mind that I am on the right track, that doubt has been removed. I couldn't ask for a better review of my efforts.

It has always been my intention to provide a platform that will give a voice to those that want to share. The books are my way of building a stage for others to share and those included in the books are the ones holding the microphone.

We come in all shapes and sizes, economic status, ages, and interests. Some of the people in the books are wealthy with large collections and some are scraping by to own one rusty old beater. But, there is a common denominator and that is a passion for old cars… and the old car stories are the fabric of our lives. The Old Car Nut Book series simply seeks to be the needle and thread that weaves them all together.

In one of the wonderful reviews I've received, a reader made the very profound observation that we are all very much alike and have been for decades. He went on to explain that the stories in these books reveal that we were all doing the same things to the same cars with the same kinds of people all across the country… without knowing each other existed.

Submissions for these books have come from all over America. A few have actually been professional writers, though they are certainly the exception. I've found that editing a story is very much like completely rebuilding a car or finding one that's almost done and getting it ready to take to a car show. Sometimes a builder starts with a real solid car that just needs some final pieces, making sure all of the body panels line up and the trim is all there, and then giving it a good detail. Sometimes it starts with a pile of parts that beg the questions… "What year, make, and model am I?"

Similarly, some of the stories shared come to me very well written and just need a final polish to really read well and sometimes I look at a submission and try to find the sentences, the paragraphs, and the real story that is begging to be told. In the end, it is always my goal to help an old car nut tell their story in the best way I can.

I never change a story, but try to enhance through asking questions of the story teller to fill in the details or do my own research about an area or event to provide a factual telling. Sometimes what gets sent to me is only a part of the story and through a bit of digging and questioning, a larger and more interesting story reveals itself.

Some of the stories in these books will make you laugh out loud and some of them will cause you to shed a tear, but they will all take you a step or two into the past. My son took a copy of the first book to a coworker that was getting ready to go on vacation and he read it on the plane headed to Hawaii. When he returned, he told about how embarrassed he got as he would read one story after another, alternating between laughing out loud and balling his eyes out, fearing that the other passengers thought he was a bit unstable.

Some of the stories have caused readers to recall certain events and write their own stories to send in and some of the stories have inspired others to rededicate themselves to a project that has lingered. Most all of the stories will affect someone in some way as they relate to their own life's experience.

For myself, I'm having the time of my life helping others share. I get the first look at each and every story, laughing the first laugh or shedding the first tear and to this day, there are a couple of stories that I cannot read without damp eyes, my emotions welled, just trying to get through them. I have reread my personal copies of the books, my proof copies, until they are now pretty worn on the edges.

This third book in the series is focused solely on Road Trips over the last century. When I began compiling this series of books, I didn't know that I would do a focused volume, but because of some personal stories I already had and some that was sent to me, it just happened.

The first story in this road trip book is one that I found in a trunk when my father passed in 1983 at 80 years old. The story was written in 1915 by his father, my grandfather, and it tells in great detail about moving the family, including my 12 year old father, from South Dakota to Oregon in a Model T Touring car. It was laying in the bottom of the trunk in a manila envelope, typed out with the same typewriter I have on display in my living room. Included, were pictures taken along the way. It was too long to fit the constraints I had placed on other submissions for the earlier books and so I held it back, wondering what I might do with it. This book is the answer.

Early in the story gathering process, Chris Kimball, eager to be a part of the books sent me several stories. He is well represented in the first book. One of the stories he sent was the daily journal of his trip to the 2012 Pantera Owners Club of America Fun Rally. Again, this was too long to fit the parameters I had set earlier, but Chris is a great writer and I wanted to use his account of the trip in a book, so there was another reason to do a Road Trips book.

So, I hope you will enjoy your ride with me as we travel some roads together in book #3 of The Old Car Nut Book series... "A century of travel across America. "

The Old Car Nut Book
Volume 3

Cross Country by Auto in 1915

by Dr. Stanley Burr Dickinson

Editor's Note: The following narrative and images are from a trip made in 1915 when my grandfather, a family doctor in Watertown, South Dakota, moved his family to Portland, Oregon in a Model T Ford.

As you read, you will find few similarities to cross country travel today. There were no major highways to speak of and you will discover the travails that these people had to endure to make the move.

In presenting this story, I have done no editing and so, it is as written in 1915. As a doctor, my grandfather was obviously a literate man, but you will see quite a different writing style than if the story was written today.

Watertown, South Dakota to Portland, Oregon

For nearly five years Queen (my wife) and I had been considering the advisability of severing our ties with South Dakota patients and friends for the purpose of spending the balance of our lives in a more moderate climate and when, in the early spring of 1915, I made arrangements to dispose of my home, we decided definitely to move to Oregon.

The question then came to our minds of the best method of travel, whether by train or auto. After a careful study of the case by correspondence, conversation, magazineoscopy, inclination, etc., we made a diagnosis of auto travel and a prognosis, complete satisfaction.

Not wishing to ship a carload, we decided to sell most of the household furniture and after packing the balance of our belongings, including my office equipment, placed it all, nearly 5,000 pounds, in pickle until we should decide just where and when we wanted it. This would give me a chance to take Queen and our two coming lights in our light popular 1915 touring car for a cross country trip with no limitation placed on time.

Our friends at Lake Kampeska

The next question to decide was what route to take: the Yellowstone Trail into Montana and thence over the National Parks Highway or to go south on the Meridian Road to Columbus, Nebraska, and then over the Lincoln Highway to Salt Lake City and over the Oregon Trail to Portland. We had about decided to take the latter route in spite of Nebraska floods, believing that there would be more travel that way because of the California Expositions, but about the last day the Queen decided it would not be treating South Dakota right to leave without seeing the Black Hills, and our friends, the Hagmans, who had never visited that beautiful section of South Dakota, decided to accompany us that far and be on hand to head us off if we attempted to turn back and remain in the state.

Stony Point at Lake Kampeska

After delaying our departure for some time and bidding goodbye to friends in town and at beautiful Lake Kampeska nearby, we finally broke away at 2 p.m., July 5th, while most of the population of Watertown was celebrating either the country's independence or our departure, I was not sure which.

Iona (Hagman's Ford) and Daisy (our Ford), the latter especially, must have looked like a gypsy outfit as we pulled out of Watertown, for after discarding a great many things at first considered necessary, she still had lashed to her side and back enough to start a good-sized second hand store.

It is always hard for relatives and longtime friends to part, or at least they think it is, and so the Queen's mother and Caroline Boggs Livingston were invited to ride with us

3

a day or two and return on the train. We drove west over fine roads and through several small towns to Redfield, 71 miles, where we arrived at 5:30 and, after calling on friends and stopping for supper at the depot lunch room, proceeded past fine fields of grain southwesterly to Miller, about 50 miles further on, where we stopped at the hotel at 10 p.m.

Leaving the hotel the next morning, we were speeding along over good roads when the first mishap overtook the party. A slough stretched across the road and for some distance into the meadow. I guided Daisy in a wide circle around to the road beyond but the Hagmans made a shorter cut and Iona came to a stop with a gasp in the greasy mire about two rods short from the desired goal.

Hagman started his engine and attempted to pull out in low gear, but the drive wheel spun in the mud like an egg beater and was soon buried to the hub in the mushy ground. The block and tackle with which I had provided myself was then brought into play and, with the assistance of a farmer who happened along, we were soon on our way.

After passing several small towns, including Harold, where we met Dr. Peabody and wife driving their car from the Black Hills to their home at Webster about 50 miles from our starting point, we stopped at Blunt for lunch. A cyclone had passed through the edge of this town a few weeks previously and we looked for evidence of it but found none. Proceeding on our journey the roads became poorer until we drew near to Pierre, where they were again in good condition, and we stopped in front of the State Capitol at 3 p.m.

After spending a pleasant hour in the building visiting the various rooms and mural paintings, we hurried to the depot where we waved a fond farewell to Mother and Caroline as the train pulled out bearing them homeward.

We decided to remain at the St. Charles over night and the next morning about 7:30 found us driving our steeds onto a flat car to be hauled across the Missouri River to Ft. Pierre, as there is no road bridge over the wide stream. Here we set our watches back one hour.

State Capitol

Leaving Ft. Pierre at 8 o'clock, we wound around up through the barren hills, following the black and yellow trail which runs west and a little north over a very thinly populated country before turning south to the railroad 100 miles west of Pierre. When about three miles out we could see the Scotty Phelps buffalo herd feeding on the hills a mile or more away. It had rained hard during the night west of us and when six miles from Ft. Pierre we were suddenly reminded of the fact that we were traveling through the gumbo country, and to one who has "been there" it is not necessary to explain what that means.

We traveled along fairly well for a mile or two but Iona, who was leading, finally refused to carry all the gumbo in that section and we proceeded with shovel and hammer to pry off enough so that our faithfuls would proceed, for what Iona had failed to pick up Daisy had accumulated. After laboring over the roads until 2 p.m. we found ourselves and a large portion of the trail at Borden's Ranch, only 25 miles from the morning's start.

We learned later that the proprietor of the ranch was a cattle rustler and at that time a fugitive from justice. It would have made little or no difference to us, however, had we known it at the time, as we were only there to satisfy our appetites, which we did in gourmand fashion when the dinner was spread by the good lady of the house.

We were glad to learn that about a mile farther on we would find dry roads and for about twenty miles we sped along, feeling that we had conquered what would have forced some travelers to turn back. We stopped at Hates, an inland store, long enough to purchase a few things for lunch in case we might need them and, while there, a couple in a Ford car passed us and we thought we would at least have a track to follow, as we learned they were going to Phillip.

We drove on several miles and, coming to a corner, we were undecided which way to go as the other parties had apparently gone straight ahead over a dim trail, while the sign pointed the other way. We decided to follow the marked road and about a mile from the corner found the entire roadway filled with water and mud for some distance. With some difficulty we turned about and followed the other car for several miles, crossing some very poor country with ditches and mud and no road or track, except from the car that had preceded us, but we pressed forward until dusk and determined to make Ottumwa, another inland station, if possible that night.

Presently we came to a slough stretching across our pathway for some distance in a forbidding manner, but as the other car had gone through I plunged into it and, as Daisy was heavily loaded, we came to a stop two rods from the edge with the rear wheels down to the hubs in water and mud and the front wheels nearly as deep "with the green grass growing all around". I climbed out in the water and proceeded to investigate but found that for ten rods ahead it was nearly as bad and at the farther side there was a ditch with a sloping bank six feet high.

We were evidently at "Sloughville" to stay until daylight, so taking an optimistic view of the situation we ate our lunch, put on the curtains to keep out the mosquitoes as much as possible and prepared to be lulled to sleep to the music of the frogs. Hagman's car was a few rods back on a little higher ground and after we had settled down they strove to improve the dampened ardor of the company by singing "Asleep in the Deep". To make things more romantic, we ordered a few flashes of lightning and rumbling thunder occasionally during the night from distant clouds.

The next morning I crawled out at daylight to survey the surroundings and, after an hour's work with block and tackle, we brought both cars to high ground and proceeded to Gillespie's ranch for breakfast. We learned there that the couple in the Ford car had passed about an hour before, so we concluded that they must have stopped overnight in the Sloughville Annex".

We proceeded across several sloughs and across country to Ottumwa, where we replenished our supplies of gas and oil and mailed some cards back home, and after driving several hours again came to a creek ten feet wide with a bridge gone and a high bank on the other side. Hagman selected a point where a car had crossed, evidently from the other direction, and charge it with fixed determination, but when nearly to the top of the grade Iona's blood ceased to circulate and she settled back pulseless and with her eyes looking heavenward as though imploring the sun god to help her out of the difficulty.

Bogged down, but on high ground

Once more the block and tackle was brought into use and, promising our better halves that we would vote for woman's suffrage at the first opportunity, they helped us pull Iona onto level ground, although Hagman's "gol darn the luck" caused spasms of laughter that nearly caused Iona to roll back into the ditch. After selecting a better crossing, having to pass through a barbed wire fence where Hagman tore his trousers with another "gol darn", I guided Daisy to the road and we stopped on a nearby hill for a picnic lunch.

We were determined to make up for lost time that afternoon as we heard the roads were good ahead of us, and we were speeding along at a 25 mile clip when Hagman attempted to drive astride a deep ditch in the road, but the wheels slid off and hung Iona on the ride like a teeter board. In the presence of ladies "Gol darn the luck" was all Hagman said, but we both removed our coats and began relief operations at once to avoid releasing the words that were on the end of our tongues.

The sun was hot but we "got out and got under" and dug the hard ridge like gophers for about an hour, the ladies assisting, of course, until finally with Daisy hitched to Iona's posterior rigging, we pulled the unfortunate victim to safety and proceeded to the town of Phillip on the railroad, where we stayed until the next morning.

Iona looking Heavenward

Proceeding westward we found dry roads but frequent sharp ditches caused by the spring rains. Hagman took most of them at a jump but in one of the worst ditches Daisy bent her radius rods in spite of a brace I had put on before starting. It was my turn to use the favorite expression which, please remember, was always said by both of us with a smile on our faces.

Before arriving in the town of Wall, it was necessary for us to traverse the famous Bad Lands where many a traveler and unfortunate animal had lost their lives before the railroad was put through. This section for miles is a succession of white hills and broken ground, in many places suddenly dropping off five or six feet, and the entire soil of a chalky whiteness that dazzled our eyes as we drove across this spooky section.

In the Badlands

When nearing Rapid City I had my first tire trouble when an old casing suddenly exploded, but a new one was soon on and we arrived at Rapid in time for the evening meal, after which we initiated our camping outfit in true Gypsy style.

The scenery began to improve from here on and we made the run to Sturgis in good time, and after purchasing an extra tire we left for Deadwood. A short distance out we saw some parties washing their car in the shallow gravelly creek so we decided to give Iona and Daisy a much needed bath. We, that is, Hagman, Robert and I rolled up our trousers and waded in while the modest ladies rendered great assistance from the edge of the stream.

We reached Deadwood, driving over the Canyon Road, at 3p.m. July 10th and, after taking in the town, drove down into beautiful Spearfish Canyon to camp and try our luck with the wiley trout. Our first attempt was crowned with success for, after trying our luck as amateurs for two hours, Hagman finally landed on six inched long. We were told there had been so much fishing there that the trout would scarcely look at bait and if we would go farther away we would have better luck, but Hagman's time was limited and the next morning we drove out of the canyon to Lead, the home of the Home of the Homestake mine and the largest gold mining plant in the world. After viewing the plant we left over the Deadwood-Denver trail for Custer and Hot Springs. Some of the road was very fine and some rather rough, but it is rapidly being brought into first class condition.

A much needed bath for Daisy

Near Hill City I noticed an occasional jerk and grind which appeared to be in the transmission but, as it was Sunday evening, we decided to go on to Sylvan Lake, were we expected to find better accommodations. It grew so dark in the mountain roads that we finally camped in front of a mountain home and proceeded up the steep but beautiful drive in the next morning to Sylvan Lake.

This is a beautiful lake at 6200 feet elevation, surrounded by rocky walls and a favorite resort for many visitors to the Black Hills. We spent about an hour there before proceeding to Custer, where I hoped to learn the cause of the grinding in my car. While waiting at Custer for the diagnosis of my car's trouble, Hagman very kindly drove Queen and myself out to the cemetery one mile from town, where my brother's remains were placed several years before, for Custer had been his home during the last years of his declining health.

Turning my back for the second time in my life on the beautiful surrounding country, we were soon back to the garage where we learned that the sound came probably from the differential but, as it was only slightly noticeable, we decided on proceeding to Hot Springs, about 40 miles away, where we had planned to spend out last day with the Hagmans.

Nothing went wrong on the run and at 2:30 p.m. we stopped at Wind Cave and while Ione and Daisy made friends with the buffalo in the pen we took and hour's stroll through the cave, the guide explaining the wonders of the many caverns. At the entrance to the cave the wind is so strong at times that one's hat is blown off and at other times the hat would be sucked in beyond rescue.

We drove on to Hot Springs twelve miles farther, where we arrived at 6 p.m. and leaving orders at the garage for Daisy's welfare and our baggage at the Gillespie Hotel we proceeded to enjoy ourselves visiting the Soldier's Home and, the next day being a hot on, we cooled off in the Evans Plunge.

At last came the time to say farewell, which we were indeed sorry to do, for in spite of the difficulties thus far encountered, we had all enjoyed the outing, and as the train pulled out bearing the Hagmans homeward—he shipped his car home—a tear dimmed Queen's eyes and I will have to admit my heart was not just where it belonged for a minute, for we were parting from friends with whom we had been closely associated for fourteen years and we were to proceed on our journey alone over 1600 miles of road we knew nothing about.

Learning there was a band concert scheduled for that evening, we climbed the hill to seats in front of the Soldier's Home overlooking the city and were cheered up by band music for a time before retiring to the hotel.

The next morning we set out for Edgemont, continuing over the Deadwood-Denver trail. We were soon away from the beauties of the Black Hills region and traveling again over thinly settled country. At Edgemont we were advised to go south to Ardmore instead of following the trail to Hat Creek as the roads were said to be very bad southwest. I did not like the idea of driving out of our course so far, but remembering our past experiences when we had companions in trouble, we took the advice offered and, on arriving at Ardmore were advised at the garage to bear east to Crawford before turning west to Harrison and Lusk.

This almost "got my goat" but I finally decided that "discretion was the better part of valor" so away we went and stopped in Crawford for lunch, then on over poor roads toward Harrison, but darkness overtook us on a dim road and we decided to pitch our tent near a farmhouse. During the day we had again driven through a stretch of the Badlands that extends down into Nebraska and after a long drive, we began to wonder how badly Daisy needed water when we saw the smoke of a train a few miles away and soon saw the train and some buildings, so concluded we were nearing a town.

The only store there was closed and I asked a small boy where I could find some water. He replied "ain't none in town but you can get some down there", pointing to a lonesome tree about three miles away. Asked what they called the place, "he did not know" so we named it "The Devil's Back Yard". I decided if that was a sample of dry towns I would never vote for prohibition.

The next day we drove west to Harrison where we took on supplies and proceeded to Lusk, stopping at a restaurant for dinner. Then on to Guernsey over some good and some very rocky roads. We arrived at 7 p.m. and after laying in a supply of groceries pitched our tent on the banks of the North Platte for the night.

Camping by the side of the road

The next morning found us at Wheatland at 10:30 and at noon we had lunch on the lawn of a large ranch home at Bordeaux, where the chickens thought they belonged at our family table and the lambs attempted to climb into the car, to the great amusement of Robert and Marian. Thirteen miles beyond we met a car from Canyon City, Colorado on a drive to Deadwood.

We reached Cheyenne at 5 p.m. July 16th, altitude 7000 feet, temperature 70, and pitched our tent that night south of town near a car party from Oklahoma.

The next morning we were ready for the first lap on the Lincoln Highway and there were dozens of cars going in both directions over the fine roads. Those that most attracted our attention were a Cadillac from Chicago and a Cole car from Maryland, for we were traveling close to them most of the time.

The morning drive took us over fine roads to the Ames monument, which marks the divide at Sherman Hill, 8000 feet above sea level, and here stood a car from Baltimore which carried a company on their way home from the exposition. The Ames monument, 65 feet high, was built of granite and erected in honor of Oakes and Oliver Ames through whose efforts mainly was due the completion of the Union Pacific railway. Pikes Peak could be plainly seen from this point.

Our next stop was Laramie where we ate dinner at the Anderson restaurant with the Chicago and Maryland parties and after a drive through town viewing the University we left for Medicine Bow, driving over winding roads across a barren, rough and uninteresting country. About five miles from Medicine Bow we saw a car standing by the roadside apparently in distress and the occupant, about "three sheets in the wind", said his pal had gone a mile to telephone for repairs.

The car appeared to be a Studebaker from the name but I found it was a 1910 Overland from Oklahoma and they had placed the first four letters of a Studebaker name plate on the radiator. They came into the hotel about 9 o'clock that night and had to wait for repairs from Denver before they could proceed. We reached Medicine Bow at 7 o'clock, about one hour after the Cadillac, and learned the Cole car had gone through about 5:30.

A pause before Medicine Bow

As the Virginia Hotel was an up-to-date house in a prairie town of 100 people, we decided to stop for the night and the Cadillac driver told me if he ever took another trip with a car it would be one like mine. This hotel was made famous by being the birthplace of that interesting novel, "The Virginian".

The next day being Sunday we did not start very early, but our Cadillac friends, who were trying to make fast time, got away at 5:30 with overcoats buttoned tight and their breaths showing in the crisp morning air, for the elevation here was 6800 feet.

After driving for a few miles out of Medicine Bow, we noticed the road was following an old railroad grade and we soon found ourselves in the deserted town of Carbon. Not a soul could be seen and the place looked as though it belonged in the war zone of Europe. The railroad had been changed a few miles to make it an easier grade and the people and business had followed the railroad. We reached Hanna, a little village, and while I repaired an inner tube that was causing a little trouble, Queen and Marian strolled over to a nearby church for a short time.

Driving on to Rawlins we took on supplies for Daisy and then appeased our own hunger at the best restaurant we could find. If you have a poor appetite, try a trip of a few hundred miles by automobile a see what effect it has on you.

We were ready to leave at 2:50 and Mr. Jensen, a traveling man who was behind on his trip requested a ride to Rock Springs and as he seemed to be a congenial sort of fellow I took him in and we proceeded by good roads but treeless country to Wamsutter, where we arrived about 5 o'clock. This was a small town with poor accommodations but, as we were not sure of reaching Rock Springs that night, Mr. J. stopped there while we moved on, following the railroad across the "Red Desert" with many miles between station and some of them without water, so we were careful to take a supply of that precious liquid at every opportunity.

A mile or two beyond Tipton we came suddenly onto two cars stopped in the road, one of them with a broken axle, and one of the passengers was a lady about 70 and another a parrot. They were from California and their destination was Indiana. They inquired the distance to water and said it was about 40 miles the way we were going but, as we had enough for our own use and they said we couldn't help them, we sped on as it was nearly sunset then.

We drove into Point of Rocks at ten o'clock, 87 miles from Wamsutter, and all the way with nothing to view but sage brush and a reddish soil. As the roads were said to be poor from there to Rock Springs and we had already driven

150 miles that day we decided to stop for the night in rooms we were able to secure. It was fortunate we did so for the next morning I found the fan belt broken and considered ourselves again lucky it had not happened in the desert.

We did not reach Rock Springs until rather late the next forenoon and while partaking of a good meal at a Chinese restaurant in walked Jensen, who had recognized Daisy standing outside. We spent a little time here replenishing our supplies and changing a tire and again took Jensen with us to Green River, where he insisted on treating us to ice cream before we parted company. Of course we did not want it.

From Rock Springs to Green River is a stretch of very fine improved highway. Green River is a pretty town with good water where most of the property owners of Rock Spring live, to Rock Springs, although about 2000 (this figure is not decipherable on original copy) is a mining town and the water is poor.

At Green River we expected to get our evening meal but we were a little early for that and this was where we must decide to go northwest following the Oregon Short Line or southwest to Evanston and Salt Lake City. Queen wished to see the famous Mormon city and tabernacle and we thought it would be a nice thing for the children so we were not long in deciding and were soon on our way to Lyman, an inland Mormon town, where we stopped for the evening meal at a Mormon home and then drove on hoping to reach Evanston that night, but the route led us through sage brush country and the road was not very good and at 10 o'clock, when we drove down into a grassy canyon 15 miles from Evanston and learned from a couple who were sleeping in blankets by their car that the road ahead was poor, we pitched out tent and crawled in.

That little tent was our best friend and we were very glad we had it along. Next morning we found a little ice in the water bag. It was a little chilly when we crawled out and Queen made breakfast by the little alcohol stove while Robert and I wasted a few cartridges firing the little twenty-two rifle at prairie dogs, which usually sat and made faces at us while we fired several shots.

At Evanston we learned that we would pass through two rather steep canyons on our way to Salt Lake City so I decided to have my brake band renewed and on removing the transmission cover I was surprised to find on top of the clutch the metal end of Robert's little flashlight, with which he had tried to help me in the Black Hills country at the time I noticed the grinding sound and endeavored to locate the trouble. It had dropped into the case at that time and I supposed it had been removed at Custer when the oil was drained from the crank case.

Again I thought luck was with us, as it might easily have given trouble and caused Daisy to halt anywhere on the road, but I suppose the reason it hadn't was because I had "knocked on wood" whenever I was told by Queen to do so.

We had traversed hundreds of miles of desert and barren table lands and seen dozens of other cars from New York to Texas doing the same thing, but now we were to see some better country and we were soon dropping down into Echo Canyon, where the road wound up and down and around with small farms crowding up on the hillsides and farther on followed the railroad past towering cliffs of different hues, out into the open for a brief period while the stage was set for a change of scenery, then down through Parley Canyon, where we stopped for lunch beside a beautiful trout stream that tumbled down over the rock and through the dense brush and trees, and out and on through open country past small Mormon villages and farms that for miles seemed like one spread out town to Wanship where we camped on a grassy spot beside the Weber River.

Starting the next day at 10 o'clock we drove through the Silver Creek canyon and over some rocky roads and about 2:30 came in sight of the great Mormon city and as we drove up through the broad streets we began to see signs of the great celebration that was on, "The Wizard of Wasatch".

As we turned the corner in front of the Capitol, Daisy as though rejoicing over our safe arrival, exploded one of her rear tires. This was the only tire trouble for several hundred miles and we dropped down from Evanston, 8500 feet, over all kinds of roads, striking many rough stones.

One of the first cars we saw on the main streets was the Cole car we had seen at Laramie and the next morning, when I saw the driver of the Cadillac, he was buying tires and said they had thirteen blowouts in the last 24 hours travel. They were endeavoring to hurry but only arrived three or four hours ahead of us.

After leaving our baggage at the hotel and putting on a new tire we drove about the city and in the evening witnessed the electrical parade. This was a fitting climax to Robert's birthday, July 21. The next morning Jensen again "bobbed up serenely" and we began to think we could not shake him but he went to Frisco so that was the last we saw of him.

Preparing Daisy for further travel and waiting for the organ recital at 12 in the Tabernacle we were again on our way over fine roads through Ogden to Brigham City, where we camped in a plum orchard at the house of a Mormon. We had stopped at an orchard during the afternoon and purchased a large pail of apricots and cherries which were much enjoyed during the drive.

Our drive to Tremonton and Snowville was over a succession of good and poor, frightfully dusty roads and through sage brush and when we reached Albion, Idaho, late in the day all were ready for a night's rest at the hotel.

The next morning we drove twenty miles before breakfasting at Burley, a prosperous little city in an irrigated section where they were having a Mormon celebration that day. By the size of the families we met as we drove out of town we decided they must all be bigamists. The irrigated section was very interesting as it showed the wonderful change made by watering land that seemed absolutely worthless. We often saw large sections of nothing but sage brush and sand and across the road nice homes and fine crops.

We made a stop of three hours at Twin Falls and will always remember the advertising spirit of its citizens for nearly every time we turned around we would see this sign—"If I spend my money out of Twin Falls and you spend your money out of Twin Falls, then what will become of Twin Falls"?

Our youngsters often repeat it and it seemed to me a very good blow at the mail order business.

We drove on to Riverside Ferry where the boat was pulled across by a gasoline launch. This was our first view of the Snake River whose waters emptied in the Columbia about 850 miles northwest. We camped at "Judge" Uhrlaub's pretty little resort and found the "Judge" very congenial. That evening some parties from Twin Falls who came out to spend the night and Sunday, went up the river to a net and soon returned with a forty pound sturgeon. I held my flashlight for the Judge to dress, or rather undress, the sturgeon and next morning we all had fish for breakfast.

That "the world is not very large after all" came to my mind when a party at this place asked me if I knew Vaud

Hopkins. Another said his father gave him some lots at Blunt, S.D. and asked what they were worth. I told him to please not give them to me.

We also learned that the Trails, whom we knew 15 years ago in Chicago, were living at Jerome about twenty miles northeast and, although it would take us a little out of our way, we decided to call on them. We arrived there shortly after noon, having stopped at Wendell for dinner so as not to trouble them, and after a pleasant visit left at three for Shoshone over the State Highway, making the run of 25 miles in 55 minutes.

We then turned west and were in Gooding for supper where we read of the Eastland disaster in Chicago, then on through Bliss to Glenns Ferry over good roads all day. The drive that moonlight evening along the Snake River near Glenns Ferry was very pretty and it was hard to realize that we were really "away out in Idaho".

Leaving the hotel next morning we drove out a mile or more before winding up a steep hill more than a mile. Having to water Daisy on the way up, and soon after reaching the top Robert discovered he had left his watch and flashlight under his pillow at the hotel. I refused to drive back but stopped at a farmhouse a little farther on and phoned the landlady to send the articles parcel-post to Boise.

That day we drove through a section lined with fine orchards and stopped at one place to get all we wished to carry of fine eating apples, finally arriving at Boise at 4 p.m. We must wait until 6 o'clock to get Robert's watch so we took on supplies, I visited the barber shop and we dined at the Grand Cafeteria. Proceeding over fine roads we stopped at Middleton for the night, pitching our tent under the trees at the edge of town.

The next day we crossed into Oregon and, after passing several small towns, again crossed the river into Idaho and lunched in a restaurant at Payette, then proceeding to Weiser, where we took on gas and Mr. Pratt, who sold the gas, informed us he was a cousin of John Ogg in Watertown. After being directed by Mr. Pratt as to the best road to Huntington, we started out and in the edge of town, when we stopped to make sure of our road, another car bearing W.H. Ambler and his father from Denver to Seattle drove alongside and said they were told at the garage to follow us. After a two hour's drive over good roads but hilly country, we crossed the ferry run by the current of the Snake River again into Oregon and were soon in Huntington, where we all stopped for supper, and after setting our watched back one hour proceeded up Burnt River Canyon, past deserted smelters for ten miles, where we all camped in a pleasant stop beside the road.

Amblers were on a hurried trip so they left at 7 o'clock the next morning for they were going by way of Walla Walla, Washington. We started at 8:30 and at 11 o'clock were in Baker City, then to Union and LeGrande over fair roads, arriving at 5 p.m.

As there was nothing to stop here for particularly we filled our water tank and water bag and being told the roads were good we started out with oil gauge full and three pints in an extra can. Ordinarily it would have been a great plenty but after driving about eight miles along a beautiful valley and stream, we started up a canyon and soon found Daisy had to climb a long steep winding grade that had to be taken mostly on low, then across rough "sheep trimmed downs" and again winding up among the fir trees that sent roots across our pathway, so it was necessary to drive on low gear until I began to wonder if we would ever reach the summit of The Blue Mountains and when we stopped to investigate the oil supply found the gauge empty.

Packing up camp and heading for Baker City

I poured in the extra three pints and as there was no water in the vicinity we did not stop to camp but drove on until an occasional down grade showed us we had reached the summit and a little farther on we came to Meacham, a small mountain town, but found there was no cylinder oil there. It was dark and we decided to camp for the night not far from the railroad. About one o'clock it began to rain and soon I heard a car. I looked out and they had stopped just beyond us, evidently wondering whether or not to proceed into LeGrande. I thought, you poor fools, to travel those roads at night in a rain. There were ladies in the car besides the driver and they soon drove on.

We left at daylight as it was getting damp around the edges and with the chains on it was rather hard work for Daisy, first up and then down over muddy roads. Finally we came out of the timber and to the top of a long down grade about ten miles from Pendleton and ahead of us could be seen fields of golden grain, but my engine seemed to be getting hot and I stopped the car for fear of doing some damage. The oil was so low I dared not run any farther so I started downhill afoot through the mud, losing a rubber nearly every step until I finally became disgusted and left them sticking in the mud and went on about two miles where, fortunately, a farmer had some extra cylinder oil.

Purchasing two quarts, I labored back up the grade, reaching the car about ten o'clock. I was ready for a "hand out" breakfast by this time. Cranking would not start Daisy as the cylinders were so dry so, with the assistance of a passer-by I pushed her a few rods to where she would run down hill of her own accord and, jumping in, threw in the clutch and we rolled down hill about 40 rods before she finally took an explosion and the engine was once more operating perfectly.

We made short work of the remaining distance in spite of mud and soon were in Pendleton, where we had a good square meal and learned that the roads were more sandy west of us. After viewing the sights in the city of "Roundup" fame, we made the run over fairly good roads through a rolling grain country to Echo, which we reached at 7 p.m. and, giving Daisy a berth in the garage, we proceeded to satisfy our inner selves at the hotel.

We here met a Mr. Hall who was driving a Ford car on his route through the state representing the Lee Tire Company. He was on his way to Portland and we traveled in company over the balance of the route.

From Echo to Ione, although through desert country, the road was fine and we spun along at a 25 mile clip, while the jack rabbits scurried out of the road every few rods and the children enjoyed themselves counting them. Now and then a badger was seen sitting beside his home. In South Dakota, Nebraska and Wyoming it was the prairie dog that dodged us.

From Ione to Olex the road was frightfully bad as heavy loads of grain had cut chuck holes in the dry ground and it was necessary to drive slow or break springs. We preferred the former and the whiter dust coated us and Daisy until she looked like a moving sandbank. This was also the case near Snowville, Utah, and we getting so we did not fell natural unless we were dirty. All tourists looked alike so we felt rather proud of it.

From Olex to the John Day Ferry was a fairly good road and the only reason I could see for a ferry was to collect the dollar charge. A horse ridden by a small boy pulled the ferry across and when I handed him the dollar told him if he cared to go back and would drive the horse into the ferry I would drive Daisy through and pull the horse across for the dollar. A good road soon brought us to Wasco and just before arriving there Mt. Hood appeared in the distance like a bold sentinel and we exclaimed "Oh, look!" The top was above the clouds and it was indeed a wonderful sight.

We had planned to reach The Dalles that day and we sped on over fine roads until we began to wind down to the Deschutes toll bridge, where another dollar was required to reach the other side. It was about six o'clock but the view of the rapids with the railroad bridge a short distance below where the Deschutes joins the Columbia was too pretty a scene to pass without a picture, so we stopped long enough for Queen to snap her camera before driving up the long hill beyond.

A little farther on we came in full view of the Celio Locks and bridge across the Columbia. We were far above and it presented another grand picture but it was too late in the day to use the camera and we drove on following the Columbia for some distance, then winding among the hills and down through a small canyon to The Dalles, arriving about 8 o'clock. Leaving Daisy at the garage we found a good restaurant and then went to The Dalles hotel for the night.

All through the state we had heard that most of the tourists shipped their cars from The Dalles to Portland but I did not like the idea of ending our tour that way and after talking at the garage with a party who had just driven over the road and expected to return the next day, I said "that settles it, we drive" and we did.

We did not leave until noon however, as we thought we could easily make it that day and winding in and out among the hills followed close to the river most of the way, Robert with Mr. Hall, and as he had no load they made better time on the hills. Not wishing to delay him I gave him instructions to leave Robert at Hood River in case we did not arrive before he was ready to leave.

As we neared Hood River the orchards in the valley below presented another beautiful scene with the river tumbling along down to the Columbia. We reached the town in a few minutes and neither Mr. Hall's Ford nor Robert could be found. Queen imagined all sorts of trouble from a kidnapper to Robert being left behind and lost in the large city of Hood River, which I verily believe contains less than one thousand souls.

After hunting for nearly an hour and unsuccessfully endeavoring to telephone ahead to learn if they had passed Mitchell's Point, we decided to move on, as I was sure they had misunderstood and would be waiting for us somewhere on the road. Mitchell's Point is a few miles west of Hood River where the Columbia Highway Association were constructing a tunnel through the hill to avoid the steep grade, which was only wide enough for one car, and it was so arranged that each autoist should telephone to the top to learn if the road was clear before starting up.

When we arrived we found a note at the telephone signed by Mr. Hall telling us they left there about 30 minutes before and Queen breathed a little easier. She had not been enjoying the scenery much and was still uneasy until we met a car near Cascade Locks, in which Robert was coming back to meet us. We had no fatted calf to kill but were ready to eat one when we arrived at Portland.

Columbia Highway Association tunnel through the hill

It would take a genius to describe the beauties of the drive over the Columbia River Highway from Cascade

Locks to Portland where many thousands of dollars have already been spent and many more will be spent the coming year to bring the highway to perfection. The drive winds around the rocky cliff with beautiful concrete work at the outer side of the drive across massive artistic concrete bridges spanning the canyons with waterfalls on one side of the bridge and the grand Columbia far below on the other. Towering fir trees and other smaller kinds with vines and flowers complete the picture, which one can only appreciate by seeing it.

Nature color photographs have been made of the highway and will be shown throughout the country during the coming year. It will pay anybody well to see them for the scenes are photographed in natural colors by a new process and are not colored photographs.

At Latourelle we were obliged to climb another steep hill about a mile long where Daisy drank all the water in the water bag. To use the old term, the scene we had just passed was like "viewing the Promised Land".

Columbia River Highway... Running with the train

It was dark when we reached the city and when we came in sight of the thousands of electric eyes lighting the city it was necessary to awaken the youngsters so they could see the beautiful sight.

We crossed the Willamette and drove to the garage, completing the tour of 2310 miles at 9:30 p.m. and, after dining, retired to our rooms at the Oregon Hotel, with a realization of our prognosis "complete satisfaction".

On the Road with Harold LeMay

by Charlie Maxwell

By the time he passed in 2000, Harold LeMay had amassed one of the largest private automobile collections in the world. But, Harold didn't just collect cars. He collected anything that had to do with cars and had one of the largest private collections of automotive memorabilia, as well.

As the owner of a variety of companies involved in sales and service, towing, trucking, and hauling garbage, Harold had access to a lot of equip- ment and he used that to his advantage when it came time to add to his collections.

I was fortunate to be Harold's friend and road trip buddy. Our annual road trips to the Fall Hershey Swap Meet would usually involve driving the roll back truck, pulling a one car trailer the 3,000 miles to our friends John and Arlene Kehl's house near Allentown, PA. If we were lucky, we would be hauling someone else's car to sell to help with the trip expenses. It was always an adventure that Harold and I looked forward to each year.

This year would be our final trip before his passing and I learned from the outset that it would not be our typical adventure. Harold had purchased some used Kenworth trucks and we would be driving one of them bob-tailed, no trailer, from his home in Tacoma, Washington all the way to Pennsylvania. We had a "sleeper", a porta-potty, and our coolers full of Harold's favorite foods. What else could two ol' car guys want on a journey?

Harold had purchased a fifty three foot Snyder trailer in Delaware and it was waiting for us at our friend's house

in PA. This was the reason for running bob-tailed. The semi-trailer would be much better to haul home the treasures he would find along the way.

We hit the road and things were going really well until we went through the scale house just beyond the Idaho-Montana border. Now, Harold had a thing about scale-houses; he didn't like them. He used to joke that if you weren't over-weight, you didn't load your truck right. We rolled over the scales with just the tractor and the lights went off saying "Bring in your paper work."

I had painted "Non-Commercial Not for Hire" on both doors. Harold, because he was a dealer, had put a dealer plate on the tractor.

The guy in the scale house says to Harold, "Where are you from?"

Harold says, "Tacoma."

The guy then asks "Where you going?"

Harold replies "Pennsylvania."

Obviously, the guy is confused at the notion of someone running bob-tailed the entire width of the country, but he recovers and then asks Harold, "Where did you get the truck?"

Harold answers "I borrowed it."

The guy asks "Who did you borrow it from?"

Harold replies "From myself."

By then, I was about to bust a gut from watching Harold run the scale guy in circles, the scale guy was doing a mental 360, and the lady behind him was laughing like mad. So, the guy behind the counter then says "I think we have a little gray area here" and tells Harold "The signs on the door say non-commercial."

He continues, and you can see he's trying to sort this out as he's talking, "The dealer plate says you're commercial. So, what are you?"

Harold replies, "What do you want me to be?"

The guy rubs his eyes and says, resignedly, "I tell you what. You are from Washington. You have passed through Idaho and now you are in Montana. If you buy a Montana fuel permit, you can hit the road." We paid the $200 and left. The lady in the back was still laughing.

We continued on our journey and just east of Hardin, Montana, Harold takes this "short cut" he knows through the Crow Indian Nation that comes out in Spearfish, South Dakota. During this time, I'm sleeping but wake up because I'm getting tossed around in the sleeper. I pull the curtains back and Harold is hunched over the steering wheel. It's raining sideways and he has the pedal to the metal, driving down through some canyons. The trip continues this way with Harold going as fast as he can until we finally arrive at our destination in Mertztown, where John and Arlene live.

The next morning, we loaded up John's camper and headed out for Olean, New York where Harold had been negotiating on a 1937 Cord Cabriolet with the daughters of

a former Gargoyle fuel dealer. We arrived at their late father's home where an auction of car parts and memorabilia was going to take place that day. Everything was in rows of
large piles in the yard, each row 100 feet long, and there were at least fifteen rows.

Well, Harold scored on the third pile and there was no stopping him. Knowing his tendency to buy a lot of stuff, I had arranged with the auctioneer to use an empty shed to amass Harold's purchases. Before long, people were asking who bidder number one was.

Things can get hectic at one of these types of auctions, because they let you take the stuff as soon as the bid is done and people will walk off with your newly acquired property if you are not careful. I was running as hard as I could to get Harold's acquisitions into that shed before they disappeared. The daughters jumped in and helped me or I never would have been able to gather it all. The irony of it all was Harold never could clinch the purchase of that Cord.

We then headed for Carlisle and then Hershey for the big swap meets. At Hershey, Harold was to meet up with the widow of a collector from whom he had purchased three

late '20s antique trucks. They all were displayed at the Eastern Region AACA car show to receive their Senior Awards. The Acme dump truck, a Chevrolet Huckster, and a Chevrolet Panel were all from the estate of the late Bobby Manweiler.

This was Harold's reason for the semi and trailer. After the two swap meets, flea markets, auctions, and yard sales we wrapped and packed all of Harold's stuff into that Snyder trailer. It was the largest haul we'd ever made.

We did stop each way in Murdo, South Dakota at the car museum there, but Harold's friend, Dave Geisler, was never in town. The rest of the way home we played "Weigh Station Closed" to see who could score the most closed. Harold always won.

Before we left on this road trip, Harold's wife, Nancy, had taken me aside and made me promise her that I would make sure Harold got a hot meal every day. At 80 years old, he was as sharp as a tack mentally, but becoming quite frail physically. The following year Harold passed away.

When I spoke at his service, I related the story of Nancy telling me to make sure he got those hot meals every day. I told those attending his service that I thought she said each way, because Harold never wanted to stop. It was pedal to the metal the whole time.

I will always miss Harold and our adventures together, but I'm still close to the family and involved with the LeMay Family Collection at the historic Marymount Military Academy. The grounds and old buildings are a perfect place to house and display Harold's passions for all things automotive and where everyone is welcome to come and share.

Road Angel

by David Dickinson

Towards the end of 1974, my enlistment in the US Navy was coming to an end and I was faced with a decision. Over a year before that, I had swapped onto a ship that was going into a yard period in Bremerton, WA, which was driving distance from my home town of Tacoma.

Having the opportunity to hang with old high school friends and sample the local economy, I realized that  there was really nothing to compel me to keep my roots buried. I had enjoyed almost four years of great travel all over the world and Uncle Sam thought I was a pretty valuable character. By that, I mean I was in what was called a critical rating. The Navy offered me some big bucks to stay in and go live in San Diego and teach school.

Having spent some time in that fair weathered, southernmost city, and finding no financial benefit to staying in Tacoma where the job market was sketchy at best, I figured I should "take the money and run!" So, I reenlisted and made plans to move south. This all happened a few months prior to my relocation date, so there was time to liquidate assets too big to pack in a box. Yes, I'm talking about cars. Future classic cars, as it turns out.

I was single, but owned four cars. My 1960 Datsun pickup was absolutely cherry and I had paid only $100 for it. Then there was the 1955 Chevy hot rod that I had pieced together on a budget and though it was far from stock or cherry, it was fun to drive. Both the Datsun and the Chevy were quickly grabbed up by friends at the shipyard.

The two other cars were a 1969 VW Bug and a 1960 Austin Healey 100/6 roadster. I had bought the VW in 1971 and it had served me well. It was paid for, ran great and looked perfect, but... it was a Bug. I had to choose a car to keep and drive down in San Diego and the Austin Healey easily won the contest when it came to cool drivers!

I had bought the Austin Healey with some of my re-enlistment money, so I already knew I'd keep it anyway, of course. That left me with the dilemma of finding a new owner for my beloved Bug. The answer, once again, came in the form of someone I knew. Her name was Denise.

To make a long story short, I had to teach Denise to drive the stick shift Volkswagen. During the lessons, two things happened. She tore up the transaxle in the car and I fell in love. After repairing the tranny, I told her that if she wanted to drive the car, she'd have to do so in California. Well, now we had two people to plan a move for!

The plan included me moving to California in June of 1975 with her finishing college classes and planning a Christmas time wedding at home in Tacoma. After the movers had hauled away all of my furniture and personal possessions, we packed the Healey for a two week road trip to San Diego. It was a very eventful trip and we had a blast. This story focuses on the beginning of that trip.

On a bright and sunny June morning, we said our goodbyes and backed out of her parent's driveway, the car loaded to the gills with everything we could get in it, including the soft top and metal framed plastic windows. It was quite a feat of sorting, stuffing, squashing and packing in general. There was absolutely no dead space when we pulled away!

Our route took us south on Interstate 5 from Tacoma to Olympia, where we turned off to Highway 101 and headed north to make that big and beautiful loop around the Olympic Peninsula that would allow us to continue right on down the coast and stay as close to the water as was possible.

The car was running great. I had done a complete service on the car after I had bought it. My instructions to the British mechanic were to make sure that every nut bolt and wire was in place and tight and all fluids were new. The guy did a complete tune up and the car purred like a kitten.

If you have traveled Highway 101 around the Olympic Peninsula, you know how remote some areas can be and around dusk of that first day, the Austin Healey chose one of the most remote areas to suddenly quit running. The engine went from a smooth and steady 2500 RPMs to dead in a heartbeat. At that point, I think my heart skipped a beat or two, as well.

Dusk, in the middle of nowhere, goes to completely dark in about a heartbeat. Remote is a very quiet place. There was no noise, unless you count the quiet buzzing of mosquitos and other life sucking pests. Being the sweet and tasty morsel that is me, I became a banquet fit for all creatures small and winged. Between the dead car, my concern for my lady, and the ever maddening bugs, I was quickly becoming distressed and had no plan.

It had all happened so suddenly that once I resigned myself to the situation and was flinging up the hood on my green example of British automotive incompetence to do my initial trouble shooting, I was astonished to see an old Ford pickup pull to a stop behind us. Whoever it was had stopped to take advantage or to help. I was hoping it was the latter.

As it turned out, the Road Angel that emerged was dirty, tired looking, and a pretty big guy, but a Road Angel none the less.

"Got trouble?" he asked. I wasn't sure what to tell him.

"Well, no, we're just feeding the bugs," I chose not to say.

"Let's take a look" he continued.

Like I said, I had just raised the hood when he pulled up, so we checked it out together and determined that it had fuel, but it didn't have spark. An inspection of the distributor revealed that the rotor was spinning freely. Of course it didn't have spark!

"Looks like the keeper pin for the gear at the bottom of your distributor shaft is gone!" our Road Angel declared. "I've seen this before. We can fix this in no time." I wasn't convinced, but he certainly had a better plan than I had, so we pulled the distributor, jumped in his truck and headed to his place just down the road.

I have to say, I was very leery of leaving the car there unattended, but I couldn't leave Denise there all alone with it. I could get another car and all the stuff in it. She was another story. So, the car sat where it died.

When we pulled up to his place, I was amazed at the size of the guy's shop. It must have been three or four times larger than the mobile home where they lived. This guy had cars, equipment, and tools up the Whazoo, so to speak. I couldn't have broken down at a better time or place than I did that evening. He was right, too. Once we had that pin fixed and got back to the car, untouched and just as I left it, the distributor slid back into the engine and it fired off in short order.

"It's kinda late to get back on the road now. If you want, we can put you up for the night and give you breakfast in the morning. May as well hit the road in the light and get a good start." his wife had said. She was every bit as nice as our Road Angel. We had certainly been blessed that night. So, back to the man cave and mini domicile we went.

We slept on the floor in the living room of their trailer. It wasn't the Ritz, but it was certainly better than the seats of the car along the side of the road and too much time had been lost to find a place to stay that night. We got cleaned up and had breakfast with our gracious hosts and then said

our goodbyes. I knew then that this was a story I would never forget.

We made our way south past Aberdeen and Hoquiam, across the Astoria Bridge, and down the Oregon coast to Seaside and stayed the night. We spent a few hours in Cannon Beach the next day, continuing our cruise south, stopping along the way at some very picturesque places along the coast. We landed the second night in Coos Bay, OR and then the third night in Lincoln City, OR. The days were filled with beautiful sites, lots of laughter and no more car troubles. We kept the travel to 100-200 miles per day and in some cases, spent two days at places when we really felt like it.

One of the places we stayed for a couple of days and nights was Mendocino, CA, which is just south of Fort

Bragg. More of a village that anything else at that time, the streets were full of shops featuring ceramics and beads, alternative lifestyle (Yep, hippie would be the word) clothing, head shops and actual hippies.

Other than having to replace the distributor cap that had gotten cracked when the rotor flew up from the keeper pin breaking, we didn't have any more mechanical car trouble.  However, after spending a couple of days in San Francisco, visiting extended family, we hopped back onto 101 and wound up getting into trouble with the CHP. That car sure did cruise nicely in overdrive! There's more to the story, but we did make it all the way to San Diego where we settled on the beach just south of the training facility where I would teach classes.

The Austin Healey? Well, it got traded for a piece of development property at a substantial dollar amount more than I paid for it and I replaced it with a Karmann Ghia convertible that was a gem of a car and lots of fun for the beach.

The Lost Washer Summer Interruption Tour

by Dennis Kent

For the past eight years, my wife, Marcia, and I have been participating in a collector car tour in Eastern Washington that is sponsored by one of three clubs. The tour is based in a different city each year and is held around July 4th. This year, the tour was based in Moscow, Idaho and was sponsored by the "Crankers Club" of Lewiston, Idaho and Clarkson, Washington.

About 10 days before the event, I discovered that the bands in our 1925 Ford Model T Touring needed to be replaced. I have done this before and am very careful not to drop anything into the pan. Not so lucky this year. While removing the reverse band, my hand slipped off the band and the washer flipped into the pan. Now, I had to get the washer out.

I started by using a flexible magnet with no success; then removed the hogshead. Still no washer. After a number of different tries, I decided that I would have to remove the engine from the car, which I did. I removed the pan and still could not find the washer. I decided to clean up the pan and engine in preparation for the re- installation and leaned the pan against the wall to clean it. While walking by, I happened to glance down and saw the washer.

The Model T pan has a cup like indentation where the oil drain is located. There is a metal cover over this area with a slot in it and the washer had somehow managed to go through the slot and landed in the drain cup. It probably would never have caused a problem, but I would have been uncomfortable leaving it in there. At this point, I put the "T" back together, made the necessary adjustments, and was ready to go.

The tour was scheduled to start on July 5th with a barbecue at 5:00 PM. The touring would take place on July 6th and 7th with lunches and dinners each day. This year, there were 85 cars registered for the tour.

Marcia and I loaded up the Model T on our trailer and headed out from Kent, Washington on Thursday morning, July 5th, planning to arrive in Moscow, Idaho around 5:00 PM. We would drive about 300 miles over Snoqualmie Pass, down through Vantage, and onto the highway to the Pullman, Washington, Moscow, Idaho destination. I planned to stop for gas in Othello, Washington.

We pulled into a Union 76 station and the Ford Expedition we use to pull the trailer just stopped. I tried to start it back up again with no luck and was thinking that the fuel pump might possibly have failed. The manager at the 76 station found one of the two repair facilities that she thought were good.

Dewey came over and pulled the Expedition, with the trailer attached, over to his facility. He confirmed that it was the fuel pump. Normally, getting that part wouldn't be much of an issue, but we were in Othello, Washington, land of very few auto parts, and we were stuck about 125 miles away from our Moscow, ID destination until the Expedition was repaired. Dewey ordered the part from Spokane and said it would be there the next morning.

At this point, we decided to unload the Model T and use it to find a motel. As soon as I started to unload the "T", I noticed that the right front tire was flat and had to put the

spare on before we could do anything. Fortunately, we found a motel and spent the night in Othello.

Dewey called the next morning to let us know that the Expedition was ready to go. So, we loaded up the "T", thanked Dewey for his help, and headed off to Moscow, arriving about 3:30 PM. We missed the Thursday night "barbecue and the Friday tour of about 125 miles, but did make it for the dinner that night and had a nice 75 mile tour the next day. The finale was the banquet that night. So, we toured 75 miles and had a nice dinner.

Sunday morning, July 8th, we loaded up the "T" and headed back home. Everything was going great until we crossed the bridge over the Columbia River at Vantage. A car came up beside us and pointed to our trailer, indicating that something was wrong with the tires. We made it over the bridge and stopped in Vantage to check on the trailer. The left rear tire had blown out and the tread had wrapped around the brake drum. The trailer didn't come with a spare and I hadn't got around to buying one. Needless to say, I was a little upset with the trailer and myself.

I then remembered that my uncle had pulled his Airstream about 1000 miles on three wheels. So, I removed the wheel and removed the jack to see what would happen. The rear drum, with wheel and tire missing, was about 5 to 6 inches off the ground.

Off we went up Vantage Hill past Ellensburg and Cle Elum and on the way to Snoqualmie Pass with a three wheel trailer. Of course, we didn't make it to Snoqualmie Pass. Coming up to the Lake Easton off ramp, I noticed smoke coming from the trailer and immediately pulled off to the right side of I-90.

I inspected the trailer and found that the bracket that holds the middle joint of the trailer springs had broken loose from the trailer frame allowing the trailer to drop down so that the tire hit the fender. Marcia was getting a little upset at this point. I called AAA for help.

It is now about 4:15 PM and we are about 100 miles from home. AAA gives us a time of 5:45. At 5:30 we call AAA and the time has now moved to 7:30 with the flatbed truck coming from Ellensburg. I decide to move a tire from the right side of the trailer to the left side. We can now tow the trailer if necessary.

At 8:00 PM, I contact the tow company in Ellensburg to find out the status. They inform me that they cannot get to us until midnight. I decide to pull the trailer with the "T" to the off ramp at Lake Easton, about 6 blocks away. Lake Easton is a state park and we went to the picnic area to consider our next move. I called a friend to see if he might have a spare that would fit. No such luck.

The figured that the trailer would pull just fine empty, so I talked to the Park Ranger to see about leaving the "T" and coming back the next day to get it. It wasn't a problem for him and so, we decide to leave the "T". Marcia and I got in the Expedition, pulling the broken trailer, and headed for home. We made it home at 11:15 PM that night.

The next morning, I went down to Les Schwab and purchased two new wheels and tires. My friend, Bill Bratrud, came over and we welded up the spring bracket for the trailer. We were ready to head up to Lake Easton to get the "T". It was an uneventful drive back home and all was good again.

Epilogue: On Tuesday, July 10th, the alternator on the Expedition failed and on the following Thursday one of the spark plugs blew out of the engine. I'm starting to think it might be time to get a new tow rig.

My Wonderful Weekend

by Will and Rhonda Johnson
Olympia, WA

O nce upon a time, on a Friday morning, me and my side kick, Rhonda, took off on a journey to Coeur d'Alene, Idaho for the annual Car d'Lane Car Show.

We needed to pick up our support group at "I'm Not Norma's Restaurant" in Nisqually. It's a quaint little place down at the bottom of a rather large hill and in a swampy piece of ground. The food ain't bad and the waitresses are sassy.

I ordered the two egg special and split the meal with Rhonda. It was OK, but I thought I would never get my toast and after looking at some of my buddies burnt sacrifices, I didn't know if I still really wanted it.

After most were headed out the door the toast showed up and as luck would have it they were out of grape jam. The waitress said they never stocked it and I would just have to tough it out. Well, was I pretty cheesed about that! Being the quiet type that everyone knows me to be, I kept my trap shut, paid the bill, and left a rather small tip as a token of my appreciation.

Having gotten fuel earlier, I was not afraid to head out on the highway and after some minor delays, we were all on the road; all six of us. The traffic was snarly and mean, but after some loud cussing and some pornographic finger gestures, we were all finally in a row together. We had us a convoy.

Heading north on the big I-5, we wound our way up to Federal Way and then headed down the valley on Hwy 18, up through the bad lands of hell and on to the pass over the Cascade Mountain range. We took a needed pit stop and re-fueled at North Bend. From there, the road looked easy and the trip was hot and fast; just the way the ol' Merc liked it.

We rolled through Wenatchee at about 2:30 pm and then motored on to our final destination, a little Podunk town called Lake Chelan; a place where the men looked tired and the women looked tough. It's the kinda place where you wonder why it hadn't fallen off the map yet. It was hot and I was hungry. Rhonda, my copilot, had hardly said a word... yet.

We rounded a corner and a tired dog walked across the street. I figured there were so few cars going by he wasn't worried much. An ample sized woman and a small child smiled and wave as I rang the Bermuda bell on the old Merc. Its ding dong chime somewhat amused them, but you could see in their hollow eyes that we were not really welcome here. The air was dry and I was thirsty. If we could find our room, I sure hoped it had cold water!

Into view came the motel we had made reservations to stay in earlier that week and we rolled in briskly. Then it happened! Scrape, Crunch, Screech, Boing! That was the sound of my lake pipes scraping on the too high curb at this damned cheap motel! For cripes sake, I have driven hundreds of miles to a crummy town where I'm not wanted and now I'm tearing the crap outta the Merc!

Inside the registration office, Rhonda takes charge and I let her. This is the place where women shine. They're good at getting a room a little cheaper than us guys ever thought of. I'm not sure why this is true, but take it from me. It is. Meanwhile, I make light conversation with the natives in the office. After Rhonda does the haggling thing, we get a lower price and move promptly to our new digs.

Well, we unpacked, got back into the Merc, and phoned the others in our herd to tell them that dinner was not far away. Ya see, this outfit kinda travels on its stomach and so they followed us to our choice of chow. We ate Mexican. It wasn't all that bad, but the hot sauce for the free chips left a lot to be desired. This time, I tipped large and after some good conversation we decided to go to the local casino. We had heard it dropped coins like the big boys down in Las Vegas, but were soon disappointed, hearing they had stopped that practice out of fear that it might draw more people to the little tumbleweed barren town.

I watched a game of craps with my friends, Rick and Chuck, and later took to the roulette table. I was winning some, but Rhonda got me out of there while I still had my shirt and was actually a cool ten spot ahead. The next day would be a hot, grueling day at the car show and we needed to be rested. Knowing that we all needed to head back to our motel for a good night's sleep, everyone claimed they were ahead when we departed. If you believe that, I've got some bridges to sell.

We arrived back at our motel only to find the other tenant's had taken all the good parking spots. Surprise, Surprise! Gee, like that's never happened before. Well, after putting the Merc to bed in a place where I couldn't really keep an eye on it, we walked quite a piece to our room. It was on the second floor and as luck would have it the only floor in the whole place that an elevator didn't go to. For crying out loud, my luck was running so bad that I felt if

I bought a cemetery people would stop dying. With that thought in mind, I faded off to sleep… a place where things usually go a lot better for me.

I awoke to the smell of coffee and a bad show on the TV. A rather grouchy person was telling me to get my lazy ass up and do something. I awoke slowly and stirred a little. After a few cups of coffee and a good dose of the Jerry Springer program, I was finally coming around. Rhonda showered while I used the growler (a ritual carried over from home… because sometimes I can get a good peek at her).

We dressed and I ate a banana as we headed for the free continental breakfast. It was everything they said it would be and more. Everyone got their fill for the morning's events and we were all quite happy.

We found a back exit from the motel that was much kinder on the old Merc's Lake Pipes and soon we were in route to the car show. The 99er's, as we are sometimes called, drove in all our glory and proper form (we always were pretty good at that sort of thing, you know). We turned down the main street where one would expect the main entrance to the show would be.

A dude with a black hat quickly corrected us, indicating that we had to drive around the block and enter on a side

road. This too was crummy, 'cause as we rolled in we could see others driving in where we were told not to. (Man, talk about piss you off… cheezzz!)

We told the next parking person that we were a group, so he could put us all on the same side of the street. Wrong! He managed to screw it up good. Being the quiet and reserved club that we are, we took our lumps and parked the cars where we were told to. It was their show, after all.

Settling in, we set up our chairs and shined up our cars. We were now ready to go look at the other cars and mingle. Out of the corner of my eye, I notice a man I recognized approaching me. I had met this moron before and would do anything to avoid contact with him. He stopped to talk to Rick and I turned quickly and motioned to Chuck with a "Follow me, so we don't have to deal with this interloper" type of gesture.

I watched from afar as Rick squirmed and tried to find a way to get away from the derelict. Actually, I was just a little happy, considering he had beaten me out of a rat rod trophy at a previous show. There was this coin toss thing and I lost, but that's another story.

We looked at countless cars and my legs were growing tired. We sat down and shot the chit with Jerry, another good old 99er in our group. He was in a good mood, but the sun was too hot on that side of the street for me. I talked some and then retreated to the shade. The day wore on like a bad chafe on your bottom side. I felt sun stroked and bored. Everyone had left to look at the old iron and I was alone. Sometimes, I kinda like it when this happens. It makes me appreciate their company.

After a while, we (the men folk) gathered and left to go get lunch at a seedy restaurant in the middle of town. It had high ceilings and higher prices. The waiter was tattooed and pierced, and he sashayed when he walked. Boy, was I glad when a female of the species came to our table. The food was filling. We ate and left. I looked for a toothpick but was shocked to fine none! Kind of reminded me of the no grape jelly at the breakfast at Norma's... CRIPE!

We returned to our cars and some went to the "candy store" for booze. I stayed and drank what I brought. I had a head start from a bar earlier. I was offered tequila, but somehow it tasted something like rubbing alcohol. The peppermint schnapps was much better. I chase both with beer. Later on, when some of us were feeling no pain, we decided to go eat dinner. It was just going to be another dinner, but this would prove to be a weird experience.

The first place of choice was Senor' Frog, a quaint little place that smelled foul and the women would not eat there. I used the men's room and left. The stench was sickening. We proceeded to a bar and grill that only had seating on the outside top floor. This was OK except for the birds on the power lines and the transformer humming.

The waitresses were in top shape, as you would expect, climbing the steps and all. They were also well tattooed and after some remarks and careful prodding, confessed to other tattoos in unmentionable places. Gee, I sure was hoping she would mention them though.

The food was OK, the company was swell, and I was in a great mood. I told my friends how well I liked them, saying something like I wanted to hold on to them as long as I could. My good friend, Chuck, reminded me that

sometimes you can't always help yourself and one just slips away.

We paid, went back to the cars, and talked about the street dance that was about to take place on the bridge later. In the meantime, there was a small cruise of the town and so, with some help from the police, we cruised. It seemed like there were more police controlling traffic than there were cars on the cruise. When we returned, we found most of the others in the car show had split. It didn't bother us any and we proceeded to the street dance.

There was a jazz band and we were in the middle of a closed main road in the center of a long bridge. They were tuning up and the lead singer, a hot broad (blonde, fat, and sassy), was getting a bit tuned up also. We helped her open her flask of cheap booze. She looked like a beauty queen that had eaten too much carrot cake, but had a voice that made Madonna sound like a mangy alley cat.

Rhonda and I danced some, but she doesn't really like jazz and we left early. Some of our group stopped by and some stayed, but all in all, I guess we're just too old to have fun like we used to. It's sad but true. Life marches on and takes no prisoners.

Meanwhile, back at the motel, we were still looking for some fun. I got on the phone and invited all I could get a hold of to come over for some mudslides. It was 8:30 pm. Well, we were mostly unsuccessful as some were already in bed and others were in pj's and couldn't make it. We drank mudslides with Rick and Chuck. The mudslides were sweet and went down easy and pretty soon we were all tired. It had been a long day and so, Chuck and Rick headed out and we went to bed.

The alarm went off early! My tongue felt like the entire Iraqi Army had marched over it in their dirty bare feet. My head was pounding and the TV (now on) was blurry. I knew, at this point, that I would have to push myself to get up and going. We had company meeting us and we were to give them a lift back to god's country (the other side of the hill where we came from).

I got up, shaved, and took some aspirins with my coffee. Rhonda, having done her womanly things and prettied up a little, looked no worse for wear (How do they do that?) and we headed for the motel's continental breakfast.

We met our guest and she had breakfast with us. My culinary skills were greatly enhanced by Pam, who help me understand how the waffle maker worked. The waffles were great, but the buzzing when they were done sounded like an air raid to me (Ya see, I'd drank some the night before and...)

I gulped my coffee while I listened to Dave tell us about Security waking him up in the middle of the night to re-park his ride, because he was a little over the line. We all thought this was very petty of the security man and left the smallest of tips in the tip jar as a way to show our discontent.

Now, loading the car to leave is always a challenge and this time was no exception. We had too many things to begin with, had bought more in town, and had a guest besides. I let Rhonda do the tight packing. It's just another of those things that women are just better at than men and I'm not going to fight it.

We got it all in and went for air and gas. I needed extra air for the shocks with the extra load and we needed to take on some fuel. The gas gauge in the Merc never did work quite right and recently, it just quit. At the station, our guest paid for our fuel and I aired up the shocks. Rhonda recorded our mileage in her little car book. The Merc gets around 20 miles to the gallon and the log book keeps us smarter than the car. It's something she started doing before the gas gauge puked and has become a normal thing she just does. I don't really know why, but she just started doing it one day and I thought it was sorta cool. Now, it's sorta needed.

It was very hard getting everyone together for the convoy back. Some were still at the motel packing up and some were ready to go. Once everyone was ready to leave, and after some discussion at high levels took place about taking a side trip to Ellensburg, we were off faster than a speeding snail.

We went down and up and around, stopped for rest areas and peaches and went up one hell of a pass and stopped at a small ghost town. There was a garage sale that worked on the honor system. It was set up where you put money in a jar for the item you took. Gee, I can't believe that would work in our neck of the woods ('cause someone would take the money) but it worked well out here in the woods. We used the out houses and left. I found them stinky and dim.

Further on down the road, we dropped into Ellensburg to a place called the "Red Horse Diner" to eat lunch. This place is an all gas station memorabilia type of place and we had a ball taking pictures. Inside, the place is extra cool. I mean, I like the signs and car stuff, but the waitresses are all under 20 and cute. I couldn't help but wonder if they would have stayed out later than 8:30 with me and danced some more. Hmm.

I sat at the counter with Chuck and Donna (old 99er's), while I had some pop and a cheese sandwich. All too soon, we bid a fond farewell to Jerry and Pam in their '33 Ford roadster as they headed back over one pass and the rest of us over another.

As God is my witness, I really don't know how, but we got lost and screwed up in our directions. It didn't seem possible, but we sure did. Luckily, we were able to use our wireless communicators for further instruction. I have an onboard navigation GPS system. I put it to the test and all I could really tell was it kept demanding I turn left! Our travel guest thought we were crazy and I was starting to wonder myself. We eventually did catch up with the others and continued on. The hills and the river were all very scenic, the road winding like a poorly tied ribbon on a Christmas gift. It was all making for a great day.

When we stopped to look at the water, Lois (Dave's wife), gave me some red licorice. It made my tongue red, but tasted good. We proceeded up the pass and stopped midway to look at some bad rapids in the river that Rick had encountered with a rubber raft. They looked tough and mean, like a good place to get killed if you couldn't read the river. Rick was a tour guide once and told us of an event. He said it was worse then, because the water was running even faster than it was on this particular day. Holy cow!

We left and soon were told of a large rock on the pass that Chuck and Donna had the misfortune of running over in their award winning Ford convertible. We saw the rock and swerved in time. When we stopped at the summit, we looked their car over. It sounded a lot louder but still ran and drove ok. It sits low and was hard to look under, but we all agreed, the rock had messed up one of the exhaust pipes or muffler. We started down the west side of the pass and the road was much like a large worm with switch backs and "runaways" just in case you lost your brakes. It's not going to happen to me in my Merc. I had that happen already and the brakes are all new now, but that's another story.

We rolled into Packwood, where we split again, some heading down Hwy 12 and the rest of us deciding to go up through a back road short cut called Skate Creek. We heard it was paved now and in tip top shape. Yeah, it started to get kinda rough and Chuck kept calling me on the walkie talkie and telling me about the sparks shooting out the back of the Merc. Rick was ahead and trying to point out high spots for us. The Merc rides pretty low.

I started to hear a squeak, then a squawk. I thought it was something loose on the dash and with this bad road anything was possible. Some places were so bad you could lose a Volkswagen in the pot holes. The noise sounded like a small mouse eating my instruments.

I hate racket in my hot rods and this was starting to bug me. Well, now the noise sounded like a chipmunk and then like a parakeet. I was running out of critters to blame when I noticed the speedometer hand flopping back in forth in a very odd way. The noise was the speedometer and as soon as we stopped, I tried to unhook it, but it was stuck badly. I decided to live with it until we got home.

After some time, we got out onto the main road and traveled onto Ashford, Elbe, and up through La Grande. We rolled onto Mountain Highway and turned toward McKenna, where we stopped for coffee and dropped our

passenger off to her waiting husband. I was going to explain why it took so long but it didn't seem necessary.

We traveled home and unloaded the Merc. I covered it where it sat and called it a day. I was tired and it would have to wait till tomorrow for me to put it away with my other babies.

The Bug and the Girl Part Deux

by David Dickinson

Editor's note: In book two of The Old Car Nut Book series, I told of my 1969 VW Bug and how it lead to getting married in the story "The Bug and the Girl". This story tells about a road trip with the same girl that was saved by that same beloved Bug.

In the spring of 1976, my wife and I were living on the beach in San Diego, California. We were down there because I was stationed in the Navy as an instructor at Fleet Combat Training Center Pacific on Point Loma. Our home was one half of a duplex in the then affordable little hamlet of Ocean Beach, located about one block from the sand and endless view of water. It was a fun community to live in during those years and still is from what I have been told. At the time, it was filled with young people and the places and activities that we found exciting.

I have always been drawn to what are considered older cars no matter what the time period. For example, when I graduated from high school in 1970, I was driving a '41 Pontiac. But during this time in San Diego, I had my cherished '69 VW Bug and a '69 Dodge van that we were in the process of finishing with carpet, paneling, and tie dyed curtains. With only a handful of years on their titles, they could hardly be considered old. I needed something that was rapidly on its way to becoming a classic.

As fate might have it, a friend at work was leaving the area and had to sell his '60 VW Karmann Ghia convertible.

There was no doubt that I had to make it mine. Shortly before we made the move to the beach, I had sold my '60 Austin Healey 100/6 and needed another old topless "cruise around our little beach community" toy to replace it. A deal was struck and it was ours. I remember paying $1300 for it.

The car was in pretty good shape, having been restored in an inexpensive manner. The interior was new, although not original style fabric, and the paint had been done by a semi-skilled amateur. It ran reasonably well and we were having a great time with it.

As that summer of fun was winding down, we decided that we wanted to make the trip back to Washington to visit family and friends before fall turned into winter. What better time could be had than by taking a classic convertible up the west coast?

Prior to any such trip, of course, vehicle maintenance and preparation are in order. I changed the oil in the Karmann Ghia and bought all new tune up parts. I started by removing the plugs. On the right side are cylinders one and two. I spun them out and inspected them. They had a medium grey color, no oil residue, and an even burn. Looking good! On the left side, I pulled number four, located up front and saw the same color and burn as the right bank. Number three wasn't the same experience at all.

As I set the socket on the plug and started turning, the resistance was not normal. It did not pop loose as it should have. As I continued to apply pressure, the plug slowly started to turn, but never really loosened up. It finally reached the end of the threads and fell free. The cause was evident the moment I held the socket and plug up to inspect it.

Whoever had last put that plug in had made a mess of things. The plug had been cross threaded and I feared the worse. I immediately grabbed one of my new plugs and tried to install it. As I suspected, it would not seat into the threads and turn in a normal fashion. The threads were toast and car was not going anywhere soon. Not without some major attention.

I called my Senior Chief, the man in charge of the instructors' team that I was part of. He was a major motor head and just happened to be the head guy in charge of the Naval Training Center auto shop, as well. It was a great facility where you could take your car to work on and there were cars coming and going all the time, with young guys doing maintenance and minor repairs. It was not a place where you could take a car and leave it unattended for very long. Spots were valuable and if you needed an extended stay while waiting on parts, you had better use your down time to prepare for up time. The word of any given day was "finish it up and get it out" because there was always someone waiting to get their car in. The chief pushed me to the head of the line and started helping me speed the process of my rebuild along.

I ordered up the rebuild parts and had my machine work done. Down time was minimal and the push was on. My bride jumped in, got greasy, and did her usual great job of cleaning. Once I had everything I needed, I bolted it all together in record time and wrapped it up. Part of the down time was spent checking brakes and suspension, fuel lines, filters, and anything else that could be an issue. Once installed, the motor fired right up and ran great. I was confident that I was now ready for the road.

We had about a week to break in the rebuild, so I drove the car at every opportunity. While it was normally just a toy, it became transportation. I drove it to work, cruised around town when I was off, and took little side trips, basking in the joy of a fresh motor and the sweet purr of

Germany's finest. I was convinced it was ready for the trip from California to Washington State.

With that confidence, we started packing and planning our route. Of course, because of the time we had, or lack of time, the interstate was the asphalt path that would carry us in the following days. There was no time to take the coastal routes we had enjoyed in the past. So, the planning was minimal. With the limited amount of room available, packing was nominal, as well. We hit the road early on a bright, sunny, fall day, anxious to see family and friends and show off our old convertible. It was going to be a fun drive, even if it was just the freeway.

The first 100 miles was uneventful. We joked and laughed, discussing who we would get to see and the things we wanted to do in our short stay. We were really enjoying ourselves and our road trip in the little convertible. The sun was shining and the car was purring, but things suddenly took a turn for the worse. One moment all was well; the next moment, not so much. The purr became a loud banging noise and the car lost power. I couldn't believe my ears or abrupt misfortune.

I immediately pulled over to the shoulder and turned off the ignition. With a deep sigh and a questioning look from my better half, I shoved the door open and crawled out. With my spirits dampened, I stepped to the back of the car and popped open the engine compartment. Nothing seemed amiss. It was the same shiny clean space I had last viewed before hitting the road. I called up to my bride, telling here to turn the key to start it. It cranked and fired up. The jackhammer sound was still there. "Turn it off!" I yelled.

It's been nearly forty years, so I don't remember quite how it all went down, but we wound up with the car on a flat bed and us riding back to San Diego with the driver. I do remember that it wasn't like today, where I would dig a cell phone out of my pocket and call AAA.

We got back home and deposited the Karmann Ghia in front of the house. We were finishing off the interior of the Dodge van and it was not ready for a trip of any kind, so we transferred our goods to my beloved bug. I had owned this car for a number of years by then. It was the car that had taken me up and down the I-5 corridor many times, so it knew its way and I had the utmost faith that it would get us there and back without issue. I had not, however, done anything to prepare it for this upcoming journey.

I checked the oil and the air pressure in the tires. I knew the brakes were good and so, doing our best to put the failure of the little convertible out of our minds and resolved to the fact that it could be dealt with upon our return home, we hit the road.

Because we were traveling on the interstate, the trip was uneventful for the most part. We were simply traveling to reach our destination. However, as we crossed over from Oregon into Washington, I began to get a whiff of rotten eggs. We had not packed any food, but I asked my wife if there was something she could think of to cause such a smell. Neither of us could come up with anything, so we continued on thinking that we had run over something that had a lingering odor.

About the time we were passing through Olympia, the state capital of Washington State, the smell grew even stronger and the car was not running and performing as well as it always did. By the time we had traveled the remaining 30 miles to her parent's home, the car seemed on its last leg and the odor was nearly intolerable.

After unloading our belongings from the car, I had the opportunity to remove the rear seat and inspect the battery. It was a small miracle that we had made it to our final destination. In fact, it's amazing that we did not suffer great injury. The battery had boiled over and had we hit any kind of large bump or been hit by another car, the possibility of a spark under that back seat would have blown the battery to smithereens!

The next day I bought a new battery and changed the oil. The car was once again running like a champ. I checked the charging system and it was fine. The trip back to San Diego should be uneventful, assuming there were no other issues that I was unaware of. I guess you can never be completely certain and the road ahead always has its way of revealing the unexpected.

Once again, my beloved bug had saved the day and survived another long distance haul up and down the left coast. We had a great visit and the trip back down the coast was, well, uneventful.

Of course, I wish I still had that car, but it was sold before we moved back Tacoma, Washington and ultimately replaced with a 1965 Impala SS, which provided its own adventures up and down the coast.

The Road to POCA
Pantera Owners Club of America

by Chris Kimball

Editor's note: Chris Kimball provided a couple of stories for the first book in The Old Car Nut Book series entitled "Pandora" and "Hot Car" about his DeTomaso Pantera. These stories were well written and very entertaining, explaining what a character in her own right that "Pandora" is. He also sent in this journal of a road trip he took in "Pandora." While it is a rather long piece, it is broken into days and as such, each day is a story unto itself. I have chosen to include the whole journal rather than edit it down in size. I hope you enjoy Chris's trip as much as I did.

The Green Pool

After spending most of Saturday evening and Sunday morning packing, I left my home in University Place at about 1:30 PM heading south. I planned on meeting my mom and younger sister at a Starbucks in Centralia, which is about an hour down the freeway from University Place. I took the scenic, back road to DuPont, planning on joining I-5 after gassing up and adding some air to my tires.

While adding air to the tires, I noticed something strange. A large pool of green liquid was slowly spreading from under my Pantera. I reasoned it could be the result of one of three things; my paint could be gradually dissolving and dripping off the car, I may have accidentally run over a Martian while pulling into the gas station (and for all I knew, part of him might still have been wedged between the cooling pipes), or I had a coolant leak.

I had conflicting emotions. On the one hand, I was very frustrated that I had only made it 20 miles before Pandora was up to her old tricks and on the other, I was glad I had only traveled 20 miles before Pandora was up to her old tricks.

I have a mechanic friend, Larry, who I've gotten to know quite well over the last few years. This bonding has occurred not only because he and Pandora have been on a first-name basis since shortly after she came into my life, but also because both my sons' first cars are classics and Larry is getting to know them, too.

I called Larry and asked if he would mind taking a look at "Piddling Pandora." Fortunately, he said he had time to do so, and I figured the leak was small enough I could make it to his shop without going dry and ruining my engine. I turned around and headed north.

I arrived at his shop and after close inspection, while utilizing a handy pump device which created pressure in the cooling system, the location of the leak was discovered. It's interesting that Pandora is now involved in Seattle's latest social debate, that being whether or not it is a fine-able offense to ask a woman not to breastfeed in public. You see, Pandora had a nipple problem. On one of the steel pipes running from the top of the radiator to the cooling tubes, there was a small nipple that had been closed off by a rubber cap and a hose clamp. Embarrassing as it is to admit, I confess that the last time I replaced the radiator I over-tightened the nipple-stopper's hose clamp, causing it to slice into the cap. The slice was just big enough so that during a spirited drive on a warm day, the coolant would leak from the faulty cap. Larry thought that the nipple may have originally been hooked to a valve and used as an air bleeder. I

just assumed anything from Italy would have as many nipples as possible.

Larry repaired the problem (or as he put it, "MacGyvered" the problem) and I departed South once again. Since the cause of the leak was diagnosed and fixed so quickly, I called my mom and sister and ended up having that Starbucks meeting we had planned, including a Venti Peppermint Mocha Frappuccino, made with breve, extra-sweet, double-pumps, two packs of white sugar, double-blended, with whip.

Driving to Hermiston was great. The scenery is fabulous and the weather was perfect; for a while. As I approached Hermiston, I noticed some bright flashes coming from over the horizon. I wasn't sure if they were caused by lightning or spotlights, but a few moments later I saw the flashes were, indeed, lightning. Huge sheet lightning, threatening clouds, and giant lightning bolts suddenly seemed only a mile or so dead-ahead. In a moment it was pouring rain, and then less than three minutes later, dry again, although the air felt like air feels right before a storm.

Nevertheless, I arrived at the Comfort Inn with no more precipitation issues. As I got out of the car in front of the hotel, I heard a voice calling my name from above. I thought maybe it was God letting me know it was a miracle I had made the first leg of the journey without any serious mechanical  malady, or without getting a ticket. I did hit 120 very briefly during my drive here, but only because the last time Larry looked at my spark plugs he said I was taking it "too easy" on the motor and needed to punch it once and awhile.

It wasn't God, however. It was Clarke Hamm, who along with his wife, Wilma, were trailering their Pantera to the Fun Rally. The idea was that I was supposed to get here first and they would catch up.

Three more days of travel to go before reaching Phoenix and then, after four days of fun, another four-day trip back. If Pandora runs as well as she did after the nipple incident was resolved, this will be a very fun trip.

Maybe I could write a song about my experiences; "By the time I get to Phoenix, she'll be dribbling... "

A Semi-terrifying Encounter

MONDAY, APRIL 23
Day Two of 2012 POCA Fun Rally Journal

On day two of the trek from University Place to Phoenix for the POCA Fun Rally, things started out well. I awoke just prior to the alarm going off, had breakfast and loaded up. I was surprised that Clarke and Wilma had already left with their truck and trailer, but then I remembered the old Aesop's fable, and had to smile. Then I stopped smiling because I remembered I wouldn't be able to use that analogy in my journal log today, because in the story of the tortoise and the hare, it was the hare that left first. D'oh! Clarke told me at dinner this evening that their Pantera only has about 9,000 miles on it, so that explains the reason it's being cosseted.

The drive out of Hermiston was beautiful. The weather was sunny, the roads relatively free from traffic, and there were numerous sweeping curves and long straightaways of the type that Panteras and their owners love. The weather was definitely getting warmer, though, and after a couple of hours I decided to forget about gas mileage. I rolled up the windows and turned on the air-conditioning! The necessity for air conditioning was made apparent when I attempted to enjoy a Rolo. Upon unwrapping said candy, instead of finding individual morsels, I found a glob of chocolate-caramel goo. Fortunately, I managed to get most of it in my mouth instead of on my clothes, or worse, my Recaros.

Although the car performed great, there was one very harrowing experience. I was driving about 70 mph and was gradually passing a semi which was on my right. It was a typical two-lane highway and I'd been passing vehicles in the slow lane all day. The truck was probably traveling at 65 or so, because I was passing him very slowly. Ahead, in the right lane was another semi which I assumed was lumbering up the hill at a rate similar to his. There were no brake lights, no emergency flashers and no turn signals to indicate otherwise. As the semi and I approached the semi ahead, however, it became apparent that the truck ahead of us was at a dead stop with mechanical problems. I think the driver of the semi I was passing realized the gravity of the situation at the same time I did, because I heard his brakes engage just at the moment I realized he couldn't avoid a rear-end collision with the disabled semi without swerving into my lane which would have put a quick end to my trip to the Fun Rally.

I thought for absolute certain that I was about to witness a horrendous crash of the semi to my right rear-ending into the semi in front of him, at 65 miles per hour. Just as I pulled ahead of the semi I was passing, he immediately swerved into the left lane, missing the back end of the disabled semi by feet. Not yards; feet. How he was able to move such a huge rig so quickly is beyond me. As I continued my drive, and as my heart rate began to get back to normal, I wondered how they would be able to move the disabled semi off the road, and if there would be a collision imminent because some other driver might not be as lucky as I.

I was 45 minutes from Twin Falls, Idaho when my stereo inexplicably went silent. I wasn't sure why, although I had noticed that my power antenna was having trouble fully extending. Sometimes it would have no problems and other times it just didn't seem to have enough energy to reach its full potential. I'm pretty sure that has a lot to do with age. It turns out my iPod may have just gotten too warm and temporarily shut down. So rather than listening to music, I began concentrating on the sounds of the Pantera.

There's a saying my wise English mother oft quotes, "Where ignorance is bliss, it is folly to be wise." Sounds

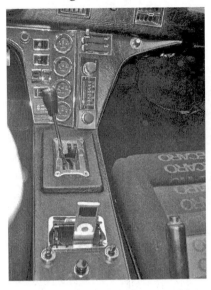

great until you own a classic car. Blissful ignorance has cost me a bundle with Pandora! So I'm listening to the sounds I don't usually hear, and all of a sudden there is a noise resembling a jet aircraft overhead. Except the sound wasn't coming from overhead; it was coming from down below. I put the car in neutral and revved the engine. That made no difference, so I surmised it wasn't a problem with the motor. I tapped the brakes, still no change. I swerved to the right and left to see if that would make a difference, but the sound remained constant.

I wasn't sure if I should take the chance to continue to Twin Falls, or pull off at the next exit. I needed a sign. I needed a miracle! At that very moment, I saw the sign, the sound stopped, and I was in Bliss.

Actually, what happened was I saw a sign that said "Miracle Hot Springs, next exit," the pavement changed from the rough surface which was causing the sound to a smooth surface so the tire noise stopped, and at that very moment I was passing through the town of Bliss, Idaho. Yes, the Lord works in mysterious ways.

Tomorrow is a long 8.5 hours (gulp!) of driving. Guess I'd better put the remaining Rolos in the cooler.

Excessive Speed Puts a Dent in My Enthusiasm

TUESDAY, APRIL24
Day Three of 2012 POCA Fun Rally Journal

I had a good sleep last night in preparation for today's journey. What Google Maps described as an 8.5 hour drive to Las Vegas from Twin Falls turned out to be 6.5 hours, including a 45-minute lunch stop. I'm not exactly sure how that happened... :)

The reason I slept so well didn't have as much to do with the drive as it did with the fact that for dinner last night, Clarke and Wilma Hamm and I ate at the "Golden Corral." Now I know some of you reading this may not be culinary experts and have not had the chance to dine at such establishments as Morton's Steakhouse, El Gaucho, The Metropolitan Grill, The French Laundry, Per Se, Aragawa, Gordon Ramsay, Acquarello, Alberto Ciarla, and other exquisite eateries, so you may not be familiar with the Golden Corral. Let me tell you, though, that place rocks! For $13.00 you get all you can eat and that includes the cost of your beverages!

I decided to have something nutritious so I could tell my wife I didn't eat only ice cream on this trip. I thought a small salad would suffice. Well, by the time I took a little of each available salad item, the plate was stacked several inches high and topped with about a half-cup of honey-mustard dressing. Once that was consumed, I just had to try the "flash-fried" shrimp and tilapia. That's right; the chef just threw some raw shrimp and fish into a pan and cooked it right there, while I watched. Such excitement defies description. I also needed to try the deep-fried Calamari, clam strips, and, yes, more shrimp. But, this shrimp wasn't "flash-fried," it was deep fried; a subtle but noticeable difference.

By the time I had eaten most of this feast, and imbibed a couple of root beer floats, I decided I was too full for dessert. Clarke, however, egged me on and I was compelled to visit the dessert table.

I marveled at the array of cakes, pies, brownies, and more, but then, suddenly, I saw it. There, standing before me as an alter to sweetness, stood a three-tiered chocolate fondue fountain! I was very close to doing an Agustus Gloop straight into the thing, but as I looked around the area, it appeared by the drips of chocolate residue sprayed everywhere, that someone had beaten me to it. Nevertheless, I did enjoy a couple of huge strawberries smothered in chocolate. And some angel-food cake.

That's why I slept so well.

I received my wake-up call promptly at 7:45 AM, showered, and went to breakfast, only to find that Clarke and Wilma had, once again, already left the building. For a moment I wondered if they purposely departed before I showed up for the complimentary oatmeal, because they couldn't bear to sit and wait forty minutes for me to finish eating what a normal person could consume in five minutes.

I jumped in the car and she started right up. I stopped at a local gas station, checked the oil, and hit the road.

And what a road it was. Clarke and Wilma did a great job of choosing the route. The scenery was fabulous with green trees, rolling fields, awesome rock formations, stunning valleys, quaint farmhouses, and best of all, long straight roads punctuated by long, sweeping curves. The temperature was, for the majority of today's drive, perfect. One window halfway down was all that was needed to fill the car with a cool breeze filled with the pleasant aromas of summer. Well, except when I was driving by those quaint farmhouses that tend to have big fields, fertilized with a substance that is anything but quaint. Odoriferous, yes; quaint, no.

Traffic was minimal. There were a few times I had no choice but to pass slower vehicles and to do so safely necessitated rather high speeds. One wants to spend as little time as possible in the wrong lane, you understand.

Although for the majority of the time the cruise control was set about 4 to 5 miles-per-hours above the conservative legal limit (they're not rules as much as... guidelines...), there were times when I drove a bit faster. Pandora is very comfortable traveling between 110 and 120 (well, that's what she told me, anyway).

I passed through a number of small towns along the way, stopping in Ely, Nevada for gas. While there, I spent a few minutes eating some more of Vicki's homemade banana bread and drinking another Frappuccino. I should note that due to the generous size of the banana bread loaf, my need to purchase food has been minimal. I've only spent about $25.00 so far. Of course, after spending a couple of hours at the Golden Corral, I'm sure I could go without any additional food for a week or more.

While sitting at the picnic table next to the Shell gas station and food mart, I noticed something I had seen in so many other small towns; empty buildings. Most of them had "for lease" or "for sale" signs in the shuttered windows. Some had no such signs, and were simply vacant; falling into disrepair. I wondered if the abandoned cafe across the street had once been owned by a family with high hopes for their business. Perhaps it had even been started by a grandparent, only to fall victim to the brutal economy of the last few years. Las Vegas has been hit especially hard by the real-estate collapse, and the many broken dreams in the shape of bankrupt businesses is a sad, silent tribute to the wretched state of the area's economy. I was glad there was a Shell gas station in that town. Without that, there would be almost no jobs for the local residents.

Fortunately, Pandora's behavior had been anything but wretched. Today she purred like a kitten... or rather a panther. So much so that I simply couldn't resist the temptation of a long, flat stretch of roadway on which I found myself.

For the record: I've always been one who has felt it important for people to accept the consequences of their actions. So I will take full responsibility for what happened. I was flirting with the redline and what I think must have happened was that a combination of strong airflow, road surface causing the car's body to flex, and the possibility I may not have fully closed my gas fill cover, caused the cover to fly open. I didn't notice it for a while, but eventually I glanced in my rear-view mirror and saw that the gas fill cover was wide open, catching the wind as if it were a kite.

I immediately pulled over to assess any damage that might have occurred.

The cover had flown open with such force that it overextended, causing the ribs on the surface to create four small dents in the pillar. Very annoying. The dents are very close to the stress cracks that seem to form on every Pantera, above the gills and toward the back. At this point, any chance that a person might not have noticed the stress cracks has been eliminated as the person will immediately notice the dents, then look closer and see the stress cracks as well.

I've been wanting to have a little body work done to get rid of those cracks, and now I guess I have an excuse to do so at the same time the dents are being removed.

I also noticed when applying brake pressure to slow down from triple-digit speeds, if I really push hard, a throbbing effect begins to occur. I'm hoping when I get to Phoenix someone will be able to help me determine if my rotors are warped.

I mentioned earlier that the weather started out perfect. Well, about an hour outside of Vegas, things started to warm up a bit. "No problem," I thought, smugly, "I have air conditioning." I had just been bragging to Clarke and Wilma that I didn't even bother having my A/C recharged for this trip, since it had been working so well. I guess you can see what's coming.

After a few minutes of being cool, I noticed I was getting warmer. Sure enough, the air coming from the vents was only about 1 degree cooler than the air outside. There's one more thing I'll need address in Phoenix.

I also think I have my stereo issue figured out. At first I thought it might be that Vicki secretly installed something in the stereo so that if I tried to listen at a volume level she thinks is inappropriate, the entire system would shut down. It appears, however, that the amplifiers have some sort of thermal overload protection circuit that has nothing to do with a concerned wife.

Since I have a bunch of tools wrapped in towels surrounding and on top of the amplifiers in the front trunk, after extended listening to classic rock at the volume for which it was, the lack of sufficient head dissipation causes the amps to go into "protect" mode. Therefore, it's no big deal. After turning off the system for about five minutes, everything resets and it's back to 38 Special.

One last thing. I'm in a very nice hotel, but they have adopted a policy that strikes me as very silly. Apparently, to help the planet, they now have a system whereby in order to operate the room's air conditioner, one must insert his or her key card into a special slot found on a control panel located on the wall just inside the door. Without the key, the cooling/heating unit will not function. The idea, of course, is to prevent a guest from leaving the room with the unit running. Heaven forbid the guest might want to come back to a room with a comfortable temperature! That might upset the entire ecological balance of the planet and cause more global warming, unless it was during the summer, in which case it would cause global cooling, since everyone would be leaving the air-conditioning on.

What is hilarious about all this is that to keep the guests happy, the friendly front-desk woman simply explains the process, and then gives each guest two keys. One key is to be used to open the door, and the other left in the control panel so the heating/air conditioning unit can keep running... Oh yes, and all the extra keys that will need to be manufactured for this? Yes, they are all made of plastic, a petroleum based product. So much for saving the planet.

But hey, I'm doing my part. I finally got Pandora to quit burning oil!

Sweaty Driver, Cool Car

WEDNESDAY, APRIL 25
Day Four of 2012 POCA Fun Rally Journal

I slept in a little this morning (Wednesday, April 24) since my Google Map indicated a drive of only about 5.5 hours from Las Vegas to Chandler. Based on recent history, I figured I could make it in about 4 hours--HA!--did I have another think coming!

The complimentary breakfast provided by the Comfort Inn was excellent, and exactly like every other breakfast at all the other Comfort Inns so far; except for the Comfort Inn located in Twin Falls. That Comfort Inn is no longer a Comfort Inn. It is now an "AmericInn." Those wacky advertising folks. It's almost like they're mad men (mad at the general public, it appears). Who can forget a name like "AmericInn." See, it's like saying "American," except the last part is "Inn," as in a place a traveler stays. Wow! That's marketing brainpower at work. What was particularly amusing was that even though it's been a year since the transition, there is still no sign indicating that the buildings have anything to do with "AmericInn," or anything else, for that matter. There is a large structure outside the hotel  that one would guess used to identify the complex as a "Comfort Inn," but now is just a blank monolith. I have a suspicion that the corporation spent so much money on research and development (let alone focus groups) coming up with the name "AmericInn" that they had nothing left over to pay for details such as signage. Confusing things further, the sign on the freeway alerting drivers that there was lodging at that exit, had both the Comfort Inn logo, as well as the "AmericInn" logo. The freeway sign was smaller than the sign in the hotel parking lot, so apparently there were enough funds to cover that expense. By the way, the breakfast at the "AmericInn" was identical to the ones at the Comfort Inns.

I didn't even look for Clarke and Wilma; I knew they were halfway to Chandler by the time I finished my Froot Loops. And bacon. And eggs. And Yoplait. And orange juice. And apple juice with Metamucil mixed in, along with another vitamin powder stuff my wife encourages me to add to my morning juice. I have no idea what the wife-recommended powder does, but ever since I took out that multi-million dollar life-insurance policy naming her as beneficiary, I've noticed the color of the powder is different than it used to be. And... now... I'm.... getting... sleepy.

I added a quart of oil (not bad, considering I'd traveled 1250 miles and started the journey a half-quart low), filled the gas tank, and got underway about 10:30 AM.

Again, the weather was relatively cool, with overcast skies and a slight breeze. As the day progressed, the air became more and more humid, which isn't a problem if one has a working air conditioner.

I promised myself I would behave better today, in terms of speed limits, and at first that was, indeed the case. It's a good thing, too, because just outside of Las Vegas, I encountered something amazing. More than 10 police officers in cars and on motorcycles were clustered along one section of road, summarily pulling over almost everyone. The speed limit was 55, but seemed as if it should have been higher. It's almost as if they planned it that way. I immediately glanced at my speedometer, and saw I was traveling at 63.

I'll never forget the image of that number displayed on the screen of my GPS.

You know how when something traumatic happens you experience that phenomenon called "Flashbulb Memory?" What happens is that when you learn of a shocking event, you remember your exact location and all sorts of details about what you were doing at the very instant you received the news. People always use "the day Kennedy was shot" as the example. I know I'll never forget that day. I was sitting in my room, playing with 1/24 scale, di-cast model of a split-window Corvette.

Today, however, I certainly was exceeding the speed limit by eight miles-per-hour in plain view of all those police officers with their fancy little radar guns. Just as I was about to reach for my wallet (literally and figuratively), yet another Pandora Miracle occurred. They may have aimed their radar guns at me, but they missed! Either that, or they took one look at me and thought, "We don't want to mess with that hombre." Understand, I hadn't shaved since I left University Place.

So, after that close call I was very mindful of the posted speed limits and drove accordingly. Until about 30 minutes later. Once again, the road beckoned and I succumbed.

Pandora is a demanding mistress. She forced me to travel at some very exciting speeds before I once again began to remind myself that I really didn't need an- other moving violation on  my record. My older sister works at Propel Insurance, and was just talking with me the other day about how in June all the "problems" would be off our collective household driving record, and she might be able to provide us insurance at a good price. Boy, would a 125 mph ticket have blown that plan!

I stopped to refuel the car with gas and me with two of the remaining four slices of home-made banana bread in the self-proclaimed "historic" town of Wickenham, or Wickedham, or Weinerham or Wickerchair or something. Whatever its name, it's in Arizona. I found a couple of vacant picnic tables and commandeered one on which to spread out my consumables and paperwork. I've been tracking my fuel economy. Pandora is returning an Obama-pleasing 20 miles-per-gallon. Sure, it's no Chevy Volt, but, that's not bad for a high performance sports car like Pandora.

In addition to the banana bread, I also enjoyed water, milk, a Yoplait I borrowed from the Comfort Inn, and a bunch more English candy. One thing I must admit about Arizona; it's very convenient when needing to use small, frozen pats of butter. In Washington, trying to spread hard butter means the bread just disintegrates. In Arizona, simply place the four pats of rock-solid, frozen butter on the surface of the bread, wait five seconds, and the butter will literally spread itself. Amazing!

Back on the road, my hard-working GPS indicated less than 60 miles to Phoenix, so I figured I'd be in Chandler a little earlier than I had originally planned. I discovered a new feature of my GPS; a little red flag appeared in the upper, left-hand corner of the screen, with a number next to it. I soon realized what that meant. It meant that there was some sort of traffic delay, and the number was the amount of minutes I should expect to be delayed.

Really, the problem could be boiled down to two words: rush hour (and I don't mean the 1998 movie starring Jackie Chan). There was something else that surprised me. I thought Bridgeport Way in University Place had the most stop lights per square inch of any road in the nation. When University Place incorporated, all the newly-elected council men and women decided to upgrade everything in town and started adding roundabouts, stop lights, plants all over the place, and worst of all, lowering all the speed limits. Surprisingly, I was in for quite an unpleasant surprise. The big surprise was that there are more stop lights on a street called "Grand Avenue" than even on Bridgeport Way. Grand Avenue is located in, where else, the town of Surprise, Arizona. Surprised? I was. Not surprisingly, I had to drive right through it to get to Chandler.

What this meant, was that it took 90 minutes to finally get to the hotel. It was stop and go and stop and go and stop and go, all the while being stuck behind semis, giant vans, or someone who is a professional landscaper and although probably being a very good landscaper is a terrible trailer-loader. There were lots of large, heavy things precariously stacked randomly on the trailer which could scratch a Pantera's paint quite badly if any of them happened to fly off the back of the trailer when accelerating toward the next stop light which was, of course, only 10 feet further ahead.

It was 95 degrees with 345 percent humidity, and I had no air conditioning. It was miserable. There was a silver lining, however. Pandora did not overheat. In fact, although for the first time on the entire trip the second of her three fans kicked on, the third, which is set to trigger at 195 degrees, stayed dormant. Indeed, the block temperature never exceeded 190, and the ultra-non-reliable original-equipment, Italian gauge never read above 210.

I, on the other hand, don't have the benefit of any fans, let alone a Dakota Digital fan relay system, so I knew by the time I get to Phoenix, she'll be running... away from me due to my smell!

I finally rolled into Chandler without incident, and the POCA and PNW Vice President, Mike Thomas, was there to greet me. Having flown in, he was fresh as a new K&N air filter, while I was more akin to a well-used, Harbor Freight shop rag. Still, seeing the four or five Panteras displayed on the patio area adjacent to the POCA hospitality suite inspired me to whip out the Griot's micro-fiber cloths and Speed Shine and get to work making Pandora as beautiful as possible.

Something I'm very proud is the fact I am doing my part in keeping the ecological balance of the planet in check. Did you ever see the 1971 film, "The Hellstrom Chronicles?" It predicts a world where insects end up taking over the entire planet. Well, as long as Pandora and I have anything to say about it, I can assure you that flying insects will never take over the world. That's because a significant percentage of them are to be found covering my Pantera's windshield. In fact, as I was driving this afternoon, something hit my arm, which was hanging out the window in a vain attempt to coerce some air to enter the cockpit and flow behind my back to evaporate the several cups of sweat that had accumulated there. The object proceeded to bounce into my lap (in a very specific place in my lap, which I don't think I need to describe), and it was then I identified the object as a bee.

I would have panicked, swerved all over the road, and probably become a statistic, except that my acute powers of observation allowed me to deduce that the beast was deceased. I flicked it to the floor and at the first stop light ejected it from the car. Another close call with a bee (ask me sometime about my motorcycle, a 70 mph bumblebee and a very swollen ear).

Currently, my overriding concern is to get my air conditioning fixed as soon as possible. To that end, I approached

"Coz." His real name is Jim Cozzolino and he is one of the event organizers. Why he goes by the nickname, "Coz" is a mystery. It must be just becoz. Anyway, he has a friend who has a shop in Phoenix that is very familiar with Panteras and can take a look at my faulty A/C. Jim actually called the guy at 6:30 PM using the guy's private phone line to get the appointment arranged for me.

Now, I know you're thinking, "Chris, you idiot! Don't you remember what happened the last time you turned your car over to someone's 'mechanic friend'? It disappeared for three months!" Yes, yes, that's true, but this time I'm not letting Pandora out of my sight! The only bummer is that the appointment had to be set for 9:00. That's AM, not PM, which is a huge sacrifice for me while on vacation. That's a sacrifice I'm willing to make, though. You know what they say, "Keep the women in your life happy, and your life will be happy." By women (plural), I'm referring, of course, to Vicki first, my mom second, and THEN Pandora!

I'm now all settled in my room, which is quite nice, although it lacks the fridge and microwave oven found in Comfort Inns, and, of course, their sign-less cousins, the "AmericInns."

Tomorrow I'll be visiting the track to watch those brave souls who risk life and limb and really expensive Italian body parts (the cars', not their own) by racing around in circles in their Panteras. Then it will be on to the Rawhide Western Town and Steakhouse for dinner. I think I'll go up to the band and request a Van Halen song, just to see how they react.

I know that all the volunteers who put on this event work very hard, but I think Judy McCartney deserves special Kudos. I watched her working the registration desk this evening, and that is a ton of work. Good job, Judy!

A Friend of a Friend Indeed

Up at 7:00 AM, way too early, so I could get to "Back to Basic Automotive", the auto repair place owned by the friend of Coz, by 9:00 AM. On the way, I dealt with a little bit of Phoenix rush-hour traffic, but still made it to the shop 15 minutes early.

Dave Hocking, the owner, was there to greet me. Before I go any further, let me give a huge "thank you" to Dave and his crew. He had planned on leaving mid-morning to get ready for a vacation in Wyoming, but agreed to see Pandora before he left. I explained the problem (too much sweat, too little cool) and he got the car on the lift almost immediately. By the time the project was completed, it was 2:30 PM.

That's the way it is with Panteras, though. You start on what seems to be a small project, and all of a sudden it becomes a huge project leading to another and another, ad  infinitum. In this case, the problem was the small coolant leak at the sight glass. I was told by someone that all that would be needed to fix that problem was a new "O" ring, which was easy to find at any hardware store. Well, it turns out there are a pair of nylon washers on either side of the sight glass, but no "O" rings whatsoever (another Pantera myth dispelled). Dave and his mechanics took care of that right away, but wait... there's more!

Next, they discovered that an A/C hose had split, causing all the R12 to split, too... into the atmosphere!

But wait, there's even more! Order now and we'll also include a cracked fitting on the condenser, some loose header bolts, a necessary clutch adjustment, and a cooling shield for the new A/C hose. Now how much would you pay? Well, don't answer, because while all this was going on, I also did a little project of my own. I covered the bottom of the ashtray/iPod dock with head shield. I've been wanting to do that for some time, and it was nice that I had the chance to do so today. I also had the chance to read an entire issue of World magazine and a complete Road and Track, too. At noon, David, his crew and I shared a lunch of Kentucky Fried Chicken. It was no complimentary "AmericInn" breakfast, but it was good, nonetheless.

I left with a properly adjusted clutch and really cold A/C, at a price that is too low to print! It pays to know the right people. Thanks, Dave! Thanks Coz!

I've often wondered if Pantera owners are nice people before they own Panteras, and that's the reason they buy them. Panteras just appeal to nice people. Or, it could be that people who buy Panteras become nicer just because they own one.

It also might be that since people who experience a shared trauma form a lifelong bond. Pantera owners have that bond. There's nothing like finding out there are others who have parts falling off their cars with some regularity to create a connection that lasts a lifetime.

After leaving Dave's shop, I drove over to the track which is a short distance from the hotel. It was great to see a number of Panteras racing around the track at speeds befitting cars of that pedigree. I ran into (figuratively, of course) Pantera guru extraordinaire, Mike Drew, but we didn't have time to talk much. I think he was in a hurry to chase after a beautiful, white car occupied by an attractive woman. It reminded me of that scene in American Graffiti with the Thunderbird and Suzanne Somers. Of course, I might be completely wrong about what I thought I saw. More than once I've made assumptions and found out later, much to my embarrassment, that my impressions were completely off base. For example, 25 years ago I saw a beautiful flute player who smiled at me, and I thought that meant she wanted to marry me and help me amass a large collection of high-dollar collector cars. OK, so sometimes I'm half-right...

When watching the cars tear around the track, I was careful to choose a seat that was in the shadow of one of the large billboards mounted to the top of the grandstand. Even though it wasn't as hot as yesterday, it was still plenty hot. At one point, the sun went behind a cloud and things were actually quite pleasant for a moment. It was then I heard a woman's voice behind me say, "When the sun goes behind a cloud is gets so cold. I should have worn layers." I couldn't believe what I was hearing! Layers? When the temperature is, like, 80 degrees? You must be kidding! I turned and introduced myself to Scott and Martha Miller. I asked where they were from, and it all made sense when they told me they lived in San Diego. They're used to being hot! I explained that when my sisters and I were young and complaining we were cold, my English mother (who "lived through a war, you know") used to always tell us to wear layers. At the time our home was heated to the extravagant temperature of 68 degrees. Remember, Jimmy Carter was President then; although I think he advocated sweaters, not layers.

After a couple of hours at the track, and consuming a couple of Twinkies and a Frappuccino (yes, the little vendor truck actually had some Starbucks drinks!) I headed back to the hospitality suite and spent a few minutes listening to John Taphorn, Bob Reid, and others discussing the particulars of trying to organize the members so that they could position their cars for a group picture. I made the hilarious observation that it was like herding cats. I only got a courtesy laugh until I explained, "You know, Panteras... cats... Pantera means "Panther" in Italian and a Panther is kind of like a big cat..." I then got two courtesy laughs.

At 6:00 PM I joined a group in the lobby to take a shuttle to the Rawhide Western Town and Steakhouse. Before dinner, I wandered around the "Western Town" part of the Western Town and Steakhouse grounds, which consists of a main street lined with buildings designed to look as if they were built in the Wild West during the mid-1800s.

One peculiarity I noticed was that no matter what any particular building was called... "Saloon," Livery," "Blacksmith," General Store," etc... the buildings were actually either food vendors of some sort or souvenir stores. Another example of marketing brilliance, no doubt. I can just imagine the advertising executives chuckling to themselves, "Yes, of course some of the guests might catch on that 'The Rawhide General Store' is filled with cheesy, western-themed trinkets, and may therefore pass by without going in. But they'll never guess that the very next building, 'Silver Spur Western Wear' is filled with exactly the same stuff!"

There was one store just devoted to toys. I wondered how long the western toy store would last if it were located in Washington DC. The entire window display was made up of dozens of realistic, toy revolvers.

I bought a rainbow sherbet ice cream cone at the "Rootin-tootin' Olde-Tyme Ice Cream Emporium" (that's not really its name--I can't remember what it was called), and then decided to pay $5.00 to see a real-live gunslinger show at the "Six Gun Theater" featuring "The Rough Riders". I was a bit bewildered as I tried to determine if the theater was named after a half-dozen weapons, or one particular style of pistol that had the capacity for six bullets. Before I could grab a bucket of paint to add the missing hyphen, however, the show started. It was the typical, fun, western-theme-park fare, and I reacted quite emotionally to the presentation. That wasn't because the performance was particularly exciting, but because I remembered that it was not so long ago that Vicki and I would take a young David, and an even younger Donny, to watch that sort of thing and share in their innocent wonderment. Time does, indeed, fly.

After the Marshall and Doc Holliday finished dispatching the bad guys, I moseyed over to the steakhouse. I went in alone, but spotted an empty seat at a table occupied by Forest and Judy Goodhart, along with a friend of Judy's who Judy has known since 6th grade. Without stopping to consider whether or not I would be horning in, I walked right up to the table and horned in. I asked the rhetorical and often risky question, "Is this seat taken?" In reality, there wasn't even a chair there; it was just the end of the table, but as anyone could see, it could easily accommodate a chair with an eating person seated in it. I think Forest recognized me, but for at least a moment, Judy looked a bit panicky as she tried to figure out who this bombastic man might be. Once she got the subliminal signals from Forest, "this is Chris, and I think we're stuck with him through dinner," she recognized me and welcomed me with open arms. We had a wonderful conversation over a great meal.

When I say "great meal" what I mean is Forest and company had already eaten their first course and were ready for dessert. I decided in the spirit of the Queen of England and the finger bowl, rather than embarrass them, I'd order dessert too; or should I say "two?" Yes, I decided the only polite thing to do would be to order as my dinner a huge piece of chocolate cake with ice cream, a generous serving of peach cobbler a la mode, a glass of milk, a large, empty cup, and four additional scoops of vanilla ice cream. "I thought you said 'two'" you might say. Well, I had two desserts (the cake and the cobbler) the rest counts as one beverage (the ice cream mixed with the milk in the empty cup). If you think about it, that was quite a nutritious meal. It encompassed four food groups; dairy, bread, fruit, and legumes (the cocoa bean counts, doesn't it?)

Following dinner, I took the shuttle back to the hotel and revisited the hospitality suite, where I had the chance to talk with some nice fellows. Jerry Brubaker, Jim Murch, and Jim Fusco chatted with me about various and sundry Pantera subjects, but then I struck up a conversation with Dale Gumm.

Dale has been to the annual POCA Fun Rallies 29 times! We started talking about his Pantera, but then veered off course and into the sordid world of politics and political-correctness. That resulted in quite the spirited conversation, mainly because I found out he and I tend to agree on a lot of things. I think he enjoyed egging me on, and I knew it was time to go when I started screaming and jumping up and down on the table.

Tomorrow, it's off to a car museum, and then on to the real reason I drove four days to get here--Karaoke!

Internal Combustion versus Saving the Planet

FRIDAY, APRIL 27
Day Six of 2012 POCA Fun Rally Journal

Today's activities began with a 40-minute drive from the hotel to what the Fun Rally program called the "Scottsdale Auto Museum." Since Mike Thomas had flown to Phoenix and didn't have a car here, he hitched a ride with me; his first trip in the legendary Pandora.

The "museum" is actually a private collection owned by, I believe, three different individuals, and it consisted of cars you have probably only seen if you've visited the Pebble Beach Concours or spend a lot of time reading the Robb Report. Many of these cars were 1950's or 1960's European one-offs or maybe one of only several that exists in the world.

Currently, the only way to have the chance to see these cars is to get a private invitation; however they are hoping to soon open the facility to the public as a museum. If they do, the first thing they should consider is adding air conditioning! I wore long pants today, thinking a museum would be cool. Well, it was really cool, except just not in terms of the ambient temperature.

The gentleman who gave us the tour was knowledgeable and entertaining. He was one of the people who worked on the cars, restoring them and keeping them in fine fettle. A full restoration shop was part of the facility.

The cars included quite a number of Zagato-bodied and other famous coachworks companies' specials, including Lancias, Ferraris, Porches, Jaguars, a Bentley, a Lamborghini, Fiats, Maseratis and more. It was absolutely unreal.

The thing that fascinates me the most, is how a car can be worth $20,000,000.00, when anyone could build 10 exact replicas for the same money. I understand the car may have an incredible history; racing provenance, famous owners or legendary features, but is that worth so many millions? I guess it is to those who can afford such "toys." All I know is that with none of the cars surrounded by any sort of stanchions or protection (we were asked not to touch them), I was terrified that I would peer into a price-less car and then sneeze all sorts of difficult-to-remove substances into the 50-year-old leather that once touched Piero Carini's bottom.

Many of these cars had raced in and sometimes won such events as the Mille Miglia or Le Mans. Just knowing I was around such rich history was an amazing sensation. This was an incredible experience that alone made this entire trip worth it.

Following the museum tour, we traveled to a restaurant called "Carlsbad Tavern." It had a few decorations depicting bats. There seems to be an ongoing theme of dodgy marketing here in Arizona; Carlsbad Tavern being a play on "Carlsbad Cavern", hence the bats. Clever, huh?

Since I've been enjoying a rather bachelor-like meal plan on this trip, I decided to order a chicken salad for lunch, along with three glasses of lemonade. At first blush, this sounds as if it is the first normal meal I've had. Well, the truth is they didn't have any ice cream, so I added a bunch of sugar to the lemonade, since it wasn't very sweet, and then had a piece of Key Lime pie and a glass of milk for dessert. Still, compared to what I normally eat, today's lunch was pretty much health food. I shared my end of the table with Mike Thomas, Dave Andreson, Steve and Kim Griffin, and John Callan.

John used to own airplanes, but doesn't own, nor ever has owned a Pantera. He was at the Rally with his Pantera-owning friend, John McIver. I asked him why he was at our table instead of his friend John's table and he told me it was "just the way it worked out." I'm a bit suspicious of that explanation, though. I remember in high school I took a girl to a dance and she ended up getting a ride home with someone else, and she used the same excuse.

After lunch we drove back to the hotel and I began to feel a headache coming on. It turned into a nasty mi-graine, and if you have ever had one you know how awful they are. If you haven't had one, you don't want to know. This proved two things: 1) the fact that I eat a lot of ice cream and sugar isn't the cause of my migraines because I had just eaten a salad (maybe eating healthy food is the problem…), and 2) stress can't be the only reason I get migraines, because right now I'm on vacation.

I got back to my room at about 3 PM and was dismayed to find the room hadn't been made up yet, so I hung a "do not disturb" sign on my door and tried to take a nap. I eventually resorted to taking my stupid, overpriced prescription migraine medicine and got a few minutes of shut-eye. Sometime later I woke up to find that it was almost 6 PM, and that's when the drag races were supposed to start. I hurried down to the parking lot and drove to the track.

I needn't have worried about being late, since the program seemed to be off a little. The races were actually scheduled to start at 7. I relaxed for a few minutes in the stands, in which there were only four other people seated. I really enjoyed the temperature, since the sun was setting and it was finally becoming less than a million degrees. Never once did I wish I had dressed in layers.

A few minutes after 7, the racing started. It was really fun to see all sorts of cars screaming down the 1/4-mile track. After a few runs, some of the Panteras were on deck. They sounded great and looked fantastic, but most of their times were only moderate. One or two did quite well, but I think many Pantera owners are reticent to push their cars very hard. It's too expensive and time-consuming to fix them when they break. I spent some time chatting with Clarke and Wilma while there, and Clarke actually ran his 9,000-mile, time-capsule Pantera down the strip. He may have achieved a nine-second run at 198 mph, but my memory seems a bit foggy on that.

At one point, a Bugatti Veyron made a pass. It did the quarter mile in just over 10 seconds, and therefore was unceremoniously booted off the track. The rules state that cars weren't supposed to run faster than 11 seconds, which sounds like a pretty dumb rule to me. I thought the whole point of a drag strip was to determine how fast one could travel in a vehicle. It probably has something to do with "safety." Ah, for the good old days when race cars had rear-only drum brakes and flimsy suspension, and the drivers wore short-sleeve shirts and caps instead of helmets. Actually, those days weren't so good after all. There have been some pretty horrific crashes throughout the history of auto racing.

After getting my fill of drag racing, I drove back to the hotel and was thrilled to see the Karaoke machine was set up. I bribed, I mean asked, the DJ if I could do a little number and I sang with all my might. Clarke and Wilma showed up poolside, where all the Karaoke action was happening, so I dedicated a song to them. I'm sure it was the highlight of their existence.

I got back to the room and found it serviced. However, I did a little experiment I'd like to share with you.

Whenever I travel, I always resent the hotels trying to get me to use the same sheets and towels over and over again. Part of the joy of staying at a hotel and paying the big bucks for the service is knowing I don't have to lie in my own filth each night, but instead, enjoy the sweet smell of fresh linens every day. On this trip, I called the front desk the first day I arrived and asked them for clean linens each day. The attendant said that would be no problem and they always change linens daily anyway. I made it a point to ask about pillowcases, since it seems to me that changing pillowcases would be one of those time-consuming jobs hotel maids would hate and therefore skip. I was assured everything would be changed each day, including the pillowcases.

I should have been suspicious when, after the nice lady told me they "always change linens daily," I found the typical "save the planet" card in my room indicating if I did not tell the staff otherwise, my sheets and towels would not be changed daily. I thought about it and realized I may not be able to tell whether or not the hotel staff were actually doing what they said they would do. I mean, I like to trust people, but I have been burned before, and now am a little more cynical. So, I marked each pillowcase and sheet with a mall blob of blue toothpaste this morning (the toothpaste should wash out without damaging the linens) so I could see if the sheets were really changed.

GUESS WHAT!!!! Same sheets, same pillowcases, same sweaty residue (I may be exaggerating a bit here). Nothing had been changed. How annoying! I told the guy at the front desk I was a little disappointed. Is it the end of the world? Of course not, but I don't like being misled. I'll be interested to see if the tell-tale toothpaste (wasn't that an Edgar Allen Poe story?) is still there tomorrow night.

Now I have to go to bed because someone came up with the brilliant idea of a group Pantera photo tomorrow morning. The photo idea is great. The fact I have to be in the parking lot at 8:00 AM isn't!

Cars, Karaoke and Camaraderie

SATURDAY, APRIL 28
Day Seven of 2012 POCA Fun Rally Journal

When preparing for a six-hour drive, getting the proper rest the night before is a very wise thing to do. A rather unwise thing to do is staying up until 12:30 A.M. singing Karaoke with a bunch of new friends you met at a POCA Fun Rally.

But allow me to begin at the beginning...

Last night (actually, Friday night; it's already Sunday, now) there were messages posted where Pantera owners were likely to be roaming, indicating there was to be a group picture the next morning. The signs showed a meeting time of 8:00 A.M. and a photo shoot time of 8:15. I had stayed up pretty late Friday night (writing the prior journal entry, as a matter-of-fact) so I wasn't too crazy about getting up at 7:00 Saturday morning, but since all car people would basically walk across hot coals to get their cars in a photo, and since I consider myself a car guy, I made the enormous sacrifice to request a wakeup call for a time far earlier than I would on any normal Saturday.

The call came, I woke up, and in a somewhat stupefied state got ready for the day. I arrived at the parking corral (as opposed to the "Golden Corral") at about 3 minutes after

8:00, only to see a group of Panteras departing from the lot... er, corral. There was, apparently, some confusion about times. I didn't realize that the picture wasn't going to be

taken in the local corral, but rather, at the Rawhide restaurant which was somewhat near the hotel. Thinking I could easily catch up to the group and not cause my early wake-up time to be in vain, I jumped in Pandora, started her up and careened through the access roads to the main intersection. I arrived at the stop sign, looked around, but found no evidence of anyone. Then it hit me. Of course I could catch up to a group of people driving normal cars, but I was trying to catch up to a group of people driving other Panteras. My speed advantage wasn't a speed advantage at all!

Somewhat nonplussed, I began to retreat to the corral (which really is just a parking lot. What is it with Arizona and corrals?) But, before doing that I went to the nearby gas station to fill up. While there, another lost Pantera owner pulled up beside me and asked where the photo shoot was supposed to be taking place. I told him I didn't have the address with me and wasn't sure. He said he was just going to go back to the hotel, and I decided that sounded like a good plan, too.

Just as he drove off, my cell phone rang. It was Clarke, wondering where I was. I had just spoken to him before I left the hotel and assumed he was still back at the corral (that would be the parking corral as opposed to the Golden Corral or even the Rawhide Corral. I'm assuming, of course, that the Rawhide restaurant actually has its own corral).

I told him I was very close to where he was (I was wrong, of course), to which he replied he wanted me to get a specific part of my anatomy to where he was right away. I jumped in the car and raced back to the hotel. In my hurry, I accidentally drove along the wrong side of one of the divided access roads leading to the hotel. Two things alerted me to this problem. The first was the arrows painted on the road surface that were pointing the wrong way. Well, actually, they were right…

The other thing that helped me deduce I might be in the wrong place at the wrong time were the other cars driving toward me. Fortunately, it was two lanes wide, and they were driving in the lane to my left, and I was to their right, so it really worked out as if it were a normal, two-lane road. At the next intersection I quickly swerved to my right, onto the correct side of the road. Since most of the cars that were going to the photo shoot had already left, there was very little traffic, about which I was very glad. The last thing I needed was for someone to see what a dork I'd been.

A few minutes later I saw Mike Drew, who said to me, "What the heck were you doing out there driving on the wrong side of the road?" or words to that effect. My wise English mother has (another) saying, "Your sins will find you out." That's for sure.

So, now I had about 40 minutes to kill before the President's breakfast began, and I wasn't sure what I should do. On the one hand, I could quickly return to my room and take a nap, but on the other hand, by the time I got back to the room, took all my clothes off, got in bed, called the front desk for a wake-up call in 30 minutes, got to sleep, got the wake-up-call and woke up again, got dressed again and went downstairs to the meeting room, a lot of energy would be spent for only a little more sleep. I didn't have to think about it for long to realize… Of course, I'd try for the nap.

I got to my room only to find the once-lackadaisical maid was now Johnny-on-the-spot, and was just entering my room to clean it. Funny how one call to a hotel manager changes everything! And speaking of changes, later when I returned to my room, all the linens had been changed (yes, even the pillow cases) and all the crumbs from the muffin I ate the night before were vacuumed. In case the maid had gotten in trouble for messing up the linen situation the day before and might do something nasty to one of my remaining candy bars; before I left the room I took a preemptive measure. I left $5 on the bed with a note that said, "Thank You!" I'll bet if Mr. Daddy had given Celie $5.00 in that particular scene in "The Color Purple" she wouldn't have had to spit into his water.

Anyway, I was forced to go back downstairs and wait for the meeting to start, which it did after 38 long minutes; minutes that could have been used for some perfectly good sleep.

Our new POCA president, Les Gray, ran the President's meeting really well. He seems like a great guy, and very dedicated to POCA. He clearly takes his position seriously, and was interested in what each person at the meeting had to say. Because the POCA President's meetings are top-secret, I cannot reveal anything that happened in that meeting, other than it turns out I am not the only person who likes ketchup on his scrambled eggs.

Following the meeting, I had just enough time to get to the parking corral to prepare for the 12:00 PM departure time for the big car show. Except it turned out that the departure time was really 12:30. Except then it was revealed that we were supposed to be at the show location at 12:30, so it would be better to depart at 12:00, but then those who thought we were supposed to leave at 12:30 might be confused, but then, weren't we already confused? We ended up leaving a little before 12:30.

The drive was only about 20 minutes, and Mike Thomas was riding along again (I think he's developing quite an affection for Pandora. I'd better keep him away from her or his beautiful Yellow Pantera might get jealous and the last thing we want is a cat fight!)

About ten minutes into the trip, I thought a little music might be nice. Despite that I told Mike I was going to turn on the stereo, he didn't seem to be quite prepared for the warm, subtle nuances of the 12", dual-voice-coil, 1200-watt-powered Pyle Driver subwoofer which was located directly behind him. This became obvious soon enough. When the music began to softly waft through the cabin, he about jumped out the window. It turns out he doesn't really like low frequencies very much.

When we arrived at the McDonald's parking lot, I realized it was part of an entire shopping mall complex, and there was space for many, many vehicles. I also realized that in Arizona, they must have some sort of special heat-resistant building material. That was the only possible explanation as to how the McDonald's was still standing in the 5000-degree heat. I mean, it was HOT! REALLY HOT! I was drenched in sweat in about two minutes. The saving grace was that I managed to park about 15 feet from the McDonalds building instead of way out in the arid hinterlands of the parking lot. Surprisingly, it was just a "lot" and not a "corral". This meant I could stand in the shade of the McDonald's' roof overhang and still be very close to my car. A few minutes later I figured out I could actually stand IN the McDonald's and be very close to my car, which was even better since the McDonald's had a fully-functioning air conditioner.

After I had consumed a Cherry-Berry frozen blast (or whatever it was called... by the time I ordered it my vision was blurry from the heat), a frozen, Caramel Mocha, and another one of those Cherry-Berry things, my body temperature had decreased all the way down to only twice what it's supposed to be. So, standing outside in the shade wasn't too bad. Not only that, but after a couple of hours, I could make brief reconnaissance missions to check out the other cars.

There was a huge amount of cars. The Panteras clearly dominated the other marques, but altogether there must have been close to 300 cars. The cars didn't necessarily stay for the entire event, either. Many came and went so that it

was possible to see a great many more cars than there were parking spots.

I stayed until after 5 PM and had a great time. Mike got too hot and went back to the hotel early, although he would have had to leave earlier than I anyway since he had to begin setting up for the big banquet.

One thing that worked out well was the mini-stereo I brought for the show. I hooked my iPod to a tiny set of portable, amplified speakers, and hooked the speakers' power input to a small, 12-volt alarm-system battery I had been saving just in case I ever needed it (see, honey? It really does make sense for me to save all these old parts you think are mostly just junk. Just because most of them are junk doesn't matter now, because I used this old alarm system battery for a cool project).

The battery had plenty of power to drive the amplified speakers, so everyone who looked into Pandora's engine compartment had the privilege of being serenaded my

Beach-Boys rip-off song "408." The iPod was set for "repeat" so the song just kept playing all day. It was great.

Something else I enjoyed was the few minutes I spent inside the McDonald's talking to Mike Drew and his lovely fiancé, Lori. I'd never really talked much with Lori, and I really enjoyed getting to know her a little better. I think Mike is definitely marrying up; just as I did 25 years ago.

I got back to the hotel just in time to shower and change clothes for the banquet. I really hate having to change clothes during the day. It is such a waste of time. Why not just get dressed once and call it good? Endlessly taking things on and off because we're all slaves to fashion probably costs our nation billions of dollars of lost GDP. People are wasting so much time worrying about whether this belt goes with these shoes, or does this tie work with this shirt, or do these Recaro seats make my butt look big...

When I got to the banquet, however, I was glad I changed into my dress jeans and dress shirt. Based on what everyone else was wearing, even I would have felt silly showing up in slipper socks. EXPLANATORY NOTE: When Vicki and I were first dating, her brother mentioned to her one day that he had seen me. His report, however, wasn't flattering. I think it was something along the lines of, "Hey Vicki, I saw your new boyfriend at the car wash today, washing his car... in his SLIPPER SOCKS!" So I guess it is possible for a wife to change her husband's behavior. It just takes 25 years.

The banquet was marvelous. I shared a table with Clarke, Wilma and Mike, among others, and Gary and Linda Herrig showed up as well (they drove up from their property in the Phoenix area). The food was absolutely delicious (note to Vicki: I had some salad and vegetables before I ate the cheesecake).

Our guest speaker was Matt Stone, who is a freelance journalist, author, broadcaster, and former editor of Motor

101

Trend Magazine. He has a bunch of other impressive credentials, but none as lofty as the fact he was once the President of POCA. His relaxed manner and appreciation of our organization made him an engaging speaker.

The raffle prizes were all given away and unfortunately, I didn't win anything. But after the banquet, I got the greatest gift of all... more Karaoke!

As was the case the previous night, everyone was too terrified to get within ten feet of the microphone, so I took it upon myself to be the first to attempt a Karaoke number (tough job, but someone's got to do it). Once I sang one song, the proverbial floodgates were opened. Tonight, I was privileged to have some extra help on some of the songs. A large contingent of women (as opposed to a contingent of large women) volunteered to help me sing "Crocodile Rock." In fact, singing that particular song was their idea. I just happen to know that song pretty well, so I figured it would be fun to sing as a big group.

Well, it was so much fun we did it again on everyone's favorite "they're trying to sound black but they're really white" song, "Play That Funky Music, White Boy." There were a number of really talented singers this evening, which was nice.

I got to know a fascinating woman during the Karaoke session. Her name is Freddie Peake (Freddie is actually a nickname). It turns out her husband was the founder of what is now the Pantera Owner's Club of America. She is an attorney (still practicing) and sings a mean Karaoke song, too! I mentioned one Frank Sinatra song that I've always wanted to sing, but since my wife hates it, I never have. Freddie was amazed. She loves that song! So for the benefit of Freddie, and because Vicki isn't here and didn't have to listen to it, I attempted to croon.

I think the spirit of Vicki was in the room, however, because for some reason the DJ lady played the song in a key so low I sounded like Frank Sinatra with a really bad cold. And flu. On his deathbed. With his mouth full of cotton.

I hated to leave on such a low note (ha), but it was getting late and I knew if I wanted to get this journal entry done by... what time is it now? Oh yes, 2:34 AM... I'd better get back to my room. Tomorrow, I start the long trip back home. I hope the air conditioning holds out!

Oh yes, one more thing... I asked Clarke and Wilma what time they were leaving tomorrow... er, today... and they said 7:00 AM. I thought they must have been kidding. How ridiculous would that be? Leaving before the sun is even really up very much? Now that I think about it, though, they really might be leaving that early. If that's true, this may be one time when they get to the motel first.

Confessions of a Teetotaler

Prologue to Sunday, April 29
Day Eight of 2012 POCA Fun Rally Journal

Before I begin this entry, I must clear up something from the last one. My wife, Vicki, read my ramblings from yesterday and sent me an advisory email. She explained that to those who may not know me, my description of my late-night activities may have led some to conclude that I had run wild in a night of wine, women, and sin.

She didn't actually write that, but she did ask if the people who read this stuff know that I am a non-drinker. What she means, of course, is that I don't drink alcohol. When I was in high school, some friends and I hid some beer in the building next to the church on a hot summer day, determined to get drunk. I took one swig of warm beer and almost puked! Other than the time a friend let me take a big gulp of apricot brandy (which scorched my throat beyond recognition), I've never had any desire for alcohol, unless it's being used to power a dragster.

Since I went to bed at 2:50 AM this morning, I thought I would have a nice rest and wake up whenever I happened to wake up. So, no wake-up call required. Check-out time was noon, so I figured I'd awaken before then. I had just drifted into R.E.M. sleep, when suddenly I was torn from my dreams by the sound of my cell phone blaring. Granted, the ringtone is "Cliffs of Dover" by Eric Johnson, one of my favorite songs of all time, but being jolted from dreamland to rock and roll at 3:45 AM isn't pleasant, no matter what the tune. I fumbled around until I found the phone; the number had an 800 prefix, so I thought it was either a stupid solicitation call for aluminum siding or something important. The phone number displayed on caller ID did ring a bell (ha!)

The call was from my alarm-monitoring company. One of the alarm codes in my office had been triggered and the monitoring company representative wanted to know what I wanted them to do. I told them I was a little too far away to do anything myself, but to call the local police and have them check it out and to call me if there really was a problem. I tried to get back to sleep, but of course, my blood had been replaced by adrenaline, so it took a while to calm down. Just as I did, the phone rang again. The police wouldn't check it out unless two codes were triggered. Since it was the interior office motion sensor that was affected, I told them not to worry about it, since unless someone dug a tunnel and accessed my office through the floor, the door or window codes would have been triggered, too. I eventually went back to sleep.

You Meet the Nicest People on a Harley

SUNDAY, APRIL 29
Day Eight of 2012 POCA Fun Rally Journal

I awoke again, bright and early at 10 A.M. and got packed up. I brought my car to the hotel entrance (in the shade) so I could check the intake manifold bolts for tightness. Most were fully tight, but a few were loose enough that I was able to tighten them an additional quarter-turn. I went to the nearby gas station, filled up, ate the last piece of banana bread, drank a carton of strawberry-flavored milk, and headed toward home.

The air conditioning system worked perfectly! That and the fact that traffic wasn't too bad made the trip out of Phoenix quite wonderful. I took a few pictures as I drove, trying not to veer off the road or into oncoming traffic. Thankfully, the trip was smooth and uneventful.

I stopped for gas about two hours out of Las Vegas, and as I was about to leave the gas station, an older gentlemen approached the car and asked me if I could give him some money. Now, if you know me, you know that I don't give away money to strangers. What I normally do is ask them to hold a sign for four hours that advertises my business, and I tell them I'll pay them $10 per hour to do so. I really do have signs pre-printed that I keep in my daily driver for just such occasions. I actually had one guy take me up on it, and I paid him for his work.

Unfortunately, I don't have those signs in the Pantera, so I asked him why he needed the money. He said he had his car fixed at the truck stop down the street and didn't have enough gas to get home. I've heard this kind of thing before, and it is usually total bunk. However, I told him if he brought his car to the station, I'd fill it up for him. He said that sounded great, and that he'd be right back. Sure he would.

To my surprise, just a few minutes later, he pulled into the station in a crusty, early-nineties four-door Mercury of some sort. I got out and started filling his tank. Interestingly, he said he only needed 7 gallons, and I didn't have to give him any more. I gave him eight, and thought perhaps his request for only seven gallons was an indication his story was true. I'll never know, of course, but at least I can rest assured I didn't give him the opportunity to take a gift of cash and blow it on some sort of sinful substance, such as ice cream, pre-sweetened breakfast cereal or chocolate milk.

I was so far ahead of schedule, even after leaving the hotel at the leisurely hour of 12:20, that I decided to stop  at one of the scenic outlooks just prior to Hoover Dam. I drove to the lookout, parked, and took the requisite scenic picture. A woman approached me and said, as she pointed to a group of motorcycle riders who were standing by their bikes, "That guy in the sleeveless shirt has a car like yours."

I was surprised, and approached the guy. He said it was true; he had a 1970 Pantera. I was a little suspicious, since Panteras were sold in the USA from 1971 through 1974, and I wasn't aware of any 1970 models. He went on to say that his car was from Mexico, and had been brought into the United States as part of a collection. The owner of the collection didn't want the Pantera, so this fellow purchased it in 1976 for $20,000. Why he would pay $20,000 in 1976 for a 1970 Pantera is beyond me, but that's what he said. He explained that since it came from Mexico, it was titled as a 1970 model. It is a push-button car, but he said since it wasn't for the U.S., it has non-D.O.T. glass and the gauges are not calibrated in miles-per-hour, U.S. gallons or Fahrenheit degrees.

The story became more interesting when he told me he also owns a number of other highly-collectible cars. I can't remember all he mentioned, but I know he said he has a Boss 429, a Cobra-Jet of some sort, and others. Then it got really weird. He said he and his business partner own an automotive shop in Renton, WA. That's about 40 minutes from where I live. I can't remember the name of his company, but I do know his first name is Dale. I gave him my card and told him to get in touch with me, since he absolutely needs to be a member of POCA. He didn't seem particularly excited about joining a club, but one never knows where such a chance encounter may lead.

Following this, I drove a few more miles and then pulled off at the Hoover Dam exit. I parked far away from everyone else in the lot and walked up the stairs to the bridge. I got to the top, and the view of the dam was pretty spectacular. I was hoping there wouldn't be an earthquake while I was there, since it was a long way down!

I was probably on the bridge for only five minutes, but when I got back to the parking lot I was disgusted to see that some idiot in a white rental car had parked about 9" away from Pandora. What is it with people? Do they think cars get lonely out there all by themselves in those far away parking spaces? Why, when there are 20 places with no cars occupying them, do people feel the need to take a spot right next to the one parking space that is occupied?

It's almost as bad as the idiotic lady who earlier today was driving 55 miles-per-hour in the left lane in a 65 zone. She was parallel to a slow truck in the right lane and refused to either speed up or slow down to let me by. Realizing she was oblivious, brain-dead, or both, I was forced to unleash the threatening sound of Pandora's horn. It made no difference, so I honked again, this time a bit longer. Still nothing. Finally, the truck slowed down enough that I could get around him and in front of her. She then slowed down again, trapping the remaining drivers who weren't as fortunate as I in escaping. In my rear-view mirror I could see the line of cars behind her was probably at least 1/4 mile long.

Lame drivers notwithstanding, I got to the Comfort Inn in Las Vegas at about 6:30 and found Clarke and  Wilma lounging by the pool. We went to "Farmer Boys Hamburgers" ("and more," according to the sign) for dinner, and it was fantastic. I had a fried egg sandwich with bacon and one of the best chocolate shakes I've had in a long time. After dinner, I retired to my room, where I had a "flake" chocolate bar and a pint of milk (remember... milk goes with chocolate). The only problem was that the flake (which for those of you who are not English candy connoisseurs, is a light, whipped cylindrical chocolate candy bar) had been with me the entire trip, and when I opened the packet, it came out as chocolate sawdust. It was still good, though.

I just received an email from Mike Drew. He said he and his travel companions got to Hoover Dam 20 minutes after I left. The security guard told them I had been there.

He must have noticed my car. Mike wanted to know if I'd like to join his group for part of the drive back home. That sounded fun, but he said they would be leaving their hotel at 8:15 A.M. I told him since I'm not in Las Vegas proper, it probably wouldn't work out. Oh yes, and I wouldn't be leaving until about 11:00! The issue of what time is appropriate for starting one's day is a prime example of the difference between someone who has a military background and someone who spent many of his formative years as a rock and roll drummer! It turns out that a person with a military background (Mike) has the same concept of time as a woman who was raised the daughter of an Assembly of God church Pastor (Vicki). I guess it's not a coincidence that they call it "The Salvation Army."

Tomorrow it's on to Twin Falls.

Your Sins Will Find You Out

MONDAY, APRIL 30
Day Nine of 2012 POCA Fun Rally Journal

In yesterday's entry, I made mention of a quote my mother likes to use, "Your sins will find you out." I was chastised by the two most important women in my life (my wife and my mom) for failing to mention the quote is actually from the book of Numbers, in the Bible. Of course, I knew that, but the last thing I wanted to do was start quoting Bible verses and have people get the idea I have a "holier-than-thou" attitude. Well, if anyone ever had that misconception, I have now done my best to eliminate that problem. Today, my sins, indeed, found me out.

For the first time while driving my Pantera, I GOT A TICKET! I can't tell you all of the details yet, because according to officer Grumpy (not his real name), the form I signed today was not an admission of guilt. That's good, because there is at least one accusation that is patently false. Granted, I was making very good time on the roads prior to my alleged transgression, so I can't complain too much, but let me explain a portion of what happened, since I love to write so many details!

But first, let me start at the beginning.

I awoke this morning in a good mood after a good sleep; no migraines to be found anywhere. I enjoyed the complimentary breakfast at the same Las Vegas Comfort Inn at which I stayed on the way to the Rally. However, this time I had a waffle that was so enormous, when I had finished consuming it along with the scrambled egg, I was forced to forego the Froot Loops. I should have known that was a foreboding sign.

I left the hotel about 11:20 AM and headed toward Ely, Nevada. I planned to stop there for lunch, but it was too far to make in one trip so I stopped at another, rather nondescript spot to fill up the tank. While there I received several favorable comments about Pandora, which is always fun, including one young man's desire to take a couple of pictures. I asked if he would like to have me take a picture of him in the car. He happily agreed, and handed me what looked like a combination game controller-portable TV-phone-Star Trek communicator. Oh, I forgot to mention "camera."

He showed me which button to push, and the pictures turned out well. I had a momentary flashback of achieving the high score at Donkey Kong sometime in the mid-eighties.

When I arrived at Ely, I drove through a couple of the neighborhoods to get a feel for the place. It's kind of a quaint little town and proud of its heritage. I took a picture of the big sign posted at the entrance of the city so I could remember just what, exactly, that heritage was.

I filled up at a local Shell station while explaining to several people what a "Pantera" is, and from whence it came. One lady thought it was a Lamborghini. Another kid asked if it cost $200,000.00. I replied to him that it depends if you include the cost of moving violations (alleged, moving violations at this point). Even the 70-something-year-old attendant took a break from ringing up pop and potato chips to come outside and inquire about it. Everyone seemed so friendly, I thought I'd stay for lunch.

I drove to the city park and did just what the name suggests, found a picnic table, and settled down to read the latest issue of Road & Track while munching on two blueberry muffins, two yogurts (those items I pilfered from the complimentary breakfast that morning... hey, I didn't get to eat my Froot Loops, so it's a break-even for the hotel chain), a bottle of some exotic mix of fruit juices (have you noticed that the big thing now is for companies to blend multiple juices together and offer the end result as some new, never-before-considered beverage? "Hey Martha, look—they took the apple juice and mixed it with the cranberry juice! Can you believe it? Genius! What do you think they'll call it?"), several chocolate digestive biscuits (for those of you who may not be English biscuit aficionados, "Digestive Biscuits" are not some sort of medically-prescribed heartburn remedy, but simply cookies with chocolate on the top and are delicious), and of course milk. Following lunch I hit the road. And here's where things went terribly wrong.

At first, I was enjoying long, straight roads with no traffic. You can guess how I was enjoying them. I was always careful to slow way down when any other traffic was present. If there's one overriding theme in the Pantera Owners Club of America, it's safety.

111

As I was passing through Elko County, Nevada, I called Clarke and Wilma to see if they had arrived at the hotel yet. Of course, they had. I used the hands-free speaker phone built into my GPS system, for safety reasons, of course, plus the fact that the stupid thing connects to my phone automatically and I don't know how to override it, even if I wanted to. The hands-free system works pretty well, as long as you can decipher "Hey Clrk, Ime llkjhjs efoiu ertppisw conbpe erlo ejtopj OK?" Actually, it wasn't that bad, and I told Clarke I'd be there in 45 minutes, unless "I get pulled over (yuk yuk)"

Five minutes later... well, I think you can guess what happened.

It was a smooth, curvy road (that sounds like that old campfire story, "It was a dark and stormy night...") and there was this car in front of me that I thought would appreciate not having me bringing up the rear, so to speak, so I passed it. Next thing you know, an innocent-looking SUV appears out of nowhere coming the other way, and I couldn't help but notice that his turn signals weren't the usual orange, but instead blue and red. And they were all flashing at the same time.

As I mentioned, I won't go into detail about the alleged infraction, only to say the officer claimed to have issues with what he thought I did. The whole situation probably could have been less financially painful, but there was a document problem. When he asked for my license and registration, I gave him the required document. So far, so good. He seemed fairly reasonable at that point. However, after spending a few minutes in his portable pokey, as I tried not to think about all the gloating going on by the drivers of all the cars I had passed who were now driving past me as I sat, humiliated, by the side of the road (that's actually worse than getting the ticket, you know), he approached me full of bluster and indignation. I think I also detected a hint of pensiveness.

The reason for his hyperventilation was that according to his "official" records, "This car hasn't been registered since 2007!" I tried to explain to him that in Washington State, collector car plates are exempt from annual registration and tags. He didn't believe me.

In fact, with a mix of bravado and nervousness (after all, for all he knew, I could be a convicted criminal) he asked me to get out of the car and look at my license plate. He asked, "Do you see a place on that plate for tags?" What I should have said was, "No, officer oblivious, I can't see anything--in fact, I'm legally blind!" Instead, I simply said, "Yes, but I never received tags for this car because it is a collector vehicle..."

He would have none of it. He told me that this wasn't Washington (thanks again, officer--maybe I should have started clicking my heels together and chanting, "There's no place like home...") and that I'd have to take it up with the court.

I then remembered all those cops and robber shows I watched as a kid, and it reminded me that the accused always got to make a phone call. Realizing this guy was nowhere near old enough to remember great shows such as "The Streets of San Francisco," I almost abandoned the idea of asking him if I could call one of my friends at the Lakewood Police Department, but then it occurred to me that he probably had watched "Who Wants to be a Millionaire?" once or twice.

"May I phone a friend?" I asked. I told him I could get verification of the tag question from one of my connections with the Lakewood PD. He told me I could call anyone I wanted, but it wouldn't make any difference.

I have a tremendous amount of respect for officers of the law. Except this one. He is an idiot.

While he was back in his paddy wagon filling out all the devilish paperwork, I phoned the same person I always call when I'm in some sort of self-imposed trouble; my wife. Since I was trying to use the ridiculous hands-free device while talking a mile-a-minute (I'm surprised officer dorky didn't give me a ticket for that, too), Vicki had great difficulty figuring out what was going on. I finally was able to convey to her that I needed the phone number for the Lakewood PD, which she found.

I called the number and had just reached a woman who could help me, when officer bloviate came back and stuck his head in the car. Before I could say anything, he informed me I could finish my call later, once he was done with me. I told the lady on the phone I needed to go, hung up, and then listened to Officer Neverwrong begin to read me all the various infractions.

I said, "Aren't you going to let me call the Lakewood PD back so they can tell you about the tags?" Proving that his powers of jerkiness were exceeded only by his inability to pay attention to anyone except himself, he replied, "What did they say?"

Rather than bursting out in laughter and saying something I might regret, I just said, "That's who was on the line when you asked me to hang up."

He again said it would make no difference and pointed to a phone number on the citation he gave me. "Call that number if (he actually said, "if") you can prove you don't need tags for your car. They'll work it out with you."

He also said although he usually lowers the speed he lists on tickets below what the driver was actually driving because, "I hate giving out big-dollar tickets," in my case he was giving me "the full boat" with no reduction whatsoever.

The moral is that one is never to argue with a crabby police officer. The problem is, however, when they are completely wrong, what is one supposed to do?

Just to show him I had no hard feelings, after he handed me the $850.00 ticket, I asked him if he'd like to take the Pantera for a quick drive. Surprisingly, he declined.

In retrospect, despite that my offer was after the citation had been issued, he'll probably try to get me for some trumped-up attempting to bribe an officer charge. I have a number of attorney clients, and I'll be checking with them on the best way to proceed. It sure is annoying, though.

By the way, "Hey, Officer Bullheaded, check this out from the Washington State Licensing website:

"License plate requirements: Collector license plates: May be assigned to currently registered passenger vehicles, motorcycles, or trucks. Are good for the life of vehicle. Aren't required to display month/year tab. Aren't renewed annually."

Too bad I didn't have David or Donny (my sons) with me. They could have pulled that info up on their phone right in front of Officer Technoboob.

The day had a happy ending, though. Clarke and Wilma, the wonderful people they are, waited to go to dinner until I arrived at the hotel at 8:00 PM. We made a beeline for our favorite corral, that's right, "The Golden Corral" and gorged ourselves silly. I was in such a mood that I ate four different desserts first.

Tomorrow, Google maps says my trip to Hermiston, Oregon should last 6 1/2 hours. Sadly, due to the snail's pace I'll now be driving, it probably will.

Misery Loves Company

TUESDAY, MAY 1
Day Ten of 2012 POCA Fun Rally Journal

Today is the first day of May, and I should be home tomorrow. I'm writing this entry much earlier in the day than usual since I got here sooner than I expected. Despite the fact I was driving like one who has recently been chastised, the trip from Twin Falls, Idaho to here (Hermiston, Oregon) took only 6 hours, including an hour lunch stop. Google maps indicated 6 1/2 hours of pure drive-time.

My wise, English mother has a saying, "Misery loves company." In the last 24 hours I've seen the truth of that sentiment. I received more responses from my fellow Panterians about yesterday's diatribe than any other entry, so far. It seems there is a lot of empathy for those who receive moving violations. There are also a lot of people who have had close calls with the State Patrol and lived to tell about it. It's kind of funny what goes through one's mind after getting a large ticket. It's not dissimilar to the five stages of loss. First, shock and denial (I can't believe that stupid SUV is a cop!), then anger (you saw that in yesterday's entry), then bargaining (I knew I should have taken Mike Drew up on his offer and joined his contingent. Then at least I wouldn't be the only one with a ticket).

I haven't gotten to the last two stages; acceptance and healing. I think I may be in a little-known 6th stage; the "I hope a good attorney can reduce the fine" stage.

I'll let you know how it works out. [Post journal note: After talking with several attorney firms, I found out the city of Jackpot, Nevada, in Elko County is notorious for NEVER reducing ANY traffic fines. I actually had an attorney tell me, "I don't want to take your money. It won't do you any good." When an attorney tells you that, you know it's bad.]

Now, about the day: This will be a (mercifully) short entry. Surprisingly, I woke up prior to the wake-up call this morning and enjoyed the "AmericInn" complimentary breakfast. Being in a nutritious state of mind, I decided to have apple juice (with that "magic powder" added, of course) and oatmeal... before the Froot Loops.

I became full more quickly than usual, probably due to the oatmeal. It's interesting how real food tends to provide more substance than the equivalent cubic foot of, say, Honeycomb cereal. Funny story about that. Not to get off on a tangent or anything, but when I was a kid, I loved Quisp cereal. I thought if some was good, a lot would be better. I realized it was pretty fluffed-up cereal, so I used my wise, English mother's grinder and transformed an entire box of the stuff to a pile of dust small enough to fit in a cereal bowl. With eager anticipation I added milk, preparing myself for a sweet, sensory overload of Quisp-ness. What it had become, however, was a facsimile of cement and wet, volcanic ash. Fail!

Since I had hoped to supplement my Froot Loops and oatmeal with other breakfast delicacies, I asked the nice attendant if I could take a little food with me. She said of course I could, and seemed a bit bemused I would even bother to ask. Now I had lunch taken care of, too!

I drove continuously until the tank was almost empty and then stopped at a small town called Baker City, Oregon. At the gas station, the attendant told me something I didn't know. Even though one is not allowed to pump one's own gas in Oregon, there is an exception made for motorcycles and collector cars. I'll bet officer blowhard in Nevada doesn't know that!

While at the station, I also added another quart of oil. That makes three quarts for about 3000 miles. That seems a bit much, although I'm not aware of the car burning or leaking oil.

The gas station attendant was a nice guy, and a self-admitted Mopar nut. When I told him my daily driver was a Magnum SRT-8, I could almost feel the bonding.

I went to the city's park for lunch. It was very nice and the weather, although cool, was sunny. It was so cool in fact, I had to put on a jacket. If only I had my leather coat with me.

I enjoyed the apple, yogurt, blueberry muffin, and raisin toast, complete with two containers of grape jelly donated by the "AmericInn" along with chocolate milk, chocolate-covered malted Easter eggs and regular milk. Did I mention the malted Easter eggs were covered in chocolate?

 Following that, I drove another 90 minutes, and now I'm here.

I called Clarke when I reached the hotel this afternoon, but he and Wilma traveled to Moses Lake today and will be taking a different route home tomorrow. That means the only lifeline I have for the rest of the trip is AAA. I think Clarke and Wilma must have figured to be efficient, they could spend time driving instead of watching me eat dinner. I eat rather slowly.

Tonight, I will begin working on my class materials for Thursday night. I had grandiose plans for preparing the lesson a little bit each night of this trip, but instead I read issues of Hot Rod, Popular Hot Rodding, Road and Track, and World magazine. But now, playtime is over.

I think in class this week I'll discuss the fact that even though Christians may be forgiven in the Heavenly sense, while here on earth, we must still pay the consequences for our actions. After all, remember that saying my wise, English mother always quotes, "Your sins will find you out!" Or, at least, the police might.

Since Clarke and Wilma had driven to Moses Lake, I spent dinner at an A&W Root Beer hamburger stand across from the Comfort Inn in Hermiston, Oregon. A&W has always been one of my favorite restaurant chains. I had a delicious chicken sandwich and their version of a milkshake, which in this case was orange pop blended with vanilla ice cream. Fantastic!

I went back to my hotel room and enjoyed a dessert of chocolate-malted Easter eggs, chocolate Digestive biscuits, and milk. All in all, very satisfying!

Enough Sugar to Get Me Home

WEDNESDAY, MAY 2
Day Eleven of 2012 POCA Fun Rally Journal

I was going to sleep in this morning, except my stupid cell phone went off early. Someone was excited to tell me about how much lower my home mortgage interest could be. I was really ticked off. Since when did solicitors start calling cell phone numbers? I laid in bed staring at the ceiling for a while, and then decided to get up.

It was too late for the complimentary breakfast, so I simply added my magic powder to water and drank that, then ate a few more chocolate Digestive biscuits and finished off the milk. I then drank a chocolate milk I had purchased last night from the convenience store attached to the A&W Root Beer stand. I guess one could argue the chocolate milk was the liquid equivalent of Froot Loops. Probably about as nutritious, too. It always cracks me up how the manufacturers of what is commonly referred to as "junk food" try to minimize the amount of calories, sugar, sodium and chemicals one is actually ingesting while eating or drinking the stuff. They do this by claiming that there are a certain number of "servings per container" instead of counting the total. For example, anyone over the height of 4'2" would drink the entire bottle of chocolate milk such as the one I had as part of my breakfast, in one go, yet the manufacturer classified the bottle as two servings, not one. What they really should have printed on the bottle was "drinking four of these will provide you with an entire day's-worth of calories." Not that it would do much good. I don't know of too many people who read the labels anyway. The only reason I did is because I didn't have Clarke and Wilma there discussing car stuff with me.

Clarke and Wilma have a number of classic Thunderbirds. They are both very active in Thunderbird car clubs, and have traveled all over the United States in their classic 'birds. We talked about how the Fun Rally compares to the Thunderbird club rallies. Basically, they are very similar except at Thunderbird rallies people have to pay for their own drinks, but get a lot of free food at the hospitality suite. The POCA Fun Rally provides complimentary drinks, but only pretzels and M&Ms.

I drove from the hotel all the way to Centralia without stopping. Other than encountering heavier traffic the closer I got to Portland, the traffic was typical freeway travel with lame-brains in the fast lane going 5 mph below the speed limit.

I got to Centralia and met my wise, English mother at Starbucks. I had a breakfast sandwich and a Venti, peppermint mocha Frappuccino, double-blended, heavy cream, double pumps (extra sweet), with two packs of white sugar and whip. Delicious.

We discussed the trip and other fun stuff and she pointed out that the ticket I received may have been a good thing, because it prevented me from continuing to drive at dangerously high speeds.

Well, most of the time she's wise!

I got home an hour later and was very happy Pandora had performed as well as she did throughout the trip. There is a little black soot or oil or something on the lower plate by the rear sway bar that reads Pantera" which I'll examine this weekend. It may just be dirt from driving in light rain conditions, experienced on the last leg of the trip.

All in all, a great experience. Now I have a year to touch up all the rock chips before the Fun Rally next year!

Oh, and by the way, due to my sedentary situation while driving and the huge amount of junk food I ate on the trip, it turns out I gained some weight... one pound, to be exact. To whip myself back into shape I guess I'll skip the milkshake today.

Chasing Roadkill

by Lee Henderson

I had been following Roadkill's progress on the GPS app Glympse and reading posts on Facebook for three days. I had an epiphany. They would be passing through my area near Atlanta, GA within the next 24 hours. I had always wanted to be an automotive journalist and this could be just my chance to have an adventure and get a story published.

I contacted Mike Spinelli of /Drive network and Jalopnik who is friend on Facebook. I had never personally messaged him before, but we'd had a few brief exchanges in the comments section and he had also answered a question of mine on an Ask Drive Anything video.

I sent him an outline of my plan and asked who I should contact to get a story published. He responded and kindly offered to help me promote it, if I pulled it off and it was quality. I immediately began typing out questions for an interview that I printed and triple spaced.

My "opus" took nearly 4 hours to write. I ran my results by a few people and the feedback I received was encouraging. I prepared my camera and truck for the trip.

Then tragedy struck. Twenty or so miles from the Alabama/Georgia border, at around 2am, Glympse was a fail. I got into my truck and drove over an hour to I20, west of Atlanta. Then I had a few realizations. What if they have gotten past me? What if they have already stopped for the night in Atlanta? How would I find them if Glympse was not restored? I decided that sleep was for the weak and cannonballed to I85 North.

Once I was clear of metro Atlanta's impending Friday morning rush hour traffic, I parked on the shoulder south of Braselton, GA to wait. It was 7am. Around 11:30am a cop "stopped" me. Yes, he pulled up behind, me, lights flashing, and approached my vehicle on foot.

I almost had heart attack. I didn't need a ticket or be told to leave my post. He allowed me to stay after reminding me of the danger and spoke with me until I calmed down. I was visibly nervous, shaking, and stuttering like I expected to be hauled off to jail. I had not packed any clothes, hygiene supplies, or food. I had only expected a quick 10-20 minutes of interview in a parking lot, if they would grant me one at all.

I had water, energy drinks, soda, and cigarettes. By 1:30pm, I had begun cursing myself and was dealing with feelings of despair, hoping I had not missed my chance. Who was I? I wasn't a quitter, I slammed a warm Red Bull, turned the radio up, and sang along to ZZ Top. By 3:30pm I had been awake for over 27 hours and had begun to smell of BO in spite of burning 9 gallons of gas running my truck's air conditioning. I decided to pull into a truck stop to buy deodorant and wash myself a little in a sink.

This is not an exaggeration, false bravado, or hyperbole. No sooner had I gotten to the bottom of the on ramp to park on the shoulder when Blasphemi  and the camera van passed me. If had taken 30 seconds longer to get back into position I would have missed my chance. I immediately took chase and about ten minutes later they pulled into a gas station. Mike Finnegan went inside to use the facilities and get snacks before I could slot my 22 foot long mastodon into a space. I got out and walked over to the sticker covered, primer black 1955 Chevy gasser that was parked at a fuel pump.

The camera guys looked at me but didn't seem concerned. After I photographed the car and took video for a few minutes, they came over and spoke with me. I learned that David Freiburger had traveled ahead to attend the long hauler dinner at Hot Rod Power Tour. They had no idea how the car rode and they had started filming for the company at the same time Mike began work with Hot Rod. Their first video together had been the controversial 'Vette Hack.

When Mike came out of the store, I shared my story with him and we talked about the car while I recorded with my camera. Here it was; my big shot. Trying my hardest to sound confident, I asked Mike for an interview and showed him the notes. He recalled my earlier messages on Facebook

 and said "OK, you're the guy with the blog."

Then things started to escalate quickly. I was invited to follow them to the Power Tour event in Charlotte so I could interview him and David, see the car show, and enjoy myself. There was absolutely no way I could turn this down. I was going to zMAX Dragway.

On the drive, Mike stopped multiple times to get fuel. I asked him how large the tank was and he explained that it was not empty. He was calculating the car's fuel efficiency and tuning the EFI system with his laptop. I told him how impressed I was by 17.9 mpg they reported in New Mexico.

He told me that the humid air had caused the economy to drop to 12 mpg and he really wanted to get it "Dialed". The most endearing thing about the trip to zMAX was seeing the reactions of others to Blasphemi.

Countless cars slowed to gawk at the car as they passed us. At every fuel stop, Blasphemi gathered inquisitive comments and looks from people of all ages, sexes, and races. The car had cache with everyone who encountered it, from a few fans of the show to laymen who were unfamiliar with Roadkill, Hot Rod Magazine, or even what kind of car it was.

I witnessed a man engage Mike in conversation and after he was told that a Hemi was under the hood, he had a moment of clarity and figured out why it was called Blasphemi. I couldn't hold back my laughter at the sight of his demeanor. Moisture on the road and scattered rain forced Mike to slow the drag tire equipped car to between 40mph and 55mph at times. The camera van and I had to activate our hazard lights. It was slow going.

The arrival of our motley convoy of nearly 1400 hp in the suburb of Concord, NC was pure bucket list. David Freiburger met us at the gate of the show grounds, shook my hand, and said "You're the guy who came all this way to see me." I pulled up next to Blasphemi and the camera van into a parking place of prominence in front of the pavilion where the Power Tour Long Hauler dinner was happening. A large crowd was forming to greet Mike and inspect the car. I stood back, filmed the enthusiastic crowd, and fed my fascination, seeing more reactions to the car.

A few minutes later Mike called me over, David shook my hand again and handed me a Corona that I two fisted with a Red Bull to David's amusement. He asked me how long I had waited on the road for Mike and how long I had been awake. 31 hours at that point.

He told me to enjoy myself and look around. They would get back to me after they mingled with the crowd of vendors and tour participants. I was completely at ease and all of my fatigue had melted away, even though I did feel like a sketchy character who had been in the same clothes for nearly a day and a half.

I walked around, taking photos of the Long Hauler's vehicles and the Chevy Performance area. Once the crowd had gotten their souvenir photos with the guys and the car and gotten autographs, I lingered nearer to the Gasser. I observed Rutledge Wood of Top Gear USA and Elana Scherr of Hot Rod in the area but, I didn't interrupt. I spoke to a few of the gentlemen who were on the tour and related my story. All were kind and wished me the best.

Around 8:30pm, David and Mike took me to the bar where long haulers and crew were playing the drinking game "flip cup" and told them to serve me. With a Miller Lite and my camera in hand, we sat at a picnic table. I asked Mike to read the questions aloud on the video as I was not comfortable with my oration skills, though I did add a few side comments verbally.

The interview went on for 20 minutes when my memory card had reached capacity. I was petrified. They were totally cool about it and I was assured that we could finish the next day. The timing was good. The camera guys were the designated drivers and they were ready to split. David inquired where I would be staying. I had asked security if it was cool to sleep in my truck in the parking lot. They had no issues with that.

Mike gave me his phone number and they were gone. I had a few more beers at the bar and with some truckers who work for Source Interlink in the parking lot until midnight. I slept with the windows down and awoke at 6am freezing. I went to Walmart and bought clothes, toiletries, snacks, beverages, and a memory card.

I showered in a latrine at the facility. I enjoyed Power Tour and finished with the guys that afternoon with another 30 minutes of questions. They signed a Roadkill hat and t-shirt off my back. I showed them the scars on my abdomen and spine from my military service.

After all was said and done, I was given a hell of an opportunity to interview and drink beer with a man I have been reading on and off, since I was a 5th grader, in Hot Rod, Car Craft, Petersen's 4 Wheel & Off Road, and a man I have been following since 2010 in Hot Rod. They were exceedingly kind in spite of my borderline insane efforts to make contact with them and my hobo appearance from the road.

It turns out that they are just normal guys who get paid to make videos of their adventures when they aren't working on the magazine. Some people say "Don't meet your heroes!" In this case, they would be wrong.

Texas to Colorado at 100MPH

by David Dickinson

In March of 1987, I moved from Washington State to Texas. Many from Washington State (God's Country, as it is called by those that are residents) have asked why I would do such a thing. Well, the answer is simple and not uncommon. It was for a woman. I was also bored with my life. I had been in Real Estate for almost a decade. The market wasn't that robust and I was simply in need of a change.

Once settled, I realized that pursuing a Real Estate career in Texas was going to be more challenging than rewarding. The market had been overbuilt and prices were sliding as quickly as the occupancy rates. I would have had to learn Texas Real Estate law and pass a state exam to get a Real Estate license just to start over in a bad market and so, I decided to seek out new opportunities. Having been in sales for many years, I responded to an ad in the local paper. It turned out to be a position as a stockbroker. This was only months before the October Black Friday of 1987, but who was to know? Of course that new position entailed a new license process, as well, not to mention the training involved, but it was a challenge that I felt like taking on. An adventure on the road during that training is the real subject of this story.

Once I had completed the studying and testing to acquire the Series 7 and Series 63 licenses required for all Stockbrokers, company training at corporate headquarters in Colorado was scheduled. Having made friends with one of my fellow trainees, we decided to make the road trip together from Fort Worth, Texas to Denver, Colorado.

Erik was the son of one of the big contractors in the Dallas-Fort Worth area and had been living the good life. He partied hardy, drinking and eating in the finest establishments, wearing the nicest clothes, and he talked the talk and walked the walk. He fancied himself a man among men. He had a new Corvette.

Preparations were made for the drive and reservations made for our stay in Colorado. We hopped into the 'Vette and departed on a sunny Saturday in September to hit the asphalt on Interstate 35W. Erik loved the idea of having a partner on this road trip. As I said, he loved to drink and he loved to drive his Corvette. By having me along, he could do both. I was more than happy to drive and so when he decided that he'd rather hold a drink than the steering wheel, I was there.

We decided to break the 700 plus mile trip into two days and had planned to stay over in Amarillo. When we got there, the first thing Erik wanted to do was find a hotel with its own bar. I couldn't tell you after all these years what the name of the place was, but Erik caught a "scent of martini" and pulled in. We quickly checked in and made our way to "the best little lounge along Route 66".

Erik was single and considered himself a "player", so while I sipped a few beers I watched him pound martinis and dance with some of the local "beauties" that were there. As I observed him move from girl to girl over the course of a couple of hours, it occurred to me that the old adage "a two at ten and a ten a two" was probably very true. He didn't get a chance to prove the theory completely, however, and before he was too drunk to walk to our accommodations for the night, Erik remembered the miles of road ahead and decided to call it a night.

The next morning took us to the complimentary breakfast of coffee and donuts, where Erik complained of a headache, stating that he should probably get his glasses checked. That made me chuckle, but I kept any snide remarks to myself. We checked out and hauled our bags to the car. I was eager to hit the road and asked if he wanted me to drive. He said he would rather go ahead and drive for a while, so I jumped into the co-pilot's seat and buckled in for the long haul.

After a couple of hours on the road, we crossed into New Mexico and arrived at historic Clayton, a small town of around two thousand people. We made use of a local gas station to fill up with gas and empty bladders. Erik declared that he was ready for a nap and asked me to drive. As we hit the highway again, Erik decided he'd rather have a cerveza instead of a siesta. As long as he was discrete, I didn't care. We made good time with the national speed limit having been increased that year from 55 to 65 and I decided to push it. The road was flat and straight and there was hardly any traffic. Before long, I was up to 80 miles an hour, the Corvette loping along at a pretty low RPM. I pressed the pedal a little more and before I knew it we were doing 100. The road was still flat, smooth, and open with barely a car in site. I mentally shrugged my shoulders and set the cruise control. With those conditions and in that car, I felt like I was doing 40. Erik was sound asleep, having hammered a few beers immediately after I took the wheel.

The stretch of highway we were on cuts across the northeast corner of New Mexico and entails about 100 miles of brown terrain. We weren't going to be in New Mexico for very long at the rate we were going. After about a half an hour, a line of cars appeared in the oncoming lane of the two lane highway. The third one in the line caught my attention because of a strange looking structure on its roof. It was round and there appeared to be an orange glow inside of it. I hadn't seen anything like it before and as it passed by, I looked in the mirror to catch site of it from the rear. As I glanced, I saw brake lights from the car that was behind it and saw the car with the alien looking orb start to do a U-turn. Crap! I suddenly had the understanding of what it must be. Moving radar. I haven't seen anything like it since.

Immediately turning off the cruise control, I settled into the speed limit. It only took a few minutes for New Mexico's finest to catch up and pull me over. The top to the Corvette was down and Erik was awake.

As the officer approached, Erik really came to life and decided it would be appropriate to engage the officer. "Nice state you got here, Officer!" I gave him a look to convey my displeasure at anything he might have to say.

"License and registration, please" were the officer's instructions. I handed them over. "This isn't your car, Mr. Dickinson?" he asked.

"No, it belongs to..."

"It's mine!" spouted Eric. "Ain't she pretty?"

"Eric, please let me take care of this" I told him.

I decided not to beat around the bush and told the officer that Erik was inebriated and I was the designated driver. I didn't use those exact words, because I don't think they had even been used together before that point in time, but it allowed the officer to understand the who and what of the two characters before him.

"Do you know why I pulled you over?"

Well duh, I thought, but said, "Yes, sir. I was speeding."

"Do you know how fast you were going?"

Again, I figured being straightforward would be best. "Yes, sir. I had the cruise control set at 100." I suspected his magic box probably told him anyway.

"We're going to Colorado!" Erik slurred. The officer shook his head and walked back to his car. I doubt that he could check my driving record from Washington as this was long before computers linked the world, but I suspect he was able to check for wants and warrants. In any event,  he came back up to the car with clipboard and pen in hand.

"Apparently, you'll be leaving us in a few minutes, because the border is just up the road, but I would advise you to do the speed limit until you leave the state", he said. With that, he handed me his clipboard and asked me to sign the citation for 100 MPH in a 65 MPH zone. I could feel the money pouring out of my wallet. "You can come back and take this to court to contest it or you can mail in the $125 fine to the address on the back." That seemed pretty cheap to me and I couldn't sign my name fast enough. I would have fallen over if I hadn't been sitting in a bucket seat about a foot off the ground already.

"Thank you, Officer!" bellowed Erik. I wanted to smack him. Instead, I put the Corvette in gear and slowly pulled away, thankful that I hadn't been treated with gestapo tactics and had been nabbed by such an understanding patrolman. He flipped another U-turn and we were both heading in our original directions, with me proceeding at a considerably slower rate.

We reached Colorado and completed our training. Our return trip to Texas wasn't nearly as eventful and I made sure that Erik was sober and driving for our journey through the little corner of New Mexico, encouraging him several times to do 100.

Don't Tell George

by Dave Darby

People whizzing across Iowa on Interstate 80 are in a rut. Perhaps they don't know it. Or perhaps they do, but are unaware that there is not only a way out, but untold treasures just a couple of miles to either side, where US Highway 6—America's longest highway dances back and forth, following the curves of the land, and paying respect to property lines laid centuries ago by some forgotten pioneers and farmers of days gone by. This is where you find the hidden treasures and the gems that are slowly fading from our collective memory banks.

One such gem is the world's oldest ice cream soda fountain. The Wilton Candy Kitchen has been in continuous operation since 1856. Built in that year for one R.A. McIntyre, this quaint little wood framed building, which leans slightly over to one side like a cartoon, has been in but two generations of the Nopoulos family since 1910. That's when Gus Nopoulos bought the business, and ran it until he turned it over to his son George, now 94, who runs it with his wife, Thelma.

George is possibly the world's oldest soda jerk! Visiting the candy kitchen is a treat, with George sharing his wry sense of humor, singing, and whistling as he scoops your ice cream. You won't find this in some chain restaurant out on the interstate.

People who've made the pilgrimage to this Iowa landmark include legendary actor Gregory Peck, Brooke Shields, Iowa governor Terry Branstad, and yours truly, who first bumped into this treasure in 2007. But this story isn't about that day. This story begins the following year, when my wife and stepsons set out for a trip across Iowa on Highway 6 in our 1999 Jeep Grand Cherokee. We were going to take the boys to see their very first drive-in movie in Newton Iowa, and we stopped by that day to visit George and Thelma and to get some ice cream.

About the time we were getting ready to leave, the air raid sirens went off, announcing a tornado watch. Thelma, took charge, herding the entire shop over to the basement of the nearby community center until the storm passed. Afterward, when we returned to the Candy  Kitchen, Thelma refused to take payment for our ice cream, instead saying, "Don't tell George". After thanking her, and saying goodbye, we started west, only to have the check engine light come on and the temperature gauge head ominously to the right after just a few miles. A check under the hood confirmed that the pulley had fallen off of the water pump.

We limped the Jeep back to the Candy Kitchen and asked Thelma if she knew anyone with any tools. Once again, she sprang into action, finding one customer to give me a ride to the auto parts store in Muscatine, and then she took me on a trip around Wilton, throughout her neighborhood, until she found someone with some tools to loan me. The Candy Kitchen was getting past closing time by then, but no matter, not only did they stay open late, but she made my wife and stepsons grilled sandwiches and root beer floats while I went about replacing the water pump.

By the time I had finished, it was nearly 9pm and when I came in Thelma sent me off to the restroom to wash my hands. When I came back, I asked how much we owed for the food, and once again, she refused to take any money from me. Instead, she pressed sixty dollars into my hand, and said "Don't tell George". I protested, saying I had a good job and that I didn't need it, but she refused to take the money back.

Thelma is that kind of pioneering spirit. When the old train depot in Wilton needed restoration, Thelma donat-ed thousands of dollars to the effort. She even found an old railroad semaphore signal and negotiated the purchase and delivery. A few years later, when my fledgling organization was raising money to put "Historic Route 6" signage along the stretch that went through Wilton, Thelma was one of the first on board. She sat in on the city council meetings and joined me in making the case for the historic signage.

With Thelma's help, Wilton was on board. As were the towns of Durant and Walcott. We were finally putting up the very first set of Historic Route 6 signs in Iowa. Later, when we set up a sign presentation at the community center with the mayors of the three towns along that stretch of road, Thelma learned that we needed to cater this historic event and she pressed two hundred dollars into my hand. I think you know by now what she said. In any case, don't tell George.

A Life on the Road

By Jim Hinckley

To say that I have an intimate knowledge of the highways and back roads of America would be akin to saying that Phoenix is a bit warm in mid-summer. Road trips and epic transcontinental journeys in vehicles best described as junkyard refugees have been an integral part of my life almost since birth and my family often used to tease me that pivotal moments of childhood development occurred along the highway.

I was born in the year of the Edsel and within spitting distance of the Atlantic Ocean. The following year we moved to Norfolk, Virginia, and two years after that to Port Huron, Michigan. In between were road trips to Arizona, much of it on U.S. 66, Utah, and a few trips to visit with family in Tennessee and north Alabama. We traveled in a battered old Chevy convertible that dad got cheap because it had spent some time under water after a hurricane.

In 1966, after spending every summer driving south on U.S. 127 to visit family in Chattanooga, Tennessee and making side trips for visits in north Alabama and Georgia, we headed west in an epic move to Kingman, Arizona that was reminiscent of the road trip immortalized forever in The Grapes of Wrath.

For the odyssey to Arizona, my dad resurrected a well-used and rusted C.O.E. truck representing the post war Advance Design series by Chevrolet. The calendar indicated that the epic westward flight of the Okies had occurred several decades prior to our move to Arizona. Still, we camped along the road on most nights, ate beans and fruit cocktail from cans, washed the dust and sweat from our faces in service station restrooms or roadside streams, and

watched the countryside drift by at speeds that occasionally were in excess of forty miles per hour, unless dad was making roadside repairs.

For reasons never fully understood, dad simply loved the life of adventures lived on the cheap. He continued such endeavors well into his late 70s with a trip to Alaska that included used tires, a twenty-year-old car, and a pup tent, as well as similar transcontinental voyages of discovery.

Five years after moving to Arizona, we packed up and moved to Silver City, New Mexico. In the period between these two moves, we made annual trips east to see family in Chattanooga, on Sand Mountain in Alabama, and in Jackson, Michigan where Hinckley Boulevard connects that city with Vandercook Lake, and one trip across Death Valley and up the west coast. With the exception of Route 66, seldom was a highway traveled twice as dad was a very big fan of seeing new country on every trip.

Early in life, I discovered the joy of personal road trip adventures, and an abiding love for a highway signed with two sixes. At first, a bicycle provided transportation for these grand adventures of discovery over a stretch of Route 66 bypassed in 1952 that snaked through the Black Mountains of Arizona west of Kingman.

As hauling water became a weekly chore by the time I was in junior high, four wheels followed two before I was old enough for a license. Behind the wheel of trucks that had rolled from the factory a decade or more before I was born, a passion for explorations on the road less traveled began to simmer as dusty, rutted trails were followed across the desert.

The next epic move, this time from Silver City to Jackson, Michigan followed a few years later. Shortly afterwards came the last family move, at least for me. That adventure involved two trips from Michigan to Arizona, each more harrowing, and exciting than the last, as they were the first in which I was behind the wheel.

Before casting my first vote for President Carter, an addiction to adventures was deeply rooted in my soul. Road trips were now as much a part of my life as breathing.

For a few years before settling down to raise a family, I flitted between Arizona and New Mexico, with occasional forays into Colorado and Mexico, and explored pioneering highways and trails along the way. Even when my dearest friend and I moved from infatuation to something a whole lot more serious, road trips, Route 66, vintage cars, and adventures on the road became an integral part of our relationship.

Weekend dates required me to drive from Ash Fork to Kingman on Route 66 in my '46 GMC. We double dated in a '26 Ford touring car. Drives to Oatman on old Route 66, a visit to Jan's Soda Fountain at the Kingman Drug, or a double date to the drive in theater in a '49 GMC consumed our time together.

After marriage, I introduced my bride to more of the thrills of road trip adventures. We traveled to the coast of Oregon, the Colorado Rockies, and into New Mexico. Still, as much as I enjoyed life lived on the open road and the people met along the way, there was a determination to ensure that my son would not spend his childhood as a gypsy. I was equally determined to instill in him a love for road trip adventures and the fascinating people who gave those exploits flavor and color.

Therefore, at least once a year our family embarked on such a journey, a road trip in search of America, and a world where the non-generic cafes and motels still reigned su-preme. Some were epic, others mundane, but none were boring trips to places such as Disneyland.

No, instead we fol-lowed dusty, rutted tracks into the Cerbat Mountains of Arizona in search of ghost towns with visions of lost treasure dancing in our head. We followed trails to the headwaters of the Gila River where cliff dwellings loom above the forest in canyon walls and made "whim of the moment" flights to Virginia to chart the evolution of America from Colonial Williamsburg to Monticello and then from the battle of Cold Harbor to Richmond in a rental car. We explored Indian reservations and Route 66, territo-rial highways in the Bradshaw Mountains of Arizona and Carlsbad Caverns, and sought out classic attractions such as Wall Drug, Rock City, and the World's Largest Hand Dug Well.

When I was not taking road trips, I planned road trips, and read about historic road trips. Soon came requests to tell tales of road trips.

Somewhere around twenty-five years ago, with gentle encouragement from my wife, I decided to pursue a child-hood goal of becoming a writer by harnessing what folks called a gift for telling people where to go and my passion for vintage vehicles. The pursuit of that goal continues, as does my love for telling folks where to go. Likewise with my passion for adventure on the road less traveled.

To date this has manifested in hundreds of feature articles and more than a dozen books. It also provides ample  fodder for my daily "Route 66 Chronicles" blog about adventures on the road less traveled.

As luck would have it, I have been out of style so long that I am now in style. Legendary Route 66 is now America's longest attraction. It has morphed into a living, breathing time capsule with just an overlay of Disneyland and as a result, a bit of time travel tinges our road trips since the past and present blend together seamlessly on the double six.

The great American road trip has been an integral part of my life for almost six decades. Fortunately, for more than three decades those adventures on the road and the memories made were shared with my best girl.

If our recent adventure on Route 66 and U.S. 54 are any indication, I am quite confident that it will continue to dominate our lives for a few decades more.

Now, I wonder how long it would take to drive Route 66, end to end, in a Model A Ford?

In the Shadow of Sputnik

by Albert Drake

I am not the kind of mechanic I once wanted to be, although I have done well on roadside breakdowns. When my '48 Ford quit in the middle of a construction site at the foot of the Cascades, I determined that the problem was fuel delivery and amid the roaring of giant machines, I installed the fuel pump that I had been carrying around for ten years. Later on that same trip, I stopped in the middle of Boise, ID. I pulled the radiator and carburetor, took them to respective shops, and soon had the old Ford underway again.

I owned, serially, three International Travelalls and I always carried an abundance of spare parts. On one occasion, I had to switch alternators in the middle of the night in the middle of Idaho. The third Travelall was an ex-ambulance. It had low miles, but the gaskets had dried out. In Iowa City, I bought gaskets, an oil pressure sending unit, and several wrenches. Off in the corner of a rest area, I tore that engine half apart.

I could go on. The examples cited are all older, pre-computer vehicles. I wouldn't know what to do if a new car quit. Whatever mechanical abilities I have evolved from the first cars I owned, 1930s cars, and whatever I know I learned from my father. He had no qualms about tearing apart a car on Saturday knowing he had to drive it to work on Monday. He did the work himself, because he had to and because he couldn't afford to pay someone else to do it. Until recently, that was pretty much my motivation. In turn, necessity shaped my life.

In 1957, my friend, Jerry Burns, and I drove to San Francisco in his nearly new MG-A and it was really a life-changing experience. The distance wasn't great, but the trip's importance was and it came at a crucial time. Jack Kerouac's novel, On the Road, had recently been published and it was widely read. It seemed like a manifesto for the postwar generation. Get behind the wheel and go, man, go! Of course, I would have been unaware of the book if I had continued my life working in garages and warehouses and screwing around with hot rods. I was entering a new phase and the trip to 'Frisco helped make the transition.

I had crap jobs for several years after I graduated from high school. Then, aware that my life was not going anywhere, I began taking evening classes at Portland State College. That was a big deal! No one in my family had gone to college and I never thought I would. But, I did okay and in the fall of 1957 I decided to quit my warehouse job and go to college full time. This was another big step for a poor boy.

Two of my close friends were Jack and Jerry Burns. They were twins and we had a lot of fun together. They dabbled in college, taking classes, flunking out, working, hanging around, and then going back. No doubt, their experiences inspired me. We also had a mutual interest in cars. I wanted to modify the cars and they wanted to meet girls in them. They would pool their money and buy a set of wheels to drive. Because there were two of them, they met twice as many girls.

When I got to know them in high school, they had a primo, one owner 1934 Lafayette sedan which they soon stripped and turned into a hot Rod. A gray 1938 Ford

144

standard followed that. It had become a real piece of crap and another friend and I bought it from the Burns brothers for $20. Then, they had a beautiful 1946 Ford four-door. That was in turn followed by a tomato red 1950 Mercury convertible; a car that attracted many girls. They figured that more cars meant more girls. I guess they were right, because they always had plenty of girls around.

We turned 21 and began to hit the taverns and bars and, of course, constantly cruised downtown Broadway with the top-down or made weekend passes at the beach. All of this continued until one day in 1957 when the Burns boys bought a nearly new MG-A roadster. By association, I was moving up in the world.

Jerry and I decided that we would kick loose and head for 'Frisco. So, two days later I quit my job and we took off. The car was gassed, the top was down, and the weather was great. In those days, the Baldock freeway (I-5) ended at Albany and although the highway narrowed it was smooth and traffic was light. We skimmed along, our hearts light with the joy of youth. This was our big adventure; something we would talk about for a long time. I'm in my 80s as I write this story.

A few miles before we reached Grants Pass, the engine made a crazy noise and the car lost power. Jerry pulled over, popped the hood, and we got out and listened. We were in the middle of nowhere, without money for a mechanic and a motel for who knew how many days. We were screwed.

It sounded to me like the noise was coming from the upper regions of the motor. We had only the toolkit that came with the car and I took a spanner wrench and removed the rocker arm cover. Once off, the problem was revealed. A rocker arm shaft support had broken. I picked out the pieces of metal, removed two pushrods, replace the cover, and we drove into Grant's Pass on three cylinders.

At the edge of town, Jerry pulled into a service station and stopped. What to do? We were midway between Portland and 'Frisco, with a car that would barely run. It was a Sunday and no garages or parts houses were open. Moreover, it was a foreign car. There were no parts for it outside of a major city. We were stuck! We pondered, quizzed the attendant, and Jerry smoked a cigarette.

When I went around the building to the restroom, I noticed a car beside the station with its hood up. I glanced into the engine compartment and saw a rod sticking through the side of the block. The attendant said that the owner had been drag racing at the local strip and the engine had thrown a rod. Suddenly, things clicked. Although this was an American car, I knew that the engine was nearly identical to the one in the MG-A.

I made a wild suggestion. I asked the attendant whether we could borrow the rocker arm shaft support, put it on our car and drop off a new one on our return. It wasn't his car, but he was agreeable. I made the switch and soon we were on our merry way. (Question: what kind of car was it? Answer at the end.)

'Frisco was everything I had hoped for. Sunny weather, steep hills with a view, cable cars, and pretty women. I'd been in the Bay Area several times. I had, in fact, spent a week at the Oakland roadster show four years earlier. But, this was different. Picture two young men, dressed in Ivy League casuals, tooling around in a sports car, top down, checking out women. We were a dynamic duo.

'Frisco was a different place in those days. Little traffic, plenty of parking spots, and interesting bistros. We stayed in a Victorian style house in an apartment owned by three airline stewardesses. They were off somewhere in the world. I never saw the girls, but there was an abundance of tiny bottles of booze they'd brought home. We sampled them. A lot of them.

At 22, I really didn't know much, but thought I did and wanted to know more. We went to a couple of museums and happened on the City Lights Books shop, which had a big sign in the window that read "Banned Books". As we entered, there was a guy reading poetry to a small group of people. We looked around and decided that the sign was misleading.

In a park in North Beach, we came upon a display of geodesic domes. The one that I remember was simply 4' x 8' sheets of plywood bolted together without support to form an igloo-shaped structure. I had some vague idea of becoming an architect and all of this was immensely interesting to me. Such displays gave me ideas and although I didn't know what to do with them, they forced me to think differently about many things.

There were few sports cars in Portland and part of the reason for the trip was to check out sports cars in the Bay Area. We talked about buying something, but we really didn't have any money. We just looked, going from agency to agency on Van Ness Avenue with its old commercial buildings with huge columns.

We checked out a variety of MGs, Austin Healeys, Jags, Triumphs, and other cars we never saw in Portland like Alpha Romeos, Porsche Speedsters, Ferraris, Lancias, Morgans, a Jowett Jupiter, and a couple racing specials. We drove along El Camino Real, checking out the used car lots and even stopped at Moss Motors where Ken Miles worked. When we pulled up in that MG-A, looking smooth, the salesman treated us like players. We didn't buy a car, but we did buy that rocker arm shaft support, which was dropped off at the station in Grants Pass on our return trip as promised.

In the evening we hit the bars. 'Frisco seemed so different from Portland that it was almost like being in a foreign city. Even the odor of cooked food that drifted along the sidewalk was like nothing I had ever experienced. In the window of the Hippopotamus, a funky restaurant, a cook was cutting thick slices of roast beef. We stopped for dinner, got a chunk of meat, a plate of spaghetti, and garlic bread. It sounds common today, but I had never had such a meal before. And when you're young your taste buds are keen.

Then, we went to the Monkey Inn and started drinking. It was noisy and funky, with peanut shells all over the floor; something one could not do in Portland. There were signs behind the bar that I've never forgotten. One said, "As Cleopatra said to Mark Anthony: I am not prone to argue." I thought that was funny. Another sign puzzled me: "IITYWYBMAB?" I asked the bartender what it meant. He replied, "If I tell you will you buy me a beer?" I had to ask him three times before I finally got the meaning.

Then, we went to other drinking places and everyone was a learning experience. We discovered the Copycat on Fillmore, the kind of dive a 22-year-old kid dreams about. The bill of fare offered beer, peanuts, pretzels, a player piano, and the promise of romance. There was a Happy Hour with cheap beer and on Wednesday night the ladies could get nickel beer.

On Sunday, there was a "Guest House Delight" with all-you-can-eat for fifty cents. We ordered pitchers of beer (illegal in Oregon) and filled up on peanuts. It was liberating to throw the shells on the floor (also illegal in Oregon.) Entertainment was supplied by the G String Strugglers. I cannot recall how it happened, but late one night, after too many beers, I was whacking away on the gut bucket and a musician said I was hip. I assumed that he was serious.

Later that night, Jerry and I met two women and the four of us crowded into the MG-A. I was driving and made a number of turns in Golden Gate Park until we were thoroughly lost. We were in a swell mood until one of the girls mentioned the Golden Gate Sadist. He was guy who would grab people, male or female, tie them up and paint their genitals red. He never raped or murdered anyone; just painted them. That was the worst thing in the news. I didn't worry until the electric fuel pump began clicking quickly, an indication that we were nearly out of gas. Scary, yes, but also rather innocent, a crime typical of the 1950s. For us it was all part of the great adventure.

I have thought about these events many times over the years and considered writing of the adventures we had on that grand excursion, but never did so until now. It amazes me how much things have changed, yet stayed the same. I'm not sure what happened to the MG-A, but I'm still around and running on all cylinders.

Have you guessed the make of the car from which we got the part? It was a Nash Metropolitan.

Road Trip in a Muscle Car

by Bill Overton

For as long as I can remember, I have been a car nut. One of my first recollections is as a toddler riding in my Grandfather's 1953 Chevy Wagon and being mesmerized by the chrome on the dash. I now own that same '53 Chevy Wagon.

As an adolescent, I collected Matchbox cars and Hot Wheel cars. I would wait for a new model to come out and

then beg my parents to buy it for me. I had quite a collection.

When I was 15 years old, I had saved up enough money to buy a 1965 VW Beetle for $150. I called my Dad at work to see if he would come home early to sign the title since I was too young to sign for it myself. This was the time when the Meyers Manx Dune Buggies first hit the market and I wanted one so bad I couldn't stand it.

The Manx kits were out of my price range, so I settled for the second best. I would build my own dune buggy using the '65 Bug as the base. I pulled the body off the VW pan, cut the pan in half, and took out 18 inches to shorten the wheel base.

My brothers, Dad, and I worked on building the dune buggy by welding a frame out of pipes. I hired a professional welder to build the roll bar since I could not bend the pipe the way I wanted to. There was a lot learned in building that dune buggy, like electrical, mechanical, and metal fabrication.

I got my driver's license when I turned 16 and had the dune buggy ready for the road. It had a rear window from a 65 Chevy truck for its wind-shield and plywood as the front hood. It was definitely a custom.

In 1973, my parents rented a building for my brothers and me to run a car repair/body and paint busi-ness. The original name for our business was "Precision Automotive". We later re-named the business to "Overton Brothers Custom Body and Paint". We had built up a good business, which lasted for about 3 years. The business ultimately failed because my brothers and I made our own cars a higher priority than our customer's cars.

During this time, a customer had brought in her 1968 Camaro for repair, but it needed so much work that we did the minimum just so she could drive it. That was all she could afford. When she paid her bill, I made the comment that if she ever wanted to sell it, she should let me know. I was interested in buying it. A few weeks went by and she showed up at the shop, asking if I was still serious about buying the Camaro. That was music to my ears! By the end of that day, I was the proud owner of a 1968 Camaro that had a 327 and a 3 speed manual.

That Camaro became my test mule for several different engine and transmission combinations. The M22 4 speed I had bought ended up staying in the car the longest since it was bullet proof. It held up to any horsepower I put through it. The Camaro had Chevy small blocks as well as big blocks between its fenders at some point in the 5 years I owned it. The original 327, which was modified for more horsepower, ended up being the most reliable.

During the school year, we had to hire people to work the shop while my brothers and I continued high school. We were known as gear heads in high school; only interested in our cars. There were a few other gear heads at school and we keep up with most of them to this day. As soon as school let out each day, we were back at the shop working on customer cars, as well as the important task of keep our own cars running and looking their best.

In those early days, my Camaro had several different paint schemes, including a light blue with flames. We had  several customers who wanted flames painted on their cars so we used my Camaro to figure out how to paint flames. The last paint scheme I had was a darker blue with white Z/28 stripes. I really liked how the stripes turned out. Only the real Z/28 connoisseurs could tell they were not factory. When graduation came for me in 1977, I was more than ready to be done with high school.

The one thing I wanted to do once I graduated was to take a road trip in my Camaro to see relatives. For graduation, my parents gave me use of their gas card and some money to take this trip. All of my relatives at that time lived in Arkansas. So, I packed up the Camaro with all the tools I thought I would need, along with some spare parts and a backpack of clothes.

I took off for the first leg of the trip to my Grandparents house near Pine Bluff, Arkansas, and settled in for the 10 hour drive. The Camaro did not have air conditioning, so the early summer air was hot. I had both door windows down which helped to keep the air a little cooler. With the windows down, I could hear the loud exhaust just under the floor boards.

The exhaust system consisted of headers and bolted on thrust mufflers with no tail pipes. As long as I was moving, the exhaust smell was not too bad, but driving through the small towns of Texas, Louisiana, and Arkansas, there was a lot of slow going which allowed the exhaust fumes to creep in.

I stayed at my Grandparents house for a day or so before I was itching to get back on the road. Most all of my cousins lived in the Ozark Mountains in a town called Mountain View. Driving the Camaro through the mountains was a blast for me, because I am used to driving the flat roads of the Texas Gulf Coast.

The wide tires, posi-trac rear end, and the 327 putting out about 400 horsepower along with the close ratio 4 speed made driving the mountains a fun time I will always remember.

One day while in Mountain View, my cousin Alex and I went to the local caves called Blanchard Springs Caverns. The Caverns had recently opened to the public and I wanted to see what they were like. We all knew about the caves, but unless you were a trained spelunker, no one could see what they were like inside until now. The roads leading to the caverns had not been paved since they were new and the drive on the hot cloudy day was dusty from the dirt roads.

The tour throughout the caverns was fascinating. When it was time to leave, the elevator doors opened in the lobby of the tour facilities and the weather had turned into a driving rain. We left the parking lot and started driving on the dirt roads which had turned to mud.

At first it was fun since every time I shifted gears, the back end of the car would go sideways in the mud. However, we eventually came to a hill that was a steep climb for almost a quarter mile and there were tow trucks at the bottom. We stopped to talk with one of the drivers to find out what they were all doing there. He said that since the road had turned to mud, no cars could make it up the hill without help from a tow truck.

About that time, a four wheel drive truck started up the hill so we watched to see if he would make it. He was barely moving by the time he made it to the top. But, he did make it. The tow truck driver smiled and said there was no way I would make it in the Camaro. I asked how much he would charge to pull me up the hill and he replied, "Forty bucks."

He might as well said $400, since I was counting every dollar on my trip. Also, since he said the Camaro would not make it, I saw that as a challenge! I turned around to go back down the road about a quarter mile, and then did a U-turn to face the hill. I told Alex to buckle his seat belt while I was fishing for my seatbelt from under the driver's seat.

I took off in first gear, trying not to spin the wheels, so I could build up as much speed as I could. With shifts to second gear and third gear, the back of the car fish-tailed because of the Posi-trac rear end. I hit fourth gear at about 100 yards from the base of the hill and we were moving about 50 miles per hour.

As we passed the tow trucks, I could see the drivers watching us with interest. We started up the hill and it was not long before I had to drop back to third gear. When I went to third gear the car started fish-tailing and throwing mud from both rear wheels. About halfway up the hill, I was moving about 25 miles per hour and had to drop back to second gear. I could hear Alex laughing and I was having fun too.

Before long, I was back in first gear and throwing mud everywhere, with the top of the hill in close sight. We kept moving, but were down to just a few miles per hour as we neared the top of the hill. We cleared the crest not a moment too soon, the momentum exhausted.

After I left Mountain View a few days later, I headed northwest and wound up taking a breather in Eureka Springs, Arkansas. Eureka Springs is a wonderful old town to visit. I also checked out John Brown University in Siloam Springs, Arkansas, which I ended up attending.

One day, as I was driving through the Ozark Mountains of North West Arkansas, I stopped for gas at a little mom and pop gas station which was also a small store. That stop was interesting in that those folks had not seen a car like my Camaro in person. As I was filling the tank, a guy walked up and started asking questions about the Camaro.

Before I left, I had the hood up and talking with several more guys about what I had done to the engine and how it performed. I must have stayed there almost an hour talking with the local folks about the car and them show-ing me their cars and trucks. It was a fun time that I remember fondly.

Later that week, as I made my way back home, I hit the flat plains of Texas wishing my air conditioner worked. Driving with the windows down, with the exhaust under my seat, the noise, fumes, and heat seemed uncomfortable at the time. With only the Thrush mufflers bolted straight to the headers, there were no tail pipes. I now recall all of that noise and heat fondly and sometimes wish I could re-live those days.

These days, the road still calls and my wife and I talk about buying a Corvette at the Corvette Museum one day and driving Route 66. I really hope that one day we can afford to do that and take the time to enjoy such a trip.

Meeting Big Daddy

by Dick Page

P robably the most fun I've ever had on a road trip was in the mid-1960s when some friends and I went to Salem Oregon for a car show. It started out kind of odd. I borrowed the Toppers Car Club two wheel trailer and loaded my Deuce Coupe on backwards so that the weight would be properly distributed. That is an invitation to disaster if you ever have a flat tire on the freeway. With it being a two wheel trailer, it could have gotten upside down pretty quickly. But, being young and dumb we didn't know the difference. We were towing it with a '54 Pontiac station wagon.

There were no incidents on the highway. The trailer and coupe followed along just the way they were sup-

posed to, but once we got down there and as I was trying to walk around the trailer in the dark, I banged my shins up pretty good on the trailer hitch. That was a little bit of a setback, personally.

One of the first people we ran into down there was Ed Roth. He was trying to back a trailer with his "Surfite" on it, hooked up to the back of a hearse. "Surfite" was a genuine surfer's car. Under its unique custom surfboard carrier body was an Austin Mini Cooper chassis. Ed tried to get the car in a movie that he heard was being filmed in Sportsman's Cove in Malibu, and even though it was only

 a split second, "Surfite" made a brief appearance in the 1965 movie Beach Blanket Bingo.

So, he asked me to help him park the trailer and I did. It was one of those things where you're yelling... "Stop... Stop... Wait... Hold it... Stop!" Well, he backs into this guy's car and says "You got to learn not to mumble, boy!" This was typical Ed Roth as I came to find out.

So, we got all settled into the show with everything unloaded and were saying goodnight to Ed when he started walking over to the hearse. I asked, "Are you sleeping in that thing?" and he says, "Yeah. Nobody's gonna bother me in a hearse!" So, we said, "No, no, no, no. We got this big room and we're having some cots brought in and we're all going to share this area." So, we talked him into joining us and he came and spent the night in there.

Well, the next night, we decided we were all going to go out and went to a variety of restaurants in Salem, Oregon and of course, Junior Nelson wasn't 21 and everyone was trying to buy a drink. A waitress would come over and ask him when his birthday was and he'd stammer and say he forgot. They'd through us out. Pretty typical deal, kids with fake ID. He had Bob Ewing's ID and it didn't work at all.

Toward the end of the evening, we ended up at a bar with sawdust on the floor. We should have realized that the sawdust was there to catch the blood and the beer and we were the only palefaces in the place. It turned out that it was an infamous Native American drinking establishment. The waitress comes over, leans in to the group of us and says, "If I were you, I'd leave now." So, we decided to leave.

We almost got out the door and Ed, being Ed, spots a Lucky Strike vending machine with a picture of Mitch Miller on it, a fellow with a goatee that was a pretty famous band leader back in those days. He turns around and starts trying to convince a bunch of drunken Indians that that's his picture. Not a good thing...

We got out of there, somehow, and the next day in the Oregonian newspaper and there was an article about somebody getting shot to death in the parking lot right after that and we were hoping that the guy didn't have a goatee.

That was my first introduction to Ed Roth. We spent a lot of time with Ed at that show and away from that show. We got to know him pretty well. He would order the most bizarre foods in a restaurant. The first time I really noticed, he was eating Chicken Chow Mein and washing

it down with a lime milkshake. Come to find out, he didn't have any taste buds. He couldn't taste, so he was going for texture and temperature.

Another thing that Ed shared with me that many people don't know has to do with his nickname. He didn't like the nickname "Big Daddy" when a promoter at Revell tagged him with it. Apparently, the boys at Revell didn't think the name Ed Roth was exciting enough to help sell models of Beatnik

Bandit, Rat Fink, Drag Nut, Mother's Worry, and Mr. Gasser. He had signed with Revell for the model kits and he told

me that once things started to take off, he didn't mind the name at all and truly embraced it.

Ed played everything up as much as he could for shock value. He liked to get up in the morning and go straight to the car show and start air brushing tee shirts and dealing with the little kids and stuff. He was a guy that was driven. We'd go out and ride around in the Pontiac station wagon after the show was over and as we were driving down the street, he'd start yelling "Wow! Look at that house! Go around the block, Dick, go around the block!"

So, of course, I went around the block and it was a Catholic church and he was just going off about what a cool house it is. I was just speechless. So, I didn't say anything. I thought, "You can't possibly think that's some dude's house." I just kept my mouth shut and kept driving. But, it was a lot of fun and a great road trip what with meeting Big

Daddy Ed Roth and getting to know him.

In later years, I helped him show the Druid Princess and some other things. Junior Nelson and I became good friends with

him and when he was going to be in the Northwest, he'd call and invite us to spend the day with him. We had a good relationship and I really miss Ed. He was a real character!

Ed shared a lot about his dad and about engineering. He took a ballpoint pen and the back of a show flyer one time and drew out a picture of a three wheeled motorcycle

with an aluminum Olds V8 in it that he intended to build and he did build it. They used to race it in the dry river beds down in L.A., the concrete basins. He was just a real wild guy.

So, meeting Ed on this trip to Salem, Oregon made for a really fun trip. You just never knew what he was going to do next. What was on or what was off... you never knew if he was putting you on or if that was really the guy underneath all that showmanship. But, that was one memorable road trip for us.

We got bored one day and Ed had a striping brush and his air brush set, so we took the car and went down

to the True Value store and bought a pint of Glidden white enamel. As a gift, Ed pinstriped the dashboard of my car. What an artist! He just got in and got to it. His artistic talent was really obvious and to watch him was an incredible experience. The hardest thing for most pinstripers is making circles. He made circles around the screws that held the dash in with no mistakes, no wipe offs, no redo's at all. He was just an amazing talent.

After the excitement of meeting what I considered a legend, the trip home was uneventful. Once again, the trailer followed along with no issues and we hauled ourselves back to the Northwest.

The trip wasn't actually over though and it did prove to be eventful before it was all over. In the aftermath of that fun trip, I unloaded the coupe off the trailer. It still had slicks on it and the street was damp from an earlier rain. As I left the trailer and turned the corner of 38th and South Tacoma Way, the boys from the auto parts store were out front and so I decided to show off.

I nailed the gas, fishtailed, and wound up with the left front tire over the concrete divider into oncoming traffic that had to swerve out of my way. I ended up far enough over that the left rear tire caught on the concrete and sheared the pin off through the center of the rear spring leafs. The whole stack of springs unstacked and the

rear end came out from under the car just enough for the right rear fender to fall down and cut a groove in the slick. That pulled the quarter panel out at the bottom.

Well, it wasn't pretty and I had to borrow a floor jack to get it all back under the car so I could drive it around the corner to a temporary repair spot and get everything back in its approximate place to make it drivable enough to get it out to my shop and not feel like an idiot. That was actually the hardest part.

Of course, any time you say "Watch this..." and your friends are watching, you just know it spells trouble and nothing good is going to come from it. In the end, it could have been a lot worse.

Sadly, Ed "Big Daddy" Roth is gone, but I still have the coupe and many fond memories of one of the most creative people I've ever met. Thanks for the good times, Ed!

Aloha Bus

by Ron Chandler

Growing up in St. Louis, I remember a neighbor who lived up the street that had an older, silver 356 Porsche. Walking to school in the mornings, I would pass by that car, hoping when I was old enough, I could drive a car like that.

Having loved German automobiles since I was young, owning Porsches, Audi's, and Volkswagens was a passion in my life. My daughters grew up learning to drive a '73 VW Beetle and my son brought the first VW Bay window bus into the family when he was old enough to drive. I became rather handy at fixing and restoring these wonderfully engineered vehicles. Our entire family owns and drives Volkswagens from all eras.

A few years ago, I discovered a very nice 1962 VW Split Window Bus for sale on the internet. A quick trip  from central Utah to Lake Havasu City, AZ with my son and we were driving the bus home on its maiden road trip.

In adding the "Aloha" theme, the '62 or "Aloha Bus" has become one of our favorite buses for automobile shows. We have driven this bus thousands of miles since we have owned it with only minor issues. For the past couple of years we have attended the Northwest Bug Run Volkswagen show in Woodburn, Oregon. Part of our family wanted to drive up and see the large west coast all-VW show that my wife and I had regis-

tered for in the previous year.

Since our 1962 Split Window Bus takes some extra time out on the road getting places, my grandson decided to join me on the trip. We brought our favor-

ite traveling companions "Michi" our Yorkie and "Gypsy" a Chorkie, Chihuahua Yorkie mix. (This is my wife's pooch).

It was the end of May and we loaded the bus for our road trip. We left two days before the rest of the family and pointed our little 40hp bus towards the Pacific Northwest. If you have never driven in an old Split Window Bus, let me authoritatively state that it is like stepping back in time. The heating system is not the best for cold weather travel so, blankets are usually readily available. It is slow and does not like wind or any steep grades.

My grandson enjoyed all the honks and thumbs up we would get as everything traveling on the highway would

pass us. Usually averaging about 50 miles per hour, even the semi-trucks would blow air horns as they swept by, sucking us across our lane of travel.

Driving a 50-year-old bus, you get used to a slower

pace of traveling and we always try to take old roads that are less traveled when possible. But, we were in a hurry for this adventure and stuck to the interstates. I add flashing LED lights and a large reflective sticker on the back of the bus to let fellow motorists know something traveling much slower is ahead.

The trip up went without incident and we arrived in Oregon. The next morning was the car show and we were eager to meet up with some friends we made at the last show. To our surprise we won the Volksters Choice Award at that show. So, they were elated to see us drive the 850 miles in the bus again this year. Our long haul meant that we were the farthest traveled entry registered in the show. That's significant, because most of these iconic buses are only pleasure driven and never get too far from home, unless trailered. Happily we drove away with more fond memories of this wonderful yearly event.

We always head for Cannon Beach and Haystack Rock when in Oregon. The crisp ocean air, tide pools, and spec-tacular scenery is a must when we get this close. It also offers the local surfers a glimpse of an earlier era when Volkswagen buses were the thing to have for hauling surf boards and your beach friends. Old buses are an icon magnet for young and old alike when they are driving the Pacific Coast Highway and this old bus has driven along Highway One, 101, and the PCH several times.

After enjoying time on the beach, we headed south into California. If you ever notice a message board in California saying the road is closed in a little over 60 miles, try to understand why they put that flashing sign up. We wanted to drive along Highway One at Big Sur and I couldn't understand why it said the road was closed so far in ad vance. Well, we understood when we got to Gorda and the

road was closed due to a landslide up ahead.

We were not the only ones with egg on our faces as we turned around, believing it was many miles of backtracking to find a road out. As we were about nine miles back, we noticed vehicles going up a narrow, roughly paved, switchback road called Nacimiento Fergusson Road.

I couldn't resist following and adding to the adventure. Very narrow, steep grades, a loaded bus, and 40 hp with a line of impolite, impatient California drivers was not a good mix and I would stop and let the line pass when possible. As far as I could see behind us on the hairpin turns were Minivans, SUV's, and other vehicles following us up into the fog shrouded mountains above the rocky coast of Big

Sur. Paved roads turned to dirt and mud. Needless to say, this bus adventure had only really just begun.

Eventually, we found our way back on our original path and met up with the rest of the family who wanted to visit Crater Lake. My wife and I had been there before and everyone wanted go. About the time we got close, a freak winter-like storm hit us and

we were pelted with hail and snow and faced slick roads.

Again, being in the old bus, we were way behind the rest of the family and opted just to pass by Crater Lake, headed for Nevada and home.

With the sleet, hail, and cold temperatures, we under stood that Safari Windows were not the thing to have in the Pacific Northwest in wet weather storms. Strategically placed towels were adorned along the dashboard to gather up the precipitation that made it past our windshield before it reached the floorboards. After the family caught  up, they told us they never did get to see Crater Lake. It was fogged in!

They decided to wave goodbye and head for home and would be there late that night. We said that we would putt along and be home in another day or so as we were going along some more scenic routes rather than Interstate 80.

Just as we were coming into Lakeview, Oregon and stopped at a light, I heard an unnerving squeal coming from the air-cooled engine in the back of the bus. Upon further inspection, there was a bearing going out in the generator on the engine.

If you have never seen a 1600cc air-cooled Volkswagen motor, the generator is connected with the shaft to the fan that spins to cool the engine. If this bearing were to fail completely the engine would overheat and we would be stranded somewhere across the Oregon-Nevada desert border with no major towns for a hundred miles in any direction.

What you need to understand about 50-year-old bus engines is that your local auto parts stores don't stock many parts that you can use. I found this out again as we visited a store in town. The man smiled and said he could special order one and have it in a couple days. That wouldn't work since I did need to get back to work by Monday.

So, I found a spot in town on a side road and proceeded to remove the carburetor, intake, and other parts to extract the generator. Having a small can of oil, I lubricated the inner bearings on the generator shaft and spun it until it was free. I figured this would buy me some time and possibly get me home. After this roadside mechanical session, I wiped all the grease and grime off me, smiled at my wife, and fired up the little power-plant.

No squeal, no noise, just the purr of a finely crafted German engine. I was feeling pretty macho as I pulled around the block to add some petrol to the tank before crossing no man's land towards Winnemucca. Then the most terrible banging and clanking sound started coming from the engine. I immediately shut it down and looked at my wife and said, "This is not going to be good!"

Everything looked fine from outside so I fired it up again to the terrible sound of internal metal banging. Something must have been dropped in the intake port and was in the combustion chamber being flogged around by the piston. I remembered seeing an auto repair shop close to the parts store, so we slowly banged and clanked about two blocks and coasted to the shop door.

It was now late Saturday afternoon. The shop owner just happened to be a VW bus lover and offered to lend me his floor jack and a slab of concrete outside his shop to remove the engine and tear it down for inspection. He was too busy to help.

I had removed an engine for a clutch replacement, but never disassembled and removed the heads. It was time to learn something new.

I dug out my tools to remove the rear bumper and all of the other components for an engine removal. Remember that freak cold storm that affected us earlier up north? Well, it had now made its way down and was dumping a rain snow mix on my engine extraction efforts. Feeling bad for me, out in the weather, the shop owner opened up a door to his shop and we pushed the bus into a drier workspace over in a corner. He was wanting to go home for the day, but said I could use the shop for another hour or so while he finished up on another project.

I pulled the engine, removed the heads on the passenger side and located the remains of a small steel washer that was supposed to be under the bolt holding the intake. It had partially embedded into the edge of the aluminum head and was easy to extract. Who could have hastily missed that out on the roadside?

I hurried and reassembled the engine, installed it back in the bus and fired it up. Quiet, pure bliss again. I made the repairs within my allotted time frame, paid my new friend a little cash for the use of his jack, torque wrench, and shop space along with a Volkswagen t-shirt that I had purchased at the car show. He was happy, I was happy, and my wife just wanted to find a place to sleep that was warm for the night.

We usually just fold down the rear cushions into a very comfortable bed, but with the cold weather and my wife sitting around while I was having such fun, I opted for a room at the nearest motel to keep that perfect smile on her face.

We still had a little over 600 miles to get home with an untested, just reassembled engine, by a novice mechanic, across some barren highways until we could get to Winnemucca, NV. I thought it best to wait until daylight before getting back on the interstate where AAA might stand a chance of finding us if required.

The next morning we left early. With 600 miles at an average speed of 50 miles per hour meant at least 13 hours in a bus, when you allot time for fuel stops. I  usually figure 40 mph to account for winds and some time to talk to interested people at gas stations.

The rest of the road trip went without incident and that little motor is still purring like a kitten, except now it's sporting a new generator. Do a magnet swipe in the intake ports before closing up the engine and identify all washers, nuts, and bolts as you remove them for reassembly. Many lessons learned.

A few thousand miles, a couple weeks living and camping in a 50+ year old bus with the family and our dogs is priceless. To be able to share this experience with others is, well, let's just say it was a road trip adventure we can all enjoy reading about.

The Sheepmobile

by Gary M Hughes

Iwas born and raised in Montana and early in my adulthood, I transplanted to Seattle, Washington for employment. Finding out where I was from, the workplace bullies were always making derogatory comments about Montana. I can't tell you how many times I heard the phrase "Montana, where the men are men and sheep are nervous", along with certain animal sounds.

I'm fairly glib and have thick skin, so I usually got the best of our childish bantering and eventually gained their respect. Even though I am from Montana, at that time I had hardly ever seen any sheep and can't remember ever seeing a nervous one. I think it was only a coincidence that I met and married a wonderful woman who was raised on a Midwestern sheep ranch. Her parents were very successful in their business ventures and my father-in-law was internationally known, having lectured and taught at many agriculture universities and colleges.

In the early 1980's my father-in-law had finished with his life. My mother-in-law had passed some years before him. Since my wife, Colette, was the oldest sibling, we traveled to Southwest Minnesota to help liquidate the properties and distribute the assets. The process was challenging, but the three siblings eventually agreed with the distribution.

Most of the assets, equipment, and farm animals were sold to co-operative neighbors and the balance of the properties were distributed to the heirs. Because of my status of "car guy", our "stash" included their prized Mercedes automobile and a U-Haul trailer load of other treasured junk. The Mercedes was a wonderful automobile. One of the things really unique about it was the vanity license plate with one word... "SHEEP". I could hardly wait to get this car home and park it in the company lot. What fun this would make for bantering with the workplace bullies.

There was one other item that we could not leave behind. It was a baby Angora Billy Goat that was the last remaining farm animal. He was born with a distinctive penile deformity and was appropriately named O'Tool. We had a couple of acres at our home in Washington and felt O'Tool would make a great pet for our children, plus we could give the angora hair to the old ladies aid society for their quilting bee. The only problem was figuring out a way to get him home with us. I took the back seat out of the Mercedes, put in some straw bedding, and covered it with a thick plastic film so it would be easy to clean.

The back seat itself was crammed into the trailer with the other treasures. Feeling a little like hillbilly's, we started our road trip home in the prized Mercedes with the vanity license plate that read SHEEP and a farm animal in the back seat, pulling a beat up U-Haul trailer. I have to admit I was glad to have been a "city slicker" most of my life.

We knew a storm was coming and felt we could make it to Montana. Then, if we had to hunker down with relatives for a day or so waiting out the storm, it shouldn't be an issue. O'Tool was a good passenger. He slept a lot and ate when he was awake. Colette fed him formula out of baby bottles, raw produce, and cigarette butts. He really loved the cigarette butts and we never had to empty the ash tray. I think Colette's maternal instincts also kicked in a little with this cute little baby animal.

Driving across North Dakota was a real challenge. I would guess the cross winds gusted close to a million miles an hour and every inch of travel was a workout to keep the car and trailer on the road. I told Colette I was determined to outrun the storm and had to keep going. She, the know-it-all smarty aleck, impolitely informed me, the idiot behind the wheel that I was driving into the storm and not running away from it!

It was dark by the time we reached the Montana border and snow was falling. Within a few miles I had to install tire chains to continue any farther. The only traffic we saw was a few eighteen wheel trucks with crusty truck drivers making fun of the idiot in the Mercedes pulling the U-Haul. Apparently they didn't know I had a CB radio and could hear them. They sounded a little like the workplace bullies back home.

Slipping and sliding down the hill into Billings, it was apparent that we were not going to make it to the relatives' house across the state. I decided to find a motel and worry about the rest of the trip after I got some much needed rest.

It was too cold for the goat to stay in the car and not many motels will allow farm animals in their rooms—even in Montana! I lied to the motel clerk and told him we were traveling with our toy poodle. After all, he was just a baby and what trouble could he be? When I wrote down the license plate number on the registration, I noticed the motel clerk raise one of his eyebrows.

Wrapping the goat in a blanket, we smuggled him past the clerk. With his white angora hair, apparently he looked enough like a toy poodle that we got away with it. We decided to put him in the shower and close the door. That way, any droppings would be easy to clean in the morning.

O'Tool had other ideas. He'd spent most of the day sleeping and was not ready to be confined. He wanted to play and we were too tired to entertain him. So, he lowered his head and repeatedly butted the glass door on the shower. While it didn't break, it made enough sound to wake most of the other travelers within the motel. We knew that from the banging on the walls in the adjacent rooms.

The bathroom floor had ceramic tile and the next plan was for me to take some of the bedding and sleep in the bathroom with the goat so he wouldn't be alone and maybe he would be quiet. That worked well, for about a minute, until the goat started making the same sort of sounds that I imagined a nervous sheep would make.

I started visualizing the Yellowstone County Sheriff showing up at our motel room and arresting us for bestiality and other sexual perversions. Oh what fun I would have telling that story to the workplace bullies. But, the Sheriff did not show up and the last resort was to take the goat back to the car and start it up every couple of hours to keep warm.

In the car, I fed him four or five packs of cigarettes and with his belly full, he finally calmed down. O'Tool and I stayed in the car and got some rest between bouts of hypothermia. Colette got a wonderful night's rest in the warm motel room. What a princess!

The next morning revealed a beautiful Montana day. We continued our journey without too many more problems. We did pass a semi truck and heard the driver announce to his CB buddies that he had just been passed by a Mercedes with farm animals in the back seat and he wondered what was in the trailer. There was quite a conversation following that in which I pretended to be another trucker. I had a good time talking like a trucker and making fun of myself.

It was great to get home. Our kids and dogs adopted the kid goat and they lived like happy hillbillies in the big city. The goat taught the dogs how to graze on the lawn and the dogs taught the goat how to chase squirrels. I went back to being a city boy and proud of it!

I kept the vanity plate on the car as long as I could until the state of Washington made me replace it. Although O'Tool and the Mercedes are long gone now, I still display the SHEEP license plate with some of the rest of the farm treasures to this day.

Memories of a Montego in the Mountains

by Mark Heller

I have always been a fan of road trips and long drives in the mountains. The first road trip that I can remember was from Kettering, Ohio to the Indianapolis Motor Speedway with my grandfather when I was seven. He had a cherry red '68 Dodge Coronet 440 with the dealer installed air conditioner and the original "Dodge Boy Sheriff" window sticker.

On the way back, we went off course through Kentucky and I remember seeing old shack type houses way up in the hills and asking my grandfather who lived there. He told me they were "Hillbillies" and for many years after that I thought "Hillbillies" came from another world. This would be confirmed in my latter years during my time living in West Virginia and visiting my in-laws in Southwestern Virginia.

Early 1985 was not good to my transportation situation. I was still living in Northern Virginia. I had totaled my '74 Mustang II in February, watched the new owner of my beloved '72 Gran Torino Sport Fastback run it into the ground, failing in a bid to buy it back from him, and having to watch it languished in his neighborhood.

In April, I finally went down to Dick Keller Autos in Fairfax. It was a "Buy Here... Pay Here" dealership where my friend Kenny and his family had bought many cars from. I gave them a down payment on a '71 Toyota Corona

Mark II and because I had never had to make payments on a car before, the $122 a month seemed like a fortune. It was very clean, great on gas and only had 60,000 miles on it, but I became bored with it very quickly. Within three weeks of taking ownership I was already looking for something different.

I opened up the local Want Ad magazine and the one ad that caught my interest was for a '72 Mercury Montego MX for $325. This was the Mercury version of my Gran Torino and I had always liked Montegos, so I called the guy named Paul that was listed in the ad. He lived in McLean, which was not far from me. According to Paul, his daughter had driven it, but she wanted something more economical. He said it was not much to look at, but ran good. I told him I would be there within the hour.

On the way to see the Montego, I came up with an idea to obtain the Mercury and dump the Corona at the same time. I had no money to buy the Montego, but since his daughter was looking for an economical car, what if I could get Paul to take over the payments on the Toyota, give me the Montego and $100 cash? I spent the remainder of the drive practicing the wording of this proposal.

The Montego was beyond what I was expecting. It was a fastback with faded yellow paint, dented and dinged with a big clump of gorilla hair in the rear quarter, but there was no rust. I opened the hood and listened to the musical sound of Paul starting the 351M/400 engine. After listening to the early 70's Toyota four banger with only an AM radio for almost a month it was like the perfect symphony.

The interior was perfect and the gauges were exactly the same as my Gran Torino. It even had the bucket seats and the console I longed for when I had my Gran Torino! I took it for a ride around the block and while the front end needed some work and the tires were bald, the engine was smooth and powerful and the transmission shifted perfectly. This was exactly what I was looking for.

When we pulled back in, I laid out my proposal to Paul. To my surprise he not only did not laugh at me, but was actually interested. He asked if we could switch cars for the weekend and he would have his daughter drive the Toyota and get the mechanic to look at it. Since it was Saturday afternoon his mechanic would not be able to look at it until the following Monday. I gladly took the Montego keys and drove off.

Since the Montego was not mine yet, my intentions were to drive it home and use it sparingly. Since I was still only nineteen, the more I drove it the more my emotions took over. The temptation, combined with a well-earned three day weekend as a result of working ten consecutive days, and I decided the Montego needed an extensive road test. Sunday morning I woke up at six and off I went.

I took it to show my dad who just shook his head. Whatever. He was never a car guy anyhow and did not understand. I then headed to work to show it off. I was working in the warehouse of Best Products at the time, so I drove to the back of the loading dock and summoned whoever I could find to look at it. Reactions were mixed ranging from "Cool!" to "Oh God not another one!" Seeing that my co-workers were not having the appreciation for this fine piece of machinery, I decided to move on.

As I took off, I punched the gas pedal so I would make my mark during the grand exit. Underestimating the Montego's power, combined with its balding tires and worn front end, it fishtailed for about 200 feet, just barely missing the wall and a nearby dumpster. Feeling my heart racing, I decided to head for the mountains.

I headed for West Virginia, which was about 70 miles away. I had been there many times before, but as a passenger, never driving by myself. I drove past Leesburg on Route 7 and eventually wound up on Route 9 until I made it to the West Virginia line. With no map and this being the days before GPS, I got lost going down the back roads. Due to the limited number of gas stations, I nearly ran out of gas. Getting lost and running out of gas in someone else's car is not a good thing. Somehow, I wound up near Maryland, got directions and gas, and eventually found my way home.

By the time I got home that early Sunday morning there were over 250 miles clocked on the odometer for the day. During this trip, the Montego and I were forming a bond. The gauges glowed just like my Grand Torino and it drove just like it, yet had even more power. The radio stations were mostly country and the Dan Seal's song "Old Yellow Car" would come on repeatedly. It was like the Car Gods were telling me that this car was to be part of my destiny.

With a newfound confidence, I called Paul on Monday afternoon. Paul told me that his daughter was not really interested in the Corona and that I would need to buy the Montego outright. My heart sank and I was nearly in tears. I didn't have the funds to purchase it and I was tied up in the Toyota payments.

Regretfully I brought the Montego back, taking the longest route possible. As I pulled up onto Paul's street, the song "Old Yellow Car" came on one last time.

I kept in contact with Paul for the next week, calling him to check on the Montego as I attempted to unload the Toyota. One my co-workers expressed interest in taking over the payments on the Toyota and I called Paul later that day to let him know that I may soon be able to buy the Montego. He informed me that he couldn't wait any longer.

The Montego was going to be sold in the next few days to a mechanic who was using the drivetrain to put into an old Volvo. To this day it infuriates me when someone takes a great piece of American Iron and scraps it to bolster an anemic import. He said if I came over he would give me the buyer's number as he would have no use for the rest of the car.

I had no interest in the Montego without the drivetrain. It would cost way more to restore it than the car was worth, but I went over to see the Montego one last time. As I left their house, I took one last look, knowing that the car that brought me joy just a short time before would be no more. While it has been many years ago, the Montego remains as one of my great road trip memories.

Some Short Cut

by Ron Limbrick

As I recall, our first trip to Grand Rapids, MN was in 1987 or very close to it. Several car friends had been talking about this beautiful little town in Minnesota that hosts two car shows on one weekend, which was always the last full weekend in July. The first time attending was in the motorhome that I had built. We parked amongst the huge white pines that the area is noted for in the fairgrounds camping area.

One of the shows, hosted by an antique car club, was located at the local fair grounds, a truly beautiful setting on a grassy area overlooking a small lake. There was a swap meet associated with that show at the fairgrounds inside the agricultural buildings and open areas.

The local Street Rod Club hosts the other show which is a Saturday only event that has been held at various venues over the years. It includes a wonderful sit down chicken dinner at the end of the afternoon trophy presentation.

During the years since our first trip to Grand Rapids, I have brought several hot rods to the show and I can only recall missing one year due to an illness. We have made numerous "Grand Rapids Friends" over these many years

and it is always wonderful renewing these friendships at the local Dairy Queen. It is a great gathering spot after a long day of checking out the neat old cars, their owners, and discovering treasures at the swap meet. I always enjoy time spent with my good friend Bob Baas (my "B" engine builder) and his co-pilot Marie.

As we come and go to Grand Rapids, The Naniboujou is a favorite spot to have a meal on the North Shore in Minnesota. However, the last time we took the '39, we decided to take a little different way home. It was decided to take the scenic route home for a change as we never have taken it. It cuts out Duluth and angles south east towards Lake Superior. I think I had heard that it was a short cut.

The road was very acceptable and took us through Iron Range towns like Hibbing, Virginia, and Ely. As we left Ely, the road was very winding and narrow, a motorcycle rider's dream. After driving on this beautiful scenic road, we unexpectedly arrived at a road closed sign and an arrow pointing to the  left that read DETOUR—GRAVEL ROAD NEXT 25 MILES.

We had come way too far on this "short cut" to turn back, so we forged onward in the little '39 on what appeared to be a seldom used logging road. Luckily, there was very little traffic, other than one heck of a large logging truck in a big hurry. After what seemed like an eternity, we finally  made it to the end of the detour and back onto pavement.

As it turned out the only damage done to the car was at one of the events in Grand Rapids where a kid on his bike ran into my rear fender and left another blemish on the old girl. We got home without any more excitement. Thank goodness! All in all, it was another very nice weekend, which I think goes to prove that getting in the car and hitting the road can always be a new adventure, even when you're going to a favorite old place.

The Greene Mille

by Mark Greene

Honest. I had no intention of purchasing another "toy" car. Really.

The phone rang and on the other end was John Willhoit, owner of Willhoit Auto Restoration in Long Beach California. John restores some of the finest 356 Porsches in the world. His shop is filled with delicious old 356 and 911 Porsches. These are the makes and models I've been in love with since childhood. But there is one old Porsche I really love. The 550 Spyder.

"Hey Mark. You interested in a Beck Spyder? You told me a while back that you would like one."

Chuck Beck has been building replica Porsche Speedsters and 550 Spyders for some time. Before he sold his business,  he was also making Porsche 904 replicas with 911 engines. I would love to have one of those, in silver, with a 2.7 liter 911 engine, please. But I digress. His Speedsters and Spyders usually run with VW engines and VW parts on board. The frames are tubular and the body is a fiberglass shell. Given the right power plant, these cars are light, quick, and a ton of fun to drive.

"Hey John. Thanks for calling. Tell me about this Beck."

"A customer of mine had me custom build the car using as many original Porsche parts as I could find. The engine is out of a 1956 Porsche Speedster and we did some modifications to give it more power, like Duel Dellorto carburetors and a Porsche transmission. The seats are Speedster seats and the gauges are from a 356. Even the steering column is out of a 356 and the steering wheel is a Werks. The wheels are 356 five-lug rims with the hubcap retentions shaved off and they are painted. The car is stunning in silver with a hint of gold, just enough to make it warm. Porsche wool, square-weave carpets, blue spears on the rear fenders, fluted headlight lenses, and rear deck leather latches make her really sweet. The owner needs money now and he's willing to let her go for a fraction of what it cost to build the car."

"Email me some photos today, John" was my quick reply.

Within a day, I was on an Alaska Airlines flight to Long Beach from Seattle International Airport. John picked me up at John Wayne Airport in his VW Thing. How cool is that? I was in a topless Thing, SoCal sunshine on my face, and on my way to see what would become my next toy.

The Beck was even better than I imagined. It was like a brand new 550 Spyder, without the 4-cam motor of course, and without the half million-dollar price tag. They are millions of dollars today, but this was over 12 years ago. The check was written and travel plans were made to return in two weeks after John did a fluid exchange, installed a new belt, checked the vitals, and got her ready for a 1,323 mile road trip. The plan was to drive up Highway 1 back to Gig Harbor, Washington.

Once back home, I knew that neither my wife, Jill, nor my daughter, Paige, had any interest in that kind of drive in an open car that had no top, no heater, no radio, no spare tire, and would ride like a race car. "My hair will get messy!" Not a problem for me. Thanks to my parents, I have no hair.

"Hey Blake. Want to go on a road trip with your ol' dad?"

Blake was 8 years old at the time and I had been taking him to vintage races, car shows, and car dealers since he was born. His eyes lit up. "Let the planning begin!"

The first thing we did was to officially title the trip as The Greene Mille. It was a tribute to the famous Mille Miglia race in Italy that was established by the young count Aymo Maggi and Franco Mazzotti. Automobile marques of all types were raced on public roadways in Italy from 1927 until 1957, from Brescia to Rome and back. Jill sewed Mille Miglia patches on our matching red Porsche caps.

We reviewed Google Maps and began planning each day, making sure our daily travels were around 300 miles and scouting out cool places to stop and visit along the route. Plus, I wanted to make sure the hotels we stayed at had safe, preferably covered, parking.

Because the Spyder sat so low and Blake was so short, I needed to come up with something to elevate him enough to be able to see out of the car. After deciding against a stack of phone books, I called John. I asked him to measure the passenger seat and to make note of any angles so Jill could fabricate a booster from whatever design I came up with. We got some think foam padding and cut it into a shape and size that would provide comfort, safety, and visibility. Jill found some dark blue gabardine to match the Spyder's dark blue vinyl and stitched it up with silver piping. Blake was now sitting tall and comfortable, the custom design three point safety harness securing him perfectly.

With Blake being 8 years old, I wanted a way to engage him in the trip and provide him with a way to participate.

187

I told him that the Mille Miglia was a race with teammates where there was a Pilota (the driver) and a Navigatore (the navigator). So, we created sheets that Blake would use to track the oil pressure, oil temperature, and calculate the gas mileage every hour while tracking our progress on a road map. The documents were adorned with the Mille Miglia logo and an easy to use check-box system. I taught him how to calculate the gas mileage and he was armed with a high-

lighter to track our progress on the map. All this on a cool, carbon fiber clipboard complete with a stopwatch! We even found a 1000 Miglia sticker on eBay for the Spyder's windshield and Pegasus horse stickers for each fender, just like the race cars had.

John picked us up at the airport in his Thing and off we went to his shop in Long Beach. There, the Spyder was waiting, ready for her road trip. We stuffed all of our things into the tiny trunk and behind the seats and climbed into the car. Pulling on my string-backed driving gloves, I addressed John, "Well, we have our cell phone, sunscreen, hats, spare parts, sunglasses, and maps. Anything else we need?"

"A great attitude!" John replied. "I can't believe you're doing this trip in that little car with your son. Call me if you have any troubles." Part of me wondered what he knew that I didn't.

Blake and I had agreed on a few Greene Mille rules:

We were going to have fun no matter what. Frankly I was expecting a break down given this car had not been driven much. Since it was a custom build, there are almost always issues.

If we saw something cool, we stopped to enjoy the pro-verbial flowers.

We keep to the speed limits. Your children are never too young to instill safe driving habits.

And off we went!

I forgot to mention our protector, the Golden Lady. The Werks style steering wheel that John had installed on the Spyder is a wheel often used in the 550 Spyder and RSK60 racecars. The center of the wheel was fitted with a special "Golden Lady" horn button. There were several optional horn button designs back in the day and this one is pretty cool. We decided she would  be our protector for the trip, kind of a St. Christopher of sorts. When I later sold the car, I kept her and she's framed and hangs in Blake's bedroom as a keepsake of our Greene Mille adventure.

Our first stop was a friend's apartment in Westwood. From there we would leave first thing the next morning and drive west on the 10 to Highway 1 in Santa Monica. My friend, Steve, had underground and secured parking and given that the car had no top and no way to lock it up, this provided me a good night's rest. One problem. The drive down into his underground garage had a steep incline off the street. The Spyder was very, very low to the ground with a clearance of only six inches. We high sided on the transition from the street to the garage. Oops! We got out and rocked the car back and forth until it was free and tried again using an angled approach. Mental note: this car is LOW!

The next morning, the sun was out in L.A. and we headed west on Highway 10 to the 1. Starting in Santa

Monica and then cruising up through Malibu is one of those iconic drives on the west coast. The combination of fresh, salty ocean air and the SoCal sunshine was absolutely blissful. We began getting thumbs up from passing drivers and Blake decided to keep track of them on his Navigatore document. One tick, two tick, three tick. It was pretty cool. As we left the craziness of Los Angeles, the traffic died down and soon we were enjoying the Pacific Ocean views to the left and the Santa Monica Mountains to the right. We stopped at a few lookout points including Leo Carillo State Park and Point Mugu State Park for photo ops and to simply enjoy the grandeur of the big blue Pacific Ocean. I had to keep pinching myself that this was real. I was actually doing this.

Our first planned overnight stop was Morro Bay. But, before we arrived there were plenty of fun places to stop and enjoy. Where Highway 1 turns away from the coast at Gaviota State park we drove up the 101 to Solvang, a beautiful little Danish town that gives you the feeling that you're in Europe. We enjoyed some delicious Danish bakery and the photo ops with the Spyder in front of the European architecture was really cool.

Back to Highway 1, also known as the Cabrillo Highway, we cruised through twists and turns, passing Vandenberg Air Force Base and eventually ending up back on the coast at the Pismo Dunes Natural Preserve. We stopped for lunch in the little beach city of Pismo Beach and it was fun to see the crowd of onlookers who would gather around the Spyder.

We soon learned that every gas stop was not a short fill-up-and-go. Almost everyone wanted to know about the car and the story about our travels. It was fun to share these stories and Blake got to add more tick marks on his "thumbs-up" tally every day.

Highway 1 cuts inland again after Pismo due to the Montana De Oro State Park, but eventually we ended up back at the Pacific Ocean in Morro Bay, our first overnight stop. I had found a hotel that had underground parking so the car would be protected. I brought a custom car cover so at night the car could be tucked in and protected from the ocean dew and prying eyes. There was a built-in battery disconnect switch; the kind where you pull the red key out to prevent would-be thieves. When we arrived I pulled out a little bottle of spray-on detailer and we proceeded to clean the day's bugs off the nose and windshield. Then I saw it. There was a paint chip on the front of the car!

Blake could see the frown on my brow and asked what was wrong.

"Our first rock chip. Darn it!" Then something really amazing happened.

Blake put his hand on my shoulder and said, "Don't worry dad. That's not a rock chip. That's a memory mark. Every time you look at that you'll be reminded what a special day today was." I about started crying right then and there. This was an eight year old teaching his old man the meaning of life. It's the adventures, not the things that count. I'll never forget that moment.

The next morning we headed out early for our next stop at Hearst Castle. We parked well away from the other cars, covered the Spyder, and went on two of the many tours at old man Hearst's little abode. It is an unbelievable place. When we returned to the Spyder there was a car parked next to ours and a family was standing there, lifting a corner of the cover, taking a peek.

"May I help you?" I asked.

The father, in a heavy German accent, apologized for taking a look. He and his family were from Stuttgart and recognized the shape under the cover. We talked cars for a bit, took pictures of each of them sitting in the car and a family photo in front of the car as well. Pretty fun making friends in a remote place, but that's what cars do. They bring enthusiasts together no matter where in the world they are from.

We motored on toward Carmel by the Sea, stopping every now and then, taking photos along the beautiful  drive at places like Big Sur and, of course, we took a photo with the beautiful Bixby Bridge at Castle Rock. When we got into Carmel by the Sea, we slipped off the highway down Ocean Avenue into town and had an early dinner. Then, we entered the iconic 17-Mile drive at the south gate and took our time along one of the most scenic drives in the world, dreaming what it would be like to live in any of the magnificent homes along that drive. It was so much fun that when we got to the exit gate past The Inn at Spanish Bay, we turned around and did the drive again going the opposite way. New views and perspectives made it well worth our while.

We left Monterey and headed toward our next nights lodging, the home of Mr. and Mrs. Adams, the gentleman who married my wife Jill and me. He and his wife have a home in Santa Cruz and were gracious enough to allow us to stay with them. He even pulled his car out of the garage and let us park the Spyder inside for the night. After a delicious homemade meal, we walked over to The Boardwalk Amusement Park, where we rode the Giant Dipper roller coaster and ate cotton candy. That evening, we sat on the beach and watched Paul Revere and The

Raiders play on the stage. Yes, the original band. They even played SS396. Perfect!

The next day we headed toward San Francisco. We were just south of Ano Nuevo Bay when closing fast in my rear view mirror was a new Porsche Turbo. He slowed down just enough to stick his hand out the sunroof and give us his thumbs up. Add another tick mark, Blake. Then he throttled up and flew into the distance. Not long after that a CHIP (California Highway Patrol) came flying by doing at least 90. Not too much longer we arrived at the scene of our friend in the Turbo pulled over with two CHIPPERs behind his car. He gave us his thumbs up as we passed, although he didn't have the same smile on his face as he had when he passed us earlier.

"I don't think I'll count that one, Dad." said Blake.

We took time to drive through Golden Gate Park and enjoyed some of the sites in San Francisco. Then, we drove over the Golden Gate Bridge and the view looking up from our open top car at the majestic towers was spectacular. We pulled off at Vista Point to enjoy the magnificent view of the bridge and San Francisco.

The Spyder had no top or heater and it didn't matter. The weather had been spectacular; sunny every day and actually a bit warm at times. The sunscreen and Greene Mille Porsche caps did their jobs. It got a bit warm in the afternoons and Blake would snap the tonneau cover in place (there was a zipper down the middle separating the driver's side from the passenger's) and it would give him some sun protection during a nap. When I told him what the tonneau was called, for some reason he heard the word "banano". So he started calling it the banano cover. We still laugh about that today.

We drove into Sausalito and found a restaurant with outdoor seating on the sidewalk. There was a parking spot right in front of the restaurant. Perfect! As we were enjoying a delicious meal a large tour bus pulled up across the street and out of the door came a large group of Japanese tourists. They immediately descended upon the Spyder. Blake looked at me with worry. I got up and walked over because a few of them were a little too close for my comfort. The tour director asked me if this was "James Dean's car". I smiled and said "Yes, sort of." One of the guys asked if he could sit in the car. "Sure, I'll take your picture."

Big mistake. I spent the next hour taking photos of every one of those tourists sitting in the Spyder. Blake ordered dessert and ate it all. I never got to finish my sandwich. But, it was worth it to see all the smiles and, once again, we had new friends from across the ocean. We enjoyed some time in Sausalito and drove north to our next nights lodging in Garberville, home of what was once the largest redwood lumber mill in the world.

When we rolled into Garberville, it was getting a little late and the hotel I had made reservations at had given away our room. Thanks a lot! The guy called around town, which is about as long as a few football fields, and found us a room at one of those places where there are a bunch of little cabins. I believe that's where the word Motel originated. Our cabin was all the way at the end of a long driveway. As we passed the other cabins, each had a big 'ol Harley Davidson motorcycle parked in front with guys wearing leather, bandanas, and big black boots, sitting out on their cabin's porch. Blake looked at me and said "Those guys look scary."

"Just look forward, we'll be okay." I replied.

When we got to our room, all the bikers were walking our way. I have to say, I was a bit concerned because these guys looked like the wild bunch. One of them walked up and asked about the car, who we were, and where we were going. Turns out it was a bunch of white collar bankers, business guys, and so forth, on their annual "Hog Ride". Cue up the movie Wild Hogs. We ended up going to a pizza parlor with them and playing pool. Blake thought it was pretty cool to be hanging out with bikers and when he called his mom that night, told her how we spent dinner. She said "Give the phone to your father right now!' Pretty funny. Looks can be deceiving. And once again, the car introduced us to a new group of friends.

The next morning was foggy and we planned on heading up the Redwood Highway to the Avenue of the Giants and the Redwood Forrest. Our biker friends were doing the same thing, so after a hearty breakfast we followed them through the trees. It was pretty amazing with all of those bikes and the majestic trees climbing up in to the fog. The whole thing was surreal. We pulled off and waved goodbye to our friends when another CHIP drove past from the other direction. He pulled over and turned around, pulling up to our car. He walked up and Blake thought we had done something wrong. The officer said "Pretty cool seeing you in that group of bikers. Tell me about your car." We talked for a bit and he gave us his business card, telling us if we had any problems while in California to call him. Again, the car brings us another friend. He gave us his thumbs up as he drove away. Add another trophy mark for Blake's tally.

Seeing the little Spyder parked next to those giant trees was really incredible. Unfortunately, the Drive Thru Tree was closed that day. How do you close a tree? Well, they did, so we missed out on that photo op.

Regardless, it was a really fun drive in a convertible, especially looking up at those huge redwoods.

We continued north to Crescent City and Blake noticed a cut off road, 199, and some caves we could go explore. So we decided to take a detour and headed up 199.

Blake had been tracking our fuel up to this point. I was told that the car had a 10-gallon tank and when we had stopped for gas I was puzzled, because our mpg calculations were not adding up. We were getting 33 mpg consistently but when the gauge read empty the car only took 8 gallons. I figured the float in the tank was not adjusted correctly. The mystery was about to be solved. As we headed up 199, Blake mentioned that the fuel gauge read empty. I told him not to worry that we still had another 66 miles or so left and we could go to the caves and then we would stop at Cave Junction. Well about 5 minutes later, the car stuttered and stopped running. We pulled off next to a beautiful river flowing alongside the highway. It was then that I noticed my cell phone had no bars showing due to the mountains. Uh-oh.

I opened up the bonnet and looked at the engine like most guys do along the road when a car quits. I was trying to figure out how far we were going to have to walk to get help and the thought of leaving the car on the side of the road was worrisome. And I wasn't about to leave Blake with the car.

Every time somebody would drive by, we would wave, and they would give us their thumbs up but, they would keep on driving. Check off another mark for Blake on his sheet.

"Maybe we are out of gas, Dad." Blake said.

"No, I don't think so. We should have at least two gallons left. It must be something else." I replied.

I stumbled about, scratching my head, wondering what was up. The fuses were all okay, nothing leaking from under the car. Hmmmm.

"What is that little glass thing dad?" Blake asked.

"That's the fuel filter."

"If we had gas, wouldn't there be gas in there?" Blake said.

Once again, the kid was smarter than me. I grabbed a flashlight, opened the gas cap and looked down into the empty tank. My "Hello" was met with an echo. Turns out the gas tank held only 8 gallons, not 10 like I was told. A wave of relief came over me because I had been starting to wonder if our journey was over.

Not long after we realized our dilemma, a guy in an old beat up car pulled over and asked if we needed help. He looked like someone from a horror movie. You know, that guy who comes out of the woods with a large, rusty machete or chain saw eager to chop off your head. He was a pretty rough looking guy.

"We're out of gas." I replied.

"Well, I live pretty close by and I have some gas in my tractor. I can get you some. Let's go."

We got in his car and drove off up the road as I looked back at the Spyder, wondering if it would still be there when I got back. Then, I started thinking why on earth didn't we just stay with the car and ask him to return with the fuel? Doh! Not far up the highway, he pulled off and drove down a dirt road lined with dense trees and into the woods. I have to say, Blake and I looked at each other with worry as we got deeper into the woods.

Every horror film I had ever watched flashed through my head. Jason and the movie Friday the 13th came to mind. We arrived at a pretty beat up old mobile home with a barn behind it and junk scattered all over the place. We got out and walked toward his barn. Hanging from the rafters were all sorts of metal chains and saws and who knows what. Yes, we had walked right into a B-rated horror film.

"If I say run, you run as fast as you can back down that road." I whispered to Blake.

It turned out that he actually had a gas can. We siphoned two gallons of gas out of his tractor and he took us back to the car. We emptied the can into the tank and offered to pay him for the gas, but he wouldn't take our money.

"Happy to help. Have fun with your son. He'll never forget this trip," said our "Jason".

My wife still frowns when I tell this part of our story.

While continuing up the Coast Highway, toward Coos Bay Oregon, I noticed the oil temperature was climbing. I had picked up the speed a bit and when I slowed down the temperature would cool. Getting a little worried, I pulled over along the Pacific Ocean at Kronenberg State Beach to enjoy the view and think about why the oil temperature kept climbing. While we sat there a guy pulled up in an older VW bug. He came over to talk about the Spyder. Then he said, "My brother has one of these cars. Have you noticed when you go over 70 mph that the oil temperature climbs?

Are you kidding me? We are in a pretty remote spot and not too many Beck Spyders were built, but a guy whose brother has one finds us. He told us his brother learned that in the original 550 Spyder design, the air inlets placement in the rear of the car didn't allow enough hot air to exit the engine compartment. His brother had installed an internal fan so he could hit a switch under the dash and suck the hot air out when he drove at higher speeds. Pretty cool chance meeting on the side of the road. Serendipity!

We spent the night and laughed about our encounter with "Jason" and told ghost stories while the Spyder slept under her cover in the hotel parking lot.

We woke up early the next day, enjoyed a robust breakfast in a local diner, made a long day out of our final leg of the journey, and pulled into our garage late that evening. We were little sunburned and a bit wind burned from 5 days in an open car, but it had been an adventure that neither of us will ever forget. The Spyder never let us down and drove like a top.

I kept the car for several years and we enjoyed participating in many tours around Western Washington with our local Porsche 356 Club. However, as time and changes in life affects our automotive buying and selling decisions, I sold the car to her next caregiver. The money went in to the kid's college fund. The last I heard, she lives in Chicago, with a retired vintage racer.

Blake has never forgiven me for selling the Spyder and I must say, after writing this story, I have to put her on the "I wish I still had that car!" list.

The End of All Roads

by Jeff Zurschmeide

North America is a really big place. You don't think of it much, because most of us move around on just a tiny part of the continent. We drive up and down the nearest coastline or maybe take a ride on old Route 66, but to really get a sense of the scale of North America, you can't rely on a map. You need a globe. Take a look at the continent without state lines or international borders. It's huge, and almost everybody lives below the 50th parallel.

So, if you want to take the ultimate road trip, I say head north to the top of the world. Furthermore, if you're going in the direction of permafrost and tundra, what's the point of going in summertime? If you want to go as far as you can, you need to go in the North's purest season—full winter. But bring some friends along, because this is not a trip to the corner grocery store.

In my case, the trip started with a conversation among friends. I had not heard of the Alcan 5000 Rally before, but the idea captured my imagination from the first word. Leaving from Seattle, participants travel north for a solid week or more, ultimately arriving at Tuktoyaktuk, Northwest Territories up at nearly 70 degrees North latitude. As the crow flies, that's about 1500 miles. If the crow is driving, however, you can tack on another thousand to account for mountain ranges you've never heard of, beautiful frozen lakes, and adventures that simply cannot be predicted. And when it's all over, you turn around and head south to Jasper, Alberta in the Canadian Rockies, or to Anchorage, Alaska; with another week to go to drive home when you're done.

To make this journey, I chose two trusted friends to share an all-wheel-drive SUV, and we teamed up with another trio in an identical vehicle for mutual support. Matt Tabor, Gary Bockman, and I did everything we could to prep the normally sedate soccer-mom car for the great white north, in-cluding a skid pan to keep the snow out, two extra spare tires, 10 gallons of gas on the roof, and a 12-volt coffee maker. We added some extra headlights to see in the land of the noonday night and the roughest studded tires we could find. And a radio, to keep in touch with the rest of the rally; perhaps the only people we could be sure would respond in an emergency.

The first four days of the rally are a steady trek north-ward through British Columbia and up to the Yukon. But from the moment you find yourself north of Vancouver, B.C., there is beauty and adventure. Maybe the Canadians are saving this all for themselves or maybe they just need a new marketing department, because the country is stunning up there. From the Blackwater highway to the Cassiar highway, past the Fraser River and Dease Lake, you just keep heading north. Eventually you get to Whitehorse, Yukon Territory. the last town big enough to have a car dealership and the site of the northernmost Starbucks in the world. Whitehorse is located at 60 degrees north latitude, about the same as Helsinki, Finland and St. Petersburg, Russia.

There are no police north of Whitehorse. That may not sound like much, but it's critical. When you get up onto the

Klondike Highway, it's a whole new world. They don't have police because there's no one there to watch over in the hundreds of miles that separate the tiny settlements. It's just you and the caribou and the ice road truckers.

Your goal when you leave Whitehorse is a town called Dawson City. Dawson is far enough up that you can rest  up there before you make the long run up to the north shore. The El Dorado Hotel in Dawson City is a slice of Gold Rush history. It's the home of the Sour Toe cocktail, for one thing. Tales grow taller with the years, but there's no denying that they've got an actual human big toe, pickled in whiskey. Order the Sour Toe and they plunk it in your drink. You're supposed to drain your glass and let the toe touch your lips. They have different ideas of fun up there. Dawson is picturesque, but it's just a jumping-off place for the real adventure.

The day that you cross the Arctic Circle begins well before dawn. It's a two-hour drive to Dempster Junction from Dawson. If you don't make it onto the Dempster Highway before 8:00 a.m., you probably won't make it to Inuvik in one day.

As we were getting ready for the trip to the Circle, several locals blessed us with the admonition, "Don't pass gas." It might sound funny, but this is a deadly serious caution. At this latitude, those who want to live to see the next summer top off their fuel tanks at every opportunity.

The reason for the fuel warning quickly becomes obvious. The Dempster Highway is little more than an extra-wide gravel road. Apart from the rudimentary path under your wheels, the gas station at the crossroads of the Klondike and Dempster highways is the last work of mankind you will see for 250 miles. Well, there is a wrecked and abandoned car down in one of the bigger ditches, but we weren't brave enough to climb down and check for skeletons.

Once you're on the Dempster, you soon pass from mountains and valleys into one of the most spectacular and remote landscapes on Earth. The tundra stays frozen almost all year long, ancient and timeless. There are trees that look like something from a science fiction movie. They can be over 50 years old and barely 6 feet tall, because that's all they can manage to grow. Frozen ponds are scrubbed and polished into diamond-bright mirrors by blowing snow. Crest a rise and you can see for 50 miles or more in every direction, and in all that space there is no evidence of humanity; not a power line or a fencepost to be seen.

The views are incredibly beautiful and delicate, but the land is also treacherous. The Canadian government plows the snow on the Dempster highway with a grader that is

about 10 feet wider than the road, and so cuts a clean, flat, inviting surface well out over the ditch on either side. And let's be clear, this is not a small ditch such as we have in the lower 48 states. The Dempster has the Grand Canyon of ditches. They're big enough to swallow your car whole under the snow. When you encounter the ice road truckers, they're moving somewhere around 80 to 90 miles per hour, dead center in the road. It's up to you to get out of the way.

Two hundred and fifty miles after your last sight of human habitation, you come to the settlement of Eagle Plains, population: 8. Eagle Plains is a bunch of portable buildings perched on a windswept ridge. It exists because it's one tank of gas away from the junction, and another tank to get to Fort McPherson. They do a steady, if sparse, business. We'll be back to stay here on our way home, but for now we push on. Our first big goal is just about 20 miles ahead.

The Arctic Circle monument is in the middle of nowhere. The kind of nowhere that makes any nowhere you've ever been seem like somewhere. But there's a monument and it's typically not all that cold, so people get naked, do stupid things, and get their pictures taken while they misbehave.

After about five minutes at the circle, you've pretty much been there and done that, so it's back on the road for another 200 miles through Fort McPherson and on to Inuvik and the treasures of the North. Inuvik is a town of about 3,500 souls and is the largest city north of the Arctic Circle in America. They have a nice hotel and the special on the dinner menu there was Elk. I asked the waitress to tell me more about it. "Grilled," she said. "Not sure if it was a Freightliner or a Peterbilt, though."

You go to bed early in Inuvik, because the next day is the big Inuksuk and the goal that brought you almost 2,500 miles to this point. The day I was there was February 20, 2008, and sunrise was due at 8:45 AM. We were up at about 5:00 AM to get started on the ice road.

Tuktoyaktuk cannot be reached by car in the summer. To get there from Inuvik, you must drive over 100 miles down the frozen McKenzie River, then about 10 miles across the Beaufort Sea to the town, which sits on a little peninsula that sticks out into the Arctic Ocean.

Something I didn't know—an ice road is nothing like an ice skating rink. You might think that ice should freeze smooth and stay solid, but it doesn't. "You gotta be careful, man," says the kid at the Petro-Canada station, "it's a full moon tonight and the tides pull on the ice, and it gets bumpy."

"Bumpy" is an insufficient term. "Bumpy" includes holes in the ice big enough to break a wheel on one of the Subarus, and to blow tires on three separate cars. But we soon work out a system: drive far enough back that you can just see the taillights of the car in front of you. That way if they stop, you've got time to avoid whatever it was that they hit.

And if you see the taillights, then the headlights, then the taillights, then the headlights again, for God's sake slow down. And this is not an uncommon sight on the road, because there's one more record you can break, if you're bold enough.

Out on the big straight path across the ten miles of Arctic Ocean that leads to Tuk, you can try for an unofficial speed record. Think of it like the Bonneville Salt Flats, only with no salt and not flat. The cherry on the sundae of this challenge is proving your top speed, but one brave soul managed to get a snapshot of his speedometer hitting 122 MPH.

We arrived in Tuk, none the worse for our adventure, and we watched the moon set and the sun rise on the frozen beach. The Canadian government has thoughtfully put up a monument to mark the north shore, almost 70 degrees north of the Equator.

If the Arctic Circle is in the middle of nowhere, then Tuk is the far edge of nowhere. Look north from this point and there's nothing but ice until north becomes south and people speak Russian. But if you made it this far, you did it. You reached the end of all roads.

Then, you turn around and drive back.

But, when you return to the land of lush green foliage, with people and towns around every curve, the fragile beauty that is the soul and magic of the Arctic just isn't there. I came back with a profound respect for the great north, its scale, its beauty, and the challenge of the journey to go and see it in its frozen glory.

It's the great, big, broad land 'way up yonder,
It's the forests where silence has lease;
It's the beauty that thrills me with wonder,
It's the stillness that fills me with peace.

There's a land where the mountains are nameless,
And the rivers all run God knows where;
There are lives that are erring and aimless,
And deaths that just hang by a hair;
There are hardships that nobody reckons;
There are valleys unpeopled and still;
There's a land—oh, it beckons and beckons,
And I want to go back—and I will.

– Robert W. Service "The Spell of the Yukon"

The Great Road Trip

by Steve Walker

Almost every summer, we would load up the Ford and set out on a Great Road Trip, visiting all our various relatives scattered across this nation. Dad was from Poplar Branch, North Carolina, where he had as a teenager worked one hellish summer in an unventilated Ford assembly plant in Norfolk, in temperatures soaring up to 120. He had remained a loyal Ford man ever since.

We lived just east of Seattle in a new suburb nestled among forests and swamps where I could find frogs and garter snakes and the occasional stray cat to bring home to be the family pet. Each sorry pet I brought home would cause Dad to reminisce about the hunting dogs he had had in his youth. I was always concerned about the care of my charges during our prolonged summer absence, but this never proved to be a problem since they all disappeared right before each annual trip.

We headed south, starting our journey with the California relatives. Dad drove with silent determination. Mom chain-smoked cigarettes and offered occasional navigation advice. The windows were kept rolled up because Mom didn't like the way the wind buffeted the maps and her hair. Billy and I sat in the back, pleading for a crack of fresh air. A disturbing rear suspension shimmy aggravated our growing nausea. Billy was first to puke.

We had barely cleared Oregon. Dad, keeping one eye on our changing color in the mirror, issued harsh warnings of the consequences, too terrible to name, for vomiting in the Ford. Billy was pressed up against his still closed window gurgling. Mom, sensing the urgency, signaled to Dad to pull over and as soon as she unlatched her door, Billy simultaneously erupted and launched himself from the still rolling car.

"Just another three hundred miles" said Mom, helpfully.

Various ads for road-side attractions, just minutes from the highway, caught our attention and then receded as Dad drove relentlessly on. Desperate to get out of the car, Billy and I begged to visit the "World's Tallest Tree" and nearby, a driveway tunnel bored right through a tree trunk. The tunnel as it turned out, might have permitted passage of a Model T if you first removed the fenders, but there was no way the Fairlane was going to make it.

Dad frowned up at the World's Tallest Tree, billed at well over two hundred feet in height. It looked less than half that. "There must be something wrong with tape measures in California" muttered Dad. There would be no further distractions along our route.

Crossing the Golden Gate Bridge on a typically foggy San Francisco day, there was no view to see but we persuaded Mom to roll the window down a little so we could at least smell the sea air, and when she did, the fog rolled out of the car and revealed that it was a lovely clear and sunny day. The view was really quite spectacular.

Arriving at last at Uncle George and Aunt Dorothy's place in San Jose, my brother and I spilled out onto the front lawn and lay there gasping for oxygen. Cousins Billy and Pam brought us sodas and sandwiches to aid our recovery, and then Cousin Billy opened the garage to reveal HIS CAR! Billy was younger than my brother or I, but Uncle George had purchased for him a gleaming Quarter Midget race car and Billy was mid-way through winning every race of that season.

When George had met with the other parents before the season and asked what engine modifications were prohibit-ed, he got only blank stares. Quarter Midgets came as kits or ready to go, provided with Kohler or Briggs and Stratton engines. Other than belt or chain tension adjust-ment, people just fired them up and ran them. There were no engine rules. Why would there be engine rules?

Uncle George, a talented truck mechanic, proceeded to bore, stroke, and port the single cylinder engine of Cousin Billy's car. Before the next season, there would be rules pro-hibiting engine modification.

In the morning, after breakfast, we loaded up for the next leg of our journey to Las Vegas. "Just another four hun-dred miles" said Mom, drawing the lighter from the Ford's dashboard. Billy wanted to stretch out across the rear seat, the first waves of nausea setting in. That was okay with me.

Remembering my school fire-safety training, I knew to get down on the floor, below the smoke. Arranging myself as comfortably as I could, draped over the hump for the drive-line, my ear pressed against the floor pan, I nodded off, lulled by the mechanical rhythm of the whining differ-ential and U-joint, warbling in time with the suspension shimmy.

After a brief visit with Grandparents Frank and Minnie in Vegas, we turned south for Frank Junior's ranch in Arizona, a dry and dusty clutch of low buildings at the end of a long dirt road. A lone horse stood sullenly in the corral, defying anyone to approach or even think of riding him. Mountains could be seen in the distance, but only desert surrounded the place. We were warned not to venture out among the scrub brush and rocks as deadly Arizona Coral Snakes lurked there. There was also a non-poisonous snake about that defended itself by mimicking the coral snake. So while the one was identified by black, yellow, and then red stripes and must be avoided, the other had yellow, red and then black stripes and was safe to catch and handle.

We pressed on for Colorado. "Just another six hundred miles" said Mom, taking a long drag on her cigarette. Dad leaned into the steering wheel, glaring hard at the road ahead. We passed signs directing "This way to the Grand Canyon!" but Dad would not be detoured to look at some culvert lined with souvenir shacks.

When we pulled into Colorado Springs to visit Gus, Melvin, and I think Pud, I could not help but notice that not only were the given names of my relatives regressing severely, but we also seemed to be drifting backwards in time, from mid-century modern California, past the Dust Bowl of the Southwest, to a turn-of-the-century mining town where my Great Grandfather Frink had been the company blacksmith, making tools and repairing mine pumps.

Mom had grown up here, the lone sister among a gaggle of brothers. The boys had worked on trucks and cars and motorcycles while to Mom fell the "women's work" of fetching water, doing the laundry, raising the vegetables and chickens, cooking the meals (this last involved beheading and butchering the chickens, and chickens really will run with their head cut off she assured Billy and I) and cleaning and probably repairing and painting the house. She had come back to relive these fond childhood memories.

There were crickets and horned toads in the garden, but I was warned not to go beyond the yard, where Diamondback Rattlesnakes lived in the rocks.

We visited the Garden of The Gods, some brilliantly colored rock formations, and there watched Native Americans perform authentic dances. Afterwards, Dad purchased authentic war bonnets from the souvenir shop for Billy and me. The headdresses were made of Native American turkey feathers dyed a range of hues, pink, yellow and blue; too garish to have ever been worn by any civilized peoples.

In the morning, Billy and I crawled into the Ford. Next stop, Poplar Branch, North Carolina. "Just another sixteen hundred miles" said Mom. I lay on the floor watching the smoke from her cigarette curl in mesmerizing art nouveau patterns. All day and long into the night Dad drove, his fists tightly gripping the wheel at ten and two, his face a mask of determination, eyes no longer blinking. On and on droned the Ford, the differential singing to me from below, Billy groaning from the bench seat above. Stopping only for fuel or vomiting, Dad drove until he could no longer hold the wheel. Then we would stop, defeated, and drag ourselves into some roadside motel and collapse until dawn revealed the true horror of our lodgings.

Taking up the challenge anew, we pressed on across endless plains. I wondered aloud… "How did the Pioneers do it?" Crawling along at a mere few miles an hour such vast distances, staring at the same mountains day after day, they must have thought they were never getting any closer. "They were going the other way" explained Dad.

Crossing the Mississippi and veering southeast, Dad picked up a new scent: barbecue! Not that ketchup-smeared cow they served in the west, but real barbecue; seasoned pork that had been aged and cooked or cooked and then aged, until it had metastasized into something of a texture and consistency unique among meats.

Eschewing clean, well-lit restaurants and diners, Dad scanned the roadside for the ancient shacks and trailers, with a broken picnic table or two out front, where the true artists of this genre mixed their jealously guarded secret seasonings into vats of aged pork. But there was a specific flavor Dad sought, like a salmon swimming home, and only the precise recipe would do. Too spicy, too flat, too fresh, too runny, too dry; none satisfied his exacting criteria.

Forewarned of our approach, the clan had gathered in Poplar Branch; Forrest and Norbert and Macon and Grady. Even Aunt Doris, come down from Bethesda. We had arrived at a time now shortly after "the War of Northern Aggression", and the locals were still pretty sore about how that had turned out.

The farmhouse was referred to as the "New House", the "Old House", built in 1735, having burned down in 1847, though the original kitchen had been saved. The square heads of hand-made nails were visible in the boards. A road passed by on the way from Elizabeth City, which was mostly a post office, to Cape Hatteras, graveyard of ships.

It was told that a Scottish ship had gone down off the coast about 1720 and a single passenger, Caleb Walker, had swum it out and made it to shore; a sole survivor from whom all us Walkers may, or may not, have been descended.

The house had originally stood on the east side of the road, next to the family cemetery, but some distant great, great, great grandmother had tired of crossing the road to fetch water and demanded that the house be moved nearer the well. This had been a daunting task as the house had consisted of a great hall flanked by two wings.

My ancestors had skimmed the job, just sawing off the wings, dragging them across the road, and patching them together into a more modest structure with a narrow hallway of unevenly abutted boards to remind one of where the great hall had been amputated. Apparently, no one thought to just dig a new well.

There was not a lot of furniture or decoration in the house. Grandpa had discovered that he need only sit out by the road, and he could get as much as five or ten dollars for one to two hundred year old chairs, dressers, and duck decoys from foolish New York tourists on their way to the Cape.

In the tiny cemetery lay generations of Walkers, alternately named William like my Dad and brother, or Samuel like my grandfather and uncle. Family lore had it that we may, or may not, be related to the famous Sam Walker who had fled arrest in North Carolina (some infraction involving a horse) to the Republic of Texas, where he founded the Rangers (before his death in the Mexican American War). And to the famous William Walker, who attempted to colonize Nicaragua (before the Nicaraguans caught and executed him).

Grandma Valeria, who prided herself in her cooking, had prepared a great feast for us all. There was goose and soft shell crab from the Sound, cured ham, fried chicken, and corn bread from the farm, and beans, black-eyed peas, yams, pickled watermelon rind, as well as fresh watermelon from the garden and pecan pie from the giant pecan tree next to the house. It was all too good and too much.

Grandpa, a tall slim fellow, kept passing platters around and helpfully shoveling the last of this or that onto everybody else's plate. There was, however, no barbecue. The pork wasn't quite ready yet. Maybe in another week or two.

Pushing off from the table in a state of digestive distress, we diners retired to the porch to try to settle our meal while gasping in the late summer heat and humidity. Just beyond the porch, the forlorn occupants of a pig pen and chicken coup silently watched us and awaited their turn on the table.

The farmhouse and pens and garden were surrounded by fields of corn and tobacco. Just beyond, a river lined by trees drained the adjoining Great Dismal Swamp. There were all manner of birds and fish and snapping turtles, but also poisonous Copperhead and Cottonmouth Snakes that would crawl up into the edge of the fields and so it was best to stay near the house.

One didn't have to actually leave the house to encounter snakes. That night, when Aunt Doris got up and made her way down the undulating hallway to the bathroom, she stepped on a six-foot Black Snake also making its way down the hall. Her shriek woke the house.

"Farmer's friend, the black snake" observed Grandpa Sam the next morning while Aunt Doris hurriedly packed. "Mice won't linger where there's a black snack about." And neither, it seems, would Aunt Doris.

Breakfast was pancakes, waffles, bacon, sausage, duck, eggs, grits, a bewildering array of preserves, plus all the leftovers from dinner. Billy and I had only begun to emerge from the breakfast food-coma when Grandma Valeria started laying out an even more epic lunch.

An outing was suggested. An excursion to Cape Hatteras and Kitty Hawk. This would complete our ocean-to-ocean crossing of the continent, and Kitty Hawk featured in the family lore. Great Grandpa Walker had been a carpenter, the nearest to Kitty Hawk and so, it was said, he had been hired by the Wright brothers to build all the structures and scaffolding and such for their experiments. Grandpa Sam, as a small boy assisting his father, might have been present to witness the World's First Powered Flight, though he wouldn't commit one way or the other about it.

The path of the First Powered Flight was marked out on the ground, near the Kitty Hawk Museum, barely over a hundred feet in length. I could have thrown a rock further. Viewing the re-creation of the elaborate catapult mechanism that the Wrights devised, I wondered if they might not have had better results launching a wheelbarrow.

"So, which of these figures in the Museum photos is you and Great Grandpa Walker?" I asked Grandpa Sam.

"We'd best get back to Poplar Branch," he replied. "Valeria will have supper on the table."

And so we left that historic place where the World's First Powered Flight may or may not have occurred and headed back to a feast that could have fed half of Africa and left us all comatose until late the following morning.

After a last breakfast of whatever creatures remained, (it was about this time that I realized there were no dogs on the farm) we loaded up the Ford and said our farewells. Billy and I fell into the back seat, too stuffed to talk. Dad started up the Ford, eased it down the drive and turned onto the road, heading west.

"Just three thousand two hundred more miles to go" murmured Mom as she tore open a fresh carton of cigarettes.

Flat Towing 101

by Tom Glide

I bought a 1949 Ford F-1 pickup many years ago that was a pretty nice truck, but it had some issues.

The previous owner had installed a 351 Windsor and B&M automatic transmission that had plenty of power and it was fun to drive, but it had a homemade wooden flat rack

box that I didn't care for, plus the rest of the truck was painted mud brown!

I wanted an original box (and a repaint) so the search began. It didn't take long to find a decent all original 1950 F-1 complete with a running flathead, which I figured I could pirate everything I wanted from, then part out. The running flattie was worth what I paid for the truck, so I stood a good chance to come out ahead on the deal.

My plans were progressing nicely. My truck looked much better with a real box and I had begun to prep the whole truck for a nice metallic blue paint job when my best friend Don heard of my parts truck.

Don and I grew up together and after high school he moved to Columbus Ohio, bought a small tract of land, and started a hobby farm. He instantly fell in love with the idea of a cool old truck to use there. He even liked the idea of the flat rack box, which would be handy for hauling stuff. So, a deal was struck.

As soon as I finished my truck, I would give the parts truck a "quickie" red paint job, install the wood box, and figure a way to get it to him some 300 miles south.

It did run, but needed quite a bit of other mechanical work which Don wanted to do himself, as funds allowed, so driving it that far was not an option. His dad had a ma-chine shop on the farm where Don grew up, so he built a tow bar and a hitch for my truck and plans were made to flat tow it there.

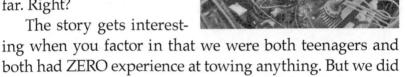

Sounds pretty simple so far. Right?

The story gets interest-ing when you factor in that we were both teenagers and both had ZERO experience at towing anything. But we did have that know-it-all attitude.

How hard could it be? It would be a cool adventure. We grew up watching Movin' On, dreaming someday we'd be Will and Sonny, seeing the country, haulin' loads and jammin' gears. I could hear Merle Haggard singing the theme song in my head... I had that steady hand to keep that load behind. [Big wheels rollin'...gotta keep 'em goin'...]

Don made the trip up to follow me back in case there were any problems, but we were sure there wouldn't be.

We bolted the tow bar to the parts truck, hooked it to my shiny, now really nice truck, and then I tied the steer-ing wheel of the parts truck with a chunk of heavy rope. "You sure we should do that?" Don asked.

"Of course we do!" I replied, remembering that the tow truck driver that delivered my '48 Chevy a few years back (that was picked up by the rear) had tied the wheel. "Otherwise, it will steer all over the place...we don't want that, do we?"

"Naw... guess not." Don answered.

And, on that nice sunny summer day, we set out for Ohio, and a lesson in towing.

I was pretty proud of myself by the time we reached Detroit. Sure, it was a flat route, with few curves, but I was doing it, and quite well. The old red truck was trailing behind mine decent enough, and life was good.

Not long after we entered Ohio, the skies began to grow a little dark, and a light rain began to fall, but there still were no problems. My confidence had grown to an all-time high, and when the rain picked up a bit, it didn't even faze me.

Halfway through Ohio, we had to change from the expressway to a two lane blacktop, and as I began to enter the freshly blacktopped cloverleaf, I felt a slight tug, and noticed I had to slightly counter steer into the curve, which caught my attention big time.

Then I found that I had to keep turning to the left, further and further. What the hell? A glance in the mirror showed the parts truck bouncing up and down and desperately trying to stay going straight, despite the curve. Shit!

I did what was probably the worst thing to do, and stood on the brakes, which sent me into a spin.

I heard an awful screeching crunch sound of twisting metal, then through my windshield, I saw Don in his car behind me, his mouth wide open, and eyes as big as saucers. Then I see the road ahead in the cloverleaf where I had previously been going, then Don again, before the cloverleaf came back into view.

I don't know why, but as I felt the truck begin to circle around again, I hit the gas, which did straighten the spin out, but now the dead end stop and very busy crossroad at the bottom of the cloverleaf were fast approaching.

Since everything was going straight again, I stood on the brakes and skidded to a stop at the bottom of the cloverleaf.

I turned onto the two lane and over to the side of the road and just sat there, shaking like a cat shitting peach seeds.

"You okay?" I heard Don ask, standing beside my truck.

"I think so..." I muttered as I got out to survey the damage.

The right rear fender of my truck was pushed in a little, and had red stripes, and the parts truck had damage to the right front fender, and some pretty metallic blue stripes, but they were still hooked together and still upright.

I felt sick to my stomach, and my knees were wobbly.

"That was some pretty fancy driving," I heard someone say. We noticed a guy walking up to us from his rusty old Chevy pickup. "You alright?" he asked.

"Yeah... just shaken up a bit." I answered.

"I'll bet," he said. "This your first time towing anything?"

How'd he know?

He took out a jack knife and cut the rope holding the steering wheel of the parts truck. "Why'd ya tie the wheel? This truck can't follow the road like that! Wonder ya weren't kilt!"

"Thanks." I said sheepishly, but he was already back to his truck and getting in.

After a while, I mustered up enough courage to finish the last hour of the trip, but every bump and noise made me jump. Needless to say, I was never as happy as I was when we finally pulled into Don's driveway.

Will and Sonny we weren't after all, but I did learn a valuable lesson.

I've towed a ton of cars since then, but will always remember the first... and I've never tied the steering wheel again!

Two Weeks in a Deuce

by Tom Bilyeu

I t all began at our January monthly meeting of the Sundown Car Club of the Yakima Valley. Our intrepid leader, Mike Morris, wanted to know if anyone was interested in driving to Pueblo, CO in our hot rods in June. Since I had completed putting my coupe together the previous May and had almost 2000 miles on it I thought, why not!

I have owned the body, an all Ford steel 1932 Ford 5 window coupe, for almost 30 years. The frame is a reproduction from the Blackboard Rod Shop in Bakersfield, CA. I run it with a Ford 351ci small block and Ford top loader 4 speed with a Ford 8" rear end. Rocket's Hot Rod Shop in Outlook, WA helped get it all together a little over a year earlier.

To be ready for the trip, there was some serious work that had to be completed before the day of departure on June 23rd. At the time, I only had the windshield installed and it had a big gap at the bottom. It seemed like a good idea to put the rest of the glass in and maybe get the old Mustang seats recovered before driving it over 3000 miles to Pueblo and back.

The question on my mind was where to start. I called my great nephew T-Jay Thomson, who had just started his own upholstery shop and arranged to get the seats done. I also contacted the local glass shop in Sunnyside, WA for new glass to be cut. Once I got the glass home and installed along with the new white diamond pleat seat covers, I was ready to get the car squared away for its first long distant cruise. To protect the new interior over the course of the trip, my wife Jean made some very stylish slip covers out of old car t-shirts to keep the white upholstery clean.

I put it up on the two-post lift and went over every nut and bolt I could find and tightened them up, installed new cotter pins, lock tight where needed, and checked and double-checked gaps, hoses, fittings, and changed the oil. I found the line fitting to the hydraulic clutch had been installed crooked and leaked, so I formed up a new fitting and line and took care of the leak. The rear seal on the transmission seeped a little, but not enough to pull the drive shaft off to fix. Of course, now the entire bottom of the frame was covered with 90 weight oil.

To help on the long stretches of highway in Wyoming and Colorado, I installed a cruise control unit from Dakota Digital, which came complete with great instructions.

At long last, the car seemed fit for travel and the day finally came to leave. Bags were packed, goody bag and cooler were filled, and it was time to meet my traveling

companions at 8:00 am for the start of the trip.

I should have been tired because I did not sleep all that well on Sunday night, too jazzed about the beginning of this great adventure, but awoke before the alarm went off. So, on that Monday morning, filled with anticipation of a great trip, I headed off to Sunnyside to fill up with mid-grade and to meet the other three cars to begin the journey.

Mike and Kim Morris were driving their green '37 Ford Tudor sedan, with a fuel injected small block Chev. Johnny and Mindy Johnson and their white '31 Ford 5 window were looking good with their matching tag along trailer. We took

a picture of the cars while waiting for Ralph and Judy Mizell with their screaming yellow, green, and black 1947 Chev custom pickup. Once Mizells arrived, we took a group photo with our "Colorado or Bust" sign. We were a rolling car show as we pulled onto the highway.

Kim Morris had planned our entire itinerary including lunch and motel stops. Mike Morris had arranged for us to visit several hot rod shops along the way. We were all eager to hit the road.

Our first stop was in Nampa, ID. Dennis and Shelley Cornish joined us for a tour of Charlie Hutten's world-class shop, where he graciously stayed open to give us a tour. There were several local hot rods there to add to the festivities. That night we stayed in probably the nicest place along the trip in Boise, ID and the next morning we all headed out to tour Kenny's Rod Shop, another well-known builder of award-winning classics. After lunch, it was back on the open roads and a chance for our cars to stretch their legs on

the highways of Idaho and Wyoming. It was a great treat to see hot rods through my windshield and in my rear view mirror.

We stayed in Rock Springs, WY that night before heading on our way

to Laramie, where we would spend another night. While on the way to Laramie, I was passing a semi and doing 80 mph when everyone else decided to turn into rest stop. I jammed on my brakes to dive in behind and experienced some serious brake fade with my four wheel drum brake system.

Under normal conditions they are quite adequate, but it had been a while since I had demanded as much from one of those antiquated systems and I held on for dear life. It felt like reigning in a pony heading for a cliff. In retrospect, it's kind of amusing, while not very funny at the time. I stretched my legs and my white knuckles, regaining my composure before hitting the road again amidst the mixed heckles and consoling of my hot rod posse.

Our third night was in a small motel around Laramie, CO. It was a welcome respite after spending nine or more hours in the hot rod. We loved every minute of the drive, but were all ready for a rest. Driving through Wyoming into Colorado was our longest day of driving. It was beautiful country, but not much to see other than the scenery.

From Laramie, we headed out for Ft. Collins, getting there in time for a late lunch and then checked into a motel on the fourth night. We a needed a break.

Early the next day we visited Pinkee's Rod Shop, just down the highway from Ft Collins in Windsor, CO. Pinkee's is another world-class builder of rods and customs and it was a great tour.

We had been dodging rain and thunder storms for most of the day. According to our motel staff, the day before it had rained so hard that the parking lot had over a foot of standing water. By the time we arrived it was sunny and dry. Could our good luck continue?

According to the evening news, rain and hail was expected in Denver about the time we were to drive through. As it turned out, we learned from friends who were coming behind us that we missed the rain in Denver

224

by about an hour. Still dry and enjoying the cruise with friends in hot rods.

Word of caution when driving through Denver: other drivers don't seem to notice street rods and tend to jump into that space you leave between you and the other cars. If they only knew how long it takes a '32 Ford with four wheel drum brakes to stop they might not be so anxious.

Making it through Denver without incident, we were on the final leg to Pueblo and the 30th NSRA Rocky Mountain Nationals. At the show, there were almost 2000 cars and we enjoyed four days of sun, cars, and great people. Pueblo is a friendly city with lots to see and do. Our motel was a few miles from the fairgrounds which gave us an opportunity to see a little bit of old town.

Of course, the NSRA show was great, but for me, it's really about the road and the people. We stayed at a Motel 6 about five miles from the fairgrounds with 30 others

and had lots of fun sitting around the parking lot with the people and their cars each evening. It was like having our own little mini car show. The cars had happily brought their people from all over the country, with one couple all the way from Pennsylvania. Everyone was really friendly, sharing the stories of their trip.

The event was cool, but for most it was all about the trip there and back and getting to know new people. I made some new friends and we still stay in touch. They are only about 50 miles from my home, so car season gets us together often.

The weather was sunny and very warm but it was a great time at the show. I was actually anticipating the return trip and the drive more than sitting around the car during the show and was anxious to hit the road again. I left right after awards were given out at 4:00 PM.

By Sunday afternoon we were all ready to load up our cars and start the return trip. We left Pueblo, ready for the long haul, but stopped to take in the Royal Gorge Bridge, the highest bridge in the U.S. It is basically a loop road that oes nowhere with the bridge crossing over a deep gorge and is part of the U.S. National Register of Historic Places.

We stayed in Leadville on the first night and cruised on to Vernal, UT on the second night, which included going up and down a mountain pass that was over 12,000 feet in elevation. Winnemucca, Nevada would welcome us after a long haul of over 500 miles on that third day. A stop at the Bonneville Salt Flats got our imaginations going and pro-

vided another photo op.

Two of the five cars were not part of the whole journey together, but three of them sat on the salt, as if ready to start a timer. It is a wide open space that boggles the mind with its vastness. I must admit the trip to Bonneville was a highlight of the return trip. It is a scene that is difficult to describe if you have not seen a group of hot rods parked on the salt. Now, on my bucket list is a trip to Speed Week with my '32.

The next stop and the final leg of the three car procession was to the 2nd annual NSRA run in Ridgefield, WA at the SW Washington Fairgrounds. I spent Thursday and Friday night in Ridgefield, but because we had been gone from home for two full weeks and I had experienced all of the sitting at fair grounds I could muster, I left the group early Saturday afternoon and headed for home before the Sunday awards ceremony.

The drive on Highway 14 through the Columbia River Gorge was beautiful. I did miss traveling with other hot rods and the friends, but it was great to be heading for home and my own bed. Not long after, I found a photo of my '32 at that NSRA run in Cruisin' Magazine.

Overall the trip went extremely well without any of our traveling companions experiencing car problems. The only rain we hit was on the return trip coming through Bend, OR, which would not have been a big deal except I am running without fenders, so the water coming off the tires was a little worrisome. Fortunately, the only equipment trouble was when my cell phone quit working, but it only took a hard shut off to get it going again. Wouldn't it be nice if fixing a car was that easy?

You never really know how the roads will be until you get on them and while there was a minimal amount of road work, I did seem to find all the deep pot holes which tested my straight axle, buggy springs, and shocks to their limits. All in all, the trip came off without a hitch and it was great to be home. I will always have great memories of the trip and the friendships and would recommend it to everyone with a classic car. Get out and drive them!

Cross Country Cadillac

by Don Homuth

While standing at State Street Auto Glass in Salem, Oregon one day, a black 1959 Cadillac pulled up and stopped right in front of me. Good or bad, an old car like this always grabs my attention and this one was no exception. This one had some issues. The windshield was cracked, the driver's side window glass was smashed, and from the sound of it the exhaust manifold gaskets were blown out. But, from 20 feet away it looked awesome! It was the fins. That's what did it.

The driver said his 83-yr-old father bought it from a guy in San Diego, but then he had a stroke and had to move in with his son. The son didn't have storage and the car had to be sold... Fast! I asked him how much and he gave me a figure. I immediately started looking much closer.

The body was straight and rust-free. Good. Interior was redone and was really nice. Good. Disc brakes had been installed up front. Really good; because the original brakes on those monsters had some serious fade from 70 mph.

Most intriguing was the claim that the engine and transmission had a recent rebuild. Good if true and there was no reason to suggest it wasn't. The generator had been replaced with an alternator and the old ignition system replaced with a modern electronic one. Good. After talking with the guy a little more we went for a test drive. There was potential here.

So, I called my friend, Mike, in Grand Rapids, MN, thinking this might be just the car for him. As I suspected, he was interested and I cut the deal on his behalf. It was decided that another friend and I would prepare the car for delivery the following year. There were things that needed to be done to get it ready for the road and for Mike.

We immediately rebuilt the front suspension and found a windshield in Ohio. We also replaced the driver's side window and all four power window switches. The dash gauges came to life once we installed a new circuit board from a fellow in Springfield, OR.

The exhaust ended up sounding absolutely sweet once we replaced the blown out manifold gaskets and re-hung and re-welded the entire dual exhaust.

The Carter AFB 4-bbl carburetor needed to be rebuilt and it ran a lot better afterwards, plus it could handle alcohol fuel. The engine still required Premium gasoline, but the rebuild sheet indicated that the valve seats had been replaced.

Drivability was a huge concern, of course, and although the bias-ply wide whitewalls were pretty, they were old and unsafe. Modern radials made by Hankook for limousines improved the handling from abysmal to livable, but still not really good by modern standards.

Getting it aligned it was tricky, but there's an old guy here in Salem who had the long alignment rack, the Bear equipment, and still knew how to do it. Handling improved greatly after that.

Missing body parts were scrounged from the same guy in Springfield. Can you say expensive? Say Cadillac and prices increase by at least 100%. But, because some miscellaneous parts, like the little chrome bits, windshield escutcheons, wiper blades and such were made of Unobtainium, there was no other source nearby and acquiring these rare pieces of automotive jewelry was no easy thing.

The car could be driven comfortably once we got the heater re-cored and the heater control valve rebuilt... and it could defrost the windshield. This was a huge improvement!

The turn signals were dodgy, but we decided not to tear into the steering column or electrical systems. The horn ring was broken off just like most of the rings in the 1959's were. This came from people pushing the horn ring too hard when angry. I guess they thought that would make it louder and more effective. I suppose not much has changed in that respect over the last fifty some years. We decreed that it was a new owner issue. After all, Mike had to have something to tinker with!

The radio, however, was a signal-seeking AM only with tubes. It was decided that the radio would be another new owner issue and it remained on the same list as the horn ring.

In the end, it took about 8 months to accomplish all of this and we put off the trip to MN until late spring. Which brings us to May 10, 2012 and our road trip from Salem, Oregon to Grand Rapids, Minnesota in the classy old Cadillac.

First Day:

This car was built before the Interstate Highways and we wanted to have the experience of travel as it was back before Eisenhower's dream of a complete interstate highway system came true. My partner for the trip was my wife and favorite co-pilot, Kathy.

We left Salem early and headed for Ontario, OR, near the Idaho border, 400 miles east by way of Bend and Burns on US 20. Travel to Bend took us across the Santiam Pass.

From Bend to Burns goes across the High Desert. There is a whole lot of nothing out there. Arid desert, huge expanses of beige land, and the endless horizon seemed somewhere "over there" far away. The roads were uncrowded—empty is a better term.

In Burns, we found RJ's Drive-In. I wanted to get out of the car and being inside for a half hour or so was a welcome change. "Bob's Burger" is one of the best we have ever had and can unconditionally recommend it. While sitting inside, we watched as most of the customers leaving stopped by to look closely at the car, peer inside, and look back as they walked away. The car got lots of attention.

Not having excess time to doddle, we got back on the road and headed out of Burns toward Ontario where we

stayed in an unremarkable motel right off I-84. Thankfully, it did have its own restaurant and the complimentary breakfast off the menu the next morning was much better than a stale croissant and bad orange juice.

And the evening and (following) morning was of the First Day, and it was Good.

Second Day:

I-84 took us into Idaho through Nampa and Boise to Mountain Home before we could take the turnoff to US 20. Our destination that day, a little over 400 miles, was Jackson, Wyoming where we would spend the evening.

On the Superslab, we got lots of horn honks, smiles, and waves. The roadway through Boise is multiple lanes and mildly confusing, but the road signs will get you through. We stopped at a rest area East of Boise* to deal with the coffee and orange juice we drank at breakfast.

US 20 runs north of and parallel to I-84 en route to the Craters of the Moon National Monument. We had taken that route in 1989 on our honeymoon trip, which we actually took several weeks before we got married. (There are no Rules!) Kathy and I spent several hours there driving and walking several parts of it. On the earlier journey, we had climbed one of the tall buttes in the area, but not this time. My right leg was starting hurt from being the only functioning cruise control. Keeping a right foot absolutely immobile is no easy thing and at my age the pain comes way too easily.

We discovered the special pass that old farts—um, Senior Citizens—can buy that provides Lifetime entrance to any national monument or park for $10. Done! It seemed like a great deal and I have felt smug about it ever since. At the gift shop and information kiosk, we each bought a T-shirt and I got a neat poster to go along with it. It was time to hit the road again.

Hopping on US 26 out of Idaho Falls, the drive was uninteresting till we got to the ID/WY border where we traveled up picturesque mountain valleys, nice mountain scenery, and some interesting terrain. We approached Jackson from the south. It's quite lovely. Finding the motel, we unpacked, and walked (still no easy thing) to a local eatery, featuring a mostly clueless waitress and a strange menu without dollar signs on the prices. After a light supper, it was time for bed. The morrow promised a long day and we'd need to leave early.

A word on eating en route: Travel stops aren't known for their great food and there's little need to eat a lot when sitting for hours at a time. Lunches were pork jerky (tasty stuff that Kathy bought at Costco), fruit/nut trail mix, and Perrier. Mildly snooty, but it sure tasted good.

The weather report said it would be chilly the next day and it was correct.

And the evening and morning were of the Second Day, and it was good.

Third Day:

It was 28F in Jackson, WY. We worried that perhaps the car, having spent most of its life in California or Oregon, might not start or run properly. It did cough and sputter, but once it caught and ran for a while it warmed up and with heater on we were off.

Heading north out of Jackson, we stopped at a roadside rest to take the obligatory picture with the Grand Tetons (I love the translation of that name from the French and suspect some bluenoses would change it if they knew what it really meant) in the background.

We travelled east across the Wind River Canyon pass at over ten thousand feet. Mid May in the Rockies includes snow still everywhere. On the long decline out of the picturesque mountains the snow disappeared entirely and again the area looked mostly beige. We passed small towns that once were, but will never again be, prosperous. There was Native American art by the side of the road here and there, but have just no idea what it meant. There was little to stop for and miles to go, so we kept going.

Coming through Shoshoni, Wyoming, I was annoyed at a car in front that was slowing for no apparent reason. I muttered something about "damned local drivers" and Kathy suggested that perhaps the driver was looking for something and she was right. Kathy had noticed a 1957 Chevrolet all turned out and said "There's a car show!" How fortuitous, considering our special ride!

I pulled into the parking lot and the entire car show migrated over to the Cadillac, giving us a pleasant 10-15 minutes chatting with gearheads. We were invited to show, but told them we were on our way to Minnesota and couldn't stay long.

To Minnesota? In that? They all thought we were nuts and I suppose they had a point, but the journey called and the road was the answer.

In Casper, we got back on the Superslab en route to a turnoff for Hot Springs, SD. We had the same experience with people flashing thumbs up (I believe it was thumbs) and waving. Although we still got passed by pretty much everyone on the road, we tried to keep the Cadillac between 65 and 70 mph most of the way. It could go 85 without too much trouble, but it just felt flakey, floating even more than normal. 65 mph was a lot more comfortable.

This is a five thousand pound car and twenty some feet long. It's not supposed to get good gas mileage and it didn't; at least when compared to modern cars. Up and down mountains, mostly at steady reasonable speeds, against headwinds and with tailwinds, our mileage varied somewhere between 16 mpg to just over 19 mpg. Across the entire trip, between 17.5 and 18mpg.

Once five thousand pounds of car gets moving along at speed, it follows Newton's Suggestions and wants to keep going at that speed. That 390 cubic inch, 325 bhp, high compression engine was just loafing along. I doubt it was turning more than about 2,000 rpm along the way.

The Caddy had an iffy gas gauge and even with a new tank sender unit got erratic readings, so we filled up every 200-300 miles. Besides, we had to stop anyway about that time. Perrier takes its toll.

After turning off the Superslab, we were back on two-lane roads across the SE portion of Wyoming. We drove for miles alongside another old railroad track bed being torn up. It was a reminder of a time when trains went almost everywhere.

Our destination was Hot Springs, South Dakota. It's an interesting old town, with which we had a connection. We used to have a rare and strange old map, from a fellow (Orlando Ferguson) who in 1893 developed what he called the Bible Map of the Earth—the "Square and Stationary Earth." It was given to me by my 8th grade English teacher. Kathy and I had it conserved professionally and hung it on one of our walls.

We had wondered if it was rare and after doing our research, discovered that it was. We offered it to the Smithsonian, but they sent us to the Library of Congress. In time, we gave it to the LOC—and thereby to the nation. The gift got worldwide (truly!) publicity and it's a great story... for another day.

Orlando Ferguson was from Hot Springs and we wanted to visit the place. Before the trip, we contacted the local Pioneer Museum which had one of the four known original copies of the map. On approaching Hot Springs, Kathy looked up the museum on her smart phone, but the website said it was closed till Tuesday. We would be coming into town Sunday night and leaving Monday morning. Things looked grim.

I suggested she call the museum anyway. Perhaps they might be preparing for the Tuesday opening. In a manner of sorts, they were and they were open because they were celebrating the gift of a 23,000 button collection. We said we would be coming in at about 5 pm Sunday and they assured us someone would be there.

We did and they were, giving us and opportunity to have a nice conversation with the museum docents. While there, we saw another original of the map. The one there is glued to a piece of cardboard and isn't in all that good a condition. But, it is there.

The book, for which the map was a giveaway advertising flyer, is also there—an original in the local community library. We got three copies of Ferguson's obituary in local papers.

Best of all, we found his gravesite! The family plot is in an old part of the Evergreen Cemetery. We took pictures of it, which we have given to the LOC with everything else. It now has complete information on an historical oddity of no real importance.

We went back to the motel to prepare for dinner and while there, in came a group of bikers, complete with full leathers and big Harleys. I walked over to say hello, but my greeting was mostly met with blank stares. Turns out they were from Poland.

Wonderful! Just plain wonderful. Polish bikers. Hoodathunk?

And the evening and (following) morning were of the Third Day. And it was not only Good—it was downright wonderful!

Fourth Day:

We got up early the next morning and the motel manager, who had a 3-4 car Cadillac collection on his own, arranged for breakfast to be ready at 6 am, rather than the usual 7 am. It was very nice of him and we left a good tip for the service.

This would be the longest day of the trip. Hot Springs to Fargo, North Dakota is 571 miles. The car was still reliable, oil consumption had dropped from a quart every 500 miles at the outset to less than half a quart for the previous thousand. I suspect the engine rebuild really was recent and it was breaking in as we drove.

Our route involved bypassing Mt Rushmore and the Reptile Gardens. (If we gave the Black Hills back to the Native Americans who owned it until Custer stole it from them after gold was discovered in 1876, I suspect they could do better than Reptile Gardens.)

At Kathy's insistence, we stopped in at Wall Drug. She wanted to go there because it's one of the few places she had been to that I had not. She was correct. Though we had stopped there briefly on our pre-marriage honeymoon in 1989, we hadn't really "stopped" there.

Wall Drug may be the best-known tourist trap anywhere. Established in the 1930's, signs and billboards for it grew up all over the nation's highways prior to WW2 and remained afterwards. Veterans are offered free donuts! Wow! Anyone could get Free Ice Water, too. Such generosity! During WW2, signs were put up by UDT on Pacific Islands indicating things like "Wall Drug—7,500 miles" with an arrow pointing east. The bumper stickers are free and all over hellandgone.

I gotta say—the donut tasted great. It was warm, right out of the oil. The ice water came from a spout, and was neither cold nor tasted good. Kathy looked and looked for something to buy, but couldn't find anything she couldn't live without. I found the entire place bizarre, the goods overpriced and the hype amusing. I was glad we stopped, but we won't stop again.

Back to the Superslab, up US 14 to Pierre, we crossed the Wide Missouri into eastern SD and slanted toward Aberdeen.

We began to notice water all over the place. There are huge shallow lakes, some of them well into former farm-yards where buildings were awash. Telephone poles 50 feet or more were out into water four feet deep. We saw drowned fence lines with the wire and posts entirely under water. In some places, the water was right up to the highway roadbeds.

Waterfowl are clearly doing very well indeed in these places, with ducks and geese all over the place.

Something important has happened. The water table is extremely high and shows no movement to go lower. This water is coming up from below, not down from above. It continued past Aberdeen toward Ellendale, then upwards from there to Fargo, where it could be seen on a number of roads.

We stopped in Ellendale to look at the Dickey County Courthouse, a lovely period structure. It's been renovated and looks quite pretty in its rural county seat setting.

Just north of Oakes, ND, there is a 1950's era F-100 Super Sabre on a static display. We took a picture of the Caddy in front of it, comparing tail fins*. The airplane has a taller fin, but the car has two which exhibit much greater style.

Eastern North Dakota is very like Eastern South Dakota, although North Dakota has more surviving shelterbelts, which are a barrier of trees and shrubs that protect against the wind and reduces erosion. Dropping down into the Red River (of the North) Valley was a gentle transition and we were on into Fargo.

I was happy to visit my sister and give her family a ride in the Cadillac, but it had been a very long day on the road and what I needed most was a decent meal and some sleep. We took my nephew's bed after he got kicked out of it to make room for a visiting uncle. That's in keeping with the Natural Order of the Universe in families. When our heads hit the pillows, we crashed and burned.

And the evening and (following) morning were of the Fourth Day, and it was also Very Good Indeed!

Fifth Day:

How much visiting can be crammed into one day? We visited with my sister and family and then my brother and his family. His wife had never met mine and I got the sense that they rather liked each other. A relief, that. We tried to see as many old friends as possible all over town.

Such visits are the very stuff of wonderfulness and were well worth the time. But, our final destination, Grand Rapids, Minnesota, beckoned us and it was still 200 miles off. We wanted to be there by the afternoon of the next day. So, once again, we climbed into bed and slept well.

And the evening and (following) morning were of the Fifth Day, and it was Wonderful.

Sixth Day:

That morning we packed, ate a good breakfast, and were off once again. We planned to travel via Detroit Lakes, MN to Park Rapids to Walker to Remer and then through Grand Rapids into the nearby town of Coleraine, where the car's new owner operates a medical clinic.

In Detroit Lakes, we visited with an old friend from past political campaigns. We would catch the return train home from there.

We stopped in Nevis to take a picture of Kathy sitting in the hand of a Paul Bunyan statue and then lost the gas cap in Remer when I forgot to replace it after the final fill-up of the trip. When you're over fifty, memory is the second thing to go.

On into Grand Rapids and through that to Coleraine to deliver the car. It was by then well adorned with dead insects, the radiator a sort of butterfly graveyard. The collected dirt from the trip was all over the car and it was beginning to look like a barn find, but it made it! A visit the local car wash was in order.

Later on, Mike's car club was having its monthly meeting and we got to the site a few minutes late. Everyone was inside. So, we went in and joined the group. The club president asked if anyone had anything else to say and I raised my hand.

Several club members thought I was trying to sell them something, so they said afterwards. I greeted them from my car club, and presented Mike with a trophy the car had received in a car show up in Portland several weeks earlier. He got a lot of congratulations about that and the group moved outside to view the Cadillac.

Pictures were taken and the PR guy for the club wanted The Story of the trip. The president thanked us for coming, telling us that he hadn't

1959 Cadillac makes long trip to Grand Rapids

Don Homuth and Kathy Cegla made a special delivery to Grand Rapids. They appeared at the May 15 meeting of the Itasca Vintage Car Club to present a special award to one of the car club members.

Don made a special presentation of a "Best Survivor Trophy" to Mike Baich, but the "rest of the story" is the best part. Don and Mike have been friends for many years. When Don discovered this beautiful black 1959 Cadillac for sale out in Salem, Oregon, he gave Mike a call. Yes, Mike wanted the classic car! This led to an adventuresome road trip for Don and Kathy.

They mapped out a "blue highway" route from Salem, Ore. to Grand Rapids, stopping along the way to see many grand sights including a stop at the infamous Wall Drug in

SUBMITTED PHOTO
Kathy Cegla, Don Homuth and Mike Baich enjoy sharing their great story about this 1959 Cadillac that Kathy and Don drove all the way from Salem, Oregon to deliver to Mike. They said the "ride was great" and they got hundreds of "thumbs up" when they met other motorists on the roads. Even though this is a "big boat" of a car, it still averaged over 18 mpg on this road trip of 2,200 miles.

South Dakota. There they bought Mike a souvenir "Wall Drug" bumper sticker! Don and Kathy drove 4 ½ days, raking up 2,300 miles to bring the car to Mike. The couple will be spending a week in Minnesota before returning to Oregon via Amtrack. That's just what good friends do! Mike's classic 1959 Cadillac plus hundreds of other classic cars will be on display at the Itasca Vintage Car Club sponsored, "Northern Minnesota Swap and Car Show" on July 28-29 at the Itasca County Fairgrounds in Grand Rapids.

The Itasca Vintage Car Club begins their Thursday Night Cruises on May 17 and will continue each Thursday evening throughout the entire summer. Look for them in area parades and at Showboat this summer. To learn more about club activities, contact Jerry Latola, Club President, (326-5910) or Tom Carpenter, Vice-President, (218-363-2510). Check out their website for more details of car shows, parades, and club events: itascavintagecarclub.com

240

planned a program for the evening, and he was pleased that we were it.

So, we made it. We were back in a place that really does feel like home, because it has so many good memories and good friends. Kathy and I had ridden together without the radio on and we talked a lot along the way. At the end, we were still talking and enjoying each other's company. Does it get any better than that? Can it?

And the evening and (following) morning were of the Sixth Day. And it was Outstanding.

Kathy went to Minneapolis to spend time with her family and later to Duluth to visit a college friend. I stayed in Grand Rapids to spend some time with a fishing buddy whose company I greatly enjoy.

We caught the train home and it was good to get back. Great memories were made, friendships were created or rekindled, and it remains of one of our greatest road trips. We have no intention of ever doing it again.

Little Orange Monster

by Troy Moore

It all began at the Goodguys Nationals Car Show in Puyallup in July of 2012. There was a couple there from Germany that put the idea in my head of taking my 1968 Opel Kadett to its birthplace someday and meet with some of the Opel folks over in Europe. So, for the rest of that year I stewed over it in my head. I had talked about it with my girlfriend, Jennifer, regarding the timing and cost associated with it.

One day in November, she brought me an Automobile magazine that described just such a trip that they had done with one of their staffers Volkswagen Scirroco's. That really got me thinking seriously about this adventure. So, come January, I decided to bite the bullet and commit to the trip. Looking at my paid time off and such, late August to early September was to be the time.

In the meantime I had proposed to Jennifer and got a definite YES. So, we set a date of July 13, 2013, which turned this car trip into a honeymoon. As it turned out, I was unable to get any shipping dates until two months prior. At the beginning of May, I got a shipping date of June 21st. After a couple months of waiting and getting the car ready for it's month long ocean voyage, we dropped him off at the Port of Tacoma on July 14th.

It was sad being without my Little Orange Monster, but I kept myself busy with trying to get my '60 Vauxhall Victor running for the wedding. I wasn't able to complete the project in time, but on July 13th, in the front yard of my grandparents' house, I married my love Jennifer.

The Little Orange Monster arrived on the shores of Belgium on July 27th. We flew out of Seattle and landed in Brussels on the morning of July 30th and caught the train into Brugges where we stored our luggage. Then, we caught another train into Zeebrugge, which was where the car was. Now, according to Garmin, Zeebrugge was between Blanenberge and Knokke-Heist, and just under six kilometers from the train stop to the port.

I offered to get us a taxi, but my lovely bride was quite tired and not really thinking straight and said let's just walk. I thanked my lucky stars that we didn't have our luggage with us and we set out. As we walked along, I suspected it was more like six miles than six kilometers. For the last two kilometers, there was not any sidewalk or biking lane so we walked along the outside of the guardrail and then on a frontage road. We found out later that walking there was not allowed.

They brought the car out to us from the secured area and found that he wasn't running too good and wouldn't idle. I quickly discovered that someone along the journey had unscrewed a hose clamp and disconnected a large vacuum hose. Why anyone would do that is still a mystery, but it was an easy fix.

Arriving back in Brugges, we picked up our bags and drove to the place where we had a reservation to stay. The website said that this was a Bed and Breakfast. It turned out to be at a private house that had four bedrooms with a shared bathroom on the ground floor in true '70's decor.

It was actually a row house, about 20 feet wide, probably 50 feet deep, and three floors up. Had we not been so tired from traveling, I might have said "don't think so, going to find someplace else to stay". But, we stayed there for two nights and our lodging decisions only got better from there. Brugges is really a very nice place to visit and they have done all that they can to preserve the medieval-looking image of the city.

On August 1st, we rolled out and headed for Caen, France. On the way, we pulled into a toll booth and heard a jingling sound followed by the alternator belt squealing. I pulled over into the rest area and found that the alternator pivot bolt had lost its nut and was running grossly out of line. Being able to rob a nut from the fuel filter bracket, I put everything back in place and we were back on the road, getting into Caen early enough to go the Caen Memorial Museum.

I have been there once before and forgot how large it is. This is a must see if your any kind of war buff or love the service. We were there for about 3.5 hours and wound up absolutely worn out by all the information taken in. After a good rest, we were off to the Normandy beaches the next morning.

Venturing down to the coast, we ended up stopping first at the Arromanches 360, which is an IMAX theatre, and then walked down to the town and onto the beach in the port. You can still see the Phoenix blocks out in the water. The Phoenix breakwaters were a set of reinforced concrete caissons built as part of the artificial Mulberry harbors developed by the British in World War II to facilitate rapid offloading of cargo onto the beaches during the Allied invasion of Normandy. On land they had a section of the bridge that ran between the artificial dock and the shore set up.

We then went on down the coast to the American Cemetery. This place will bring a tear to your eye. Then, Jennifer and I went down to see the Ranger Memorial. By now, thunderstorms had rolled in and we headed back for the hotel.

The next morning of August 3rd, had us headed for Versailles, France. If anyone wants to know why the French Revolution started, go see the palace of Versailles. There was much pomp and circumstance inside that happened during a time when the rest of the country was starving. In addition to the palace, there is the huge Queen's Gardens and the Marie Antoinette house.

Next, we were back on the road in the direction of Switzerland with a night stay in Becanson, France. At about 200 km out, I noticed that the alternator had quit charging. With a stop to ensure that the belt was still in good condition, we made it to our hotel. This was on a Saturday afternoon in "not tourist" France where just about everything closes at 3pm and doesn't open back up until Monday morning.

I took the alternator out and apart to see if I could fix it and found that the little bracket that holds the capacitor down had broken free and been pinched between the rotor and the case. With a small bit of coat hanger, I made a hold down for the capacitor and tried to make it work. McGuyver would have been proud… if it had worked. But, it was still dead. So, we had to spend an extra day in Becanson.

Monday morning, August 5th, found us investigating where we could get the alternator repaired. The best answer I could get was five days minimum. So, under much duress, I purchased an extra battery. I knew that getting it fixed once we got to Switzerland would be easy. So, we set out on the original battery and drove for about three hours. Once the engine started to run strange, I pulled into a Burger King which was very similar to what you might find in the US. Jennifer had a milkshake and I changed the battery out with the new one.

Once back on the road, we motored over Klausen Pass into Altdorf, Switzerland. There, we scored a hotel and once secured in our accommodations, I started asking about the alternator repair. The hotel desk directed me to an Opel facility that told me about a man in town who rebuilt alternators and so the next morning we set out to get the car back on the road. While it took all day long to get fixed, we got a new rebuilt alternator that was a quality unit and we headed out for Mustair, Switzerland. We stopped for dinner in a small town on the way and there was a group of guys that were amazed that we came all the way from Seattle with our Opel Kadett.

The morning of August 7th had us up bright and early, headed for the Stelvio Pass, which at over 9,000 feet above sea level is the second highest pass in the Alps. The television show Top Gear has aired a segment of them running up this pass and I have posted a video of Jennifer and me going up on my YouTube channel. We made the run up and had a blast in all of the twists and turns of what has been called the "greatest driving road in the world." It was quite the fun experience.

Arriving at the top, a beer seemed in order, even though it was only 0930. In the shop, I purchased my dad a biking jersey and then we headed down the Umbrail Pass and back into Switzerland. There are some really good downhill twists in that one. Being two days behind schedule, we decided to push through and get back on track up to Wachenheim, Germany, which made for a long day.

On the morning of August 8th, we set out for the Opel museum in Russelsheim, Germany. However, it is a little difficult to find and it was closed the week that we were there and the next. It seems they forgot to plan for our arrival. So, we just bumped along the country side down to Trier, Germany on the banks of the Moselle River. Some say that it may be the oldest city in Germany, founded sometime around 16 BC. Trier is the home of Porta Nigra, the oldest defensive structure in Germany, built by the Romans just prior to 200 A.D. After seeing the old city, we took the easy cruise up the Moselle Valley.

The next morning we headed up the Moselle Valley for Bad Bertrich, Germany. It is another old town steeped in history and we got to run some more nice twists and turns as we followed the Mosel River along. The driving was fantastic and we had a chance to wander around after taking in the flavor of the old town.

The next day was without a doubt one of the best days of driving when we toured, to put it mildly, on the Nurburgring Nordschleife, the Holy Grail of driving. This racetrack is a German toll road during nonevent times and with its 14.1 miles of high speed turns, it makes for a great time behind the wheel of your favorite automobile. On that day, the Oldtimer Grand Prix was happening on the GP track. Featuring vintage race cars, this event draws 60,000 spectators and a friend of mine from California had his Opel GT in the event. Had I known what was in store for me on that Friday, I could have been part of this. I didn't get to run, but it was an opportunity to see his car on the track with all of the others.

At the end of the day, we headed out towards the Amsterdam area where we had plans to meet up with a member from the local Kadett C club in Zandvoort, Netherlands for a car show. It was fun to be there and see some of the old European classics and even some American rigs, not to mention discovering some cars that I hadn't even heard of.

We then spent a day in Delft and two days in Amsterdam. It was so nice to have a couple days of downtime and not being on the road. On August 11th, we dropped the Little Orange Monster back off at the port in Zeebrugge and caught the train on into Brussels for a good day of sightseeing. It was from there that Jennifer and I flew back home. It had been a long trip, but one we will never forget.

We had crammed a lot into a month. Between getting married and running at full speed on one of the world's most noteworthy race courses, we were both worn out. It had been a big huge experience for the Monster, as well, and he deserved a rest.

He got it as he made his way back over the Atlantic during the course of the next six weeks, arriving home in Tacoma, WA safe and sound on September 27th. He's currently hanging out in the garage, watching as I work on his stablemate, my '60 Vauxhall Victor.

On the Road with Otto

by Janet Ehli Fairchild

It all started out as an out of state summer job. I was going to be one of two life guards and the assistant arts and crafts instructor at a Northern California dude ranch for kids. Not a bad gig for a 20 year old woman.

So, I packed up my '67 Datsun station wagon and hit the road. Keep in mind, my seven year old import was never what would be considered a hot car. It had only an AM radio, no AC, and just the bare basics. But, it was all mine. It also had an unusual feature. For some reason, that year and that year only, Datsun made their station wagon with hanging leaf springs.

My friends had all named their cars and insisted I name mine. I thought giving this very basic vehicle a name was a bit silly, but I finally buckled. So, one early June morning, "Otto" and I set off. My parents were worried that Otto wouldn't make it all the way to Petaluma, CA. Ha! Otto was a champ all summer long, though there were a few mornings that I had to talk him into starting.

Those hanging leaf springs came with an unexpected surprise. Everywhere I went, they became the opening line for guys who wanted to start a conversation. Almost all of my talks with young men on that drive started with, "Excuse me, but your leaf springs are hanging."

I spent my first night out at a cute little motel right on the Rogue River. I didn't find out until later that the reason the manager was so nice to me, and checked on me before

I crashed for the night, was that as soon as my mom found out where I was staying she called the motel and asked them to keep an eye on me. Sheesh!

After two weeks at the dude ranch, two friends and I quit. The situation had become intolerable. I had become the only lifeguard, they demoted the head arts and crafts instructor to be my assistant because they liked my work better. I was suddenly the head girl's counselor and the day I quit they wanted me to work with the horses, also. Never mind that I knew nothing about horses. Extra duties were being added on with no increase in pay and with a serious deduction in my time off.

So, the other Janet, Joey, and I packed up our cars and left. Poor Otto looked like a humble orphan compared to the rich gal cars being driven by my friends. Janet drove a new Camaro and Joey's car was of similar stature.

Janet had a nice roomy tent, so we found a campground and moved in. The next morning, we each took off to find jobs. Both Janet and Joey were looking to work with horses. I was looking for anything that would keep me from returning home a failure.

On beautiful Pt. Reyes, I found a job stringing oyster seed shells at Johnson's Oyster Farm. The next day, both Janet and Joey joined me at the oyster farm. We made a whopping nickel a string and Charlie paid us cash at the end of each day.

Our campground had a ten day limit. On the tenth morning, we woke up to a flooded tent. It was pouring! For Joey, it was the last straw. She left that morning to return to the comforts of Pasadena, never to be heard from again. Everything we owned was soaked, so Janet and I packed up our cars and headed to my aunt's home in Palo Alto. Dear Aunt Barbara took us in and got us set up with her washer and dryer, then she took off. She returned later with enough food to keep an army going for a while. She and my uncle spoiled us rotten that weekend! All of the fresh fruit was worth the trip alone.

The following Monday, we found the campground that was to be our home for the next seven weeks and it was back to the oyster farm. Charlie, the owner, approached us and told us he was going to have to let us go at the end of the day because he was running out of shells. I told him we needed to leave at noon to get cleaned up and get out to find another job. He returned around 10:00 and asked if we had found a job yet. Funny man! Then, he offered us another job; painting the outbuildings on the farm. He paid us $2 an hour, which was a considerable raise. Keep in mind, minimum wage at the time was $1.65. Of course we accepted.

We spent the rest of the summer painting and having a blast! Janet had a battery operated radio and in the mornings, she got to listen to her country western music. In the afternoons, I got to choose Rock n Roll. There were some great songs in the summer of '74!

The crew at the oyster farm kept us in the freshest possible seafood all summer. At least twice a week, they'd bring us something tempting. Often, it was something I hadn't tried before. Abalone and shark made great impressions on both of us. Every Friday, Charlie gave us a dozen oysters from that days' harvest and they were delicious cooked over an open fire.

Janet's fiancé would spend the weekends at our campsite. That meant I had to make myself scarce for a few hours on Friday and Saturday evenings. In a campground, there's always a campfire surrounded by young people. Back then, it was unusual not to be invited to join in. I met people from all over the world that summer.

At a campfire one night, a guy asked me out for dinner and a movie the next night, so I got all spiffed up in the only dress I had with me. Little did I know, his idea of dinner and a movie and mine certainly didn't match. He took me to McDonalds and a drive-in!

Toward the end of August, we finished painting the last outbuilding. After some tearful good-byes at the oyster farm, Janet and I decided it was time for us to take a vacation of our own to Mexico. Once again, we packed up the cars. We left Janet's car at my aunt's house. She didn't want to take her pristine Camaro into Mexico and no one wanted to steal my Otto.

Good ol' Otto took us to the border. We got there pretty late in the evening and decided to spend the night in the car before crossing into Mexico. It was a good thing Otto was a station wagon. All our stuff went into the front seat so we could lower the back seat and have room to stretch out. Little did we know, we were sleeping in the car in one of the most dangerous neighborhoods in the U.S.

The next morning, we crossed the border and drove to Lagunitas. We actually paid for a motel room for two nights. Neither of us had slept in a real bed since we got rained out. Then we hit the town.

I got all my Christmas shopping done in August! I remember getting a leather jacket for my two-year-old nephew and an onyx chess set for my big brother.

We started getting really hungry and couldn't find a burger joint anywhere. So, we stopped a young man and asked if he knew where we could grab a burger. He laughed and told us we weren't in the US anymore and pointed us to a sandwich shop.

Before we could finish our sandwiches, he came into the restaurant and up to our table. He invited us to have dinner with him and his roommates. What a memorable

252

evening it was. While dinner was among the poorest I've eaten, spaghetti with browned oil and bottled water, the company was memorable.

One of the roommates had a guitar. We sat in their living room and sang for hours. To this day, when I think of the song "Time in a Bottle", I hear it sung with a Mexican accent.

After a couple of days in Mexico, it was time to head back home. I had to laugh when Janet expressed concern over Otto's ability to make it all the way to Tacoma. He may have needed some parental inspiration to start in the mornings, at which times I used his full and proper name of Otto Mobile like a frustrated mother might, but once his motor kicked off and he began purring like a kitten there was no stopping him! At these times, when he was at his best, I lovingly referred to him as Ott.

I had no problem making it home and arrived with a pile of Christmas presents, $14, and memories to last a lifetime.

A Journey Down Memory Lane

by Gregory Hasman

Trips down memory lane often take the form of meta-phors and clichés. This past Christmas Eve I took an excursion with Maybelline, my 2009 Navy Blue Chevy Colorado, to my Godparents in Rosharon, TX, just a half hour south of Houston. In the process, it became more than a trip to visit some family; it was a portal back in time.

In February of 2006, I relocated from Brooklyn, NY to Houston, TX to be on my own, yet I was close enough to where if I needed something there were some friendly faces to comfort me (my Godparents). At the time, I had just received my driver's license. In New York City, due to high insurance premiums and a great public transporta-tion system, my driving ambitions were dim. Furthermore, when I moved to Houston, I didn't own a vehicle and my Godmother drove me around in her white 1995 Saturn. At this juncture my experience behind the wheel was exclu-sive to streets. So, one afternoon, along with my Godfather, she told me to get in the driver's seat. We wound up driving across parts of US 59 that traversed the I-610 Loop inter-change and several lanes of traffic. It felt like going down the first drop of a roller coaster sitting in the front seat without a seat belt. The nerves were intense as was the traffic, but we eventually made it to a mall in Sugarland, southwest of Houston. From there, she slowly gave me the reins after I got a job as an Office Services Clerk in down-town Houston.

Traveling to and from work on the conveyor belt known as Texas Highway 288 enabled this grasshopper to learn the lay of the land and to become more confident. A couple of months later, on my 25th birthday, mom drove down from Brooklyn and brought some stuff I needed. In the process, she provided me with her own  vehicle, a burgundy 1999 Buick Century. She flew back a few days later, but not without my eternal gratitude. A parent provides in many ways and she has always given me the ultimate gift of her love.

For the next couple of years I took that Buick across many parts of Texas, including a Christmas drive through sawmill communities of Soda and Woodville in east-central Texas. In 2009, my mom helped me again when I decided to get a truck. After deciding on Maybelline, I knew the limits were lifted. From Clayton, NM to Vicksburg, MS the truck drove like a dream, stopping on a dime whenever I wanted to get out and shoot some old buildings, neon signs, or vast landscapes.

Maybelline was with me in 2012 when I decided to pursue a Master's Degree at the University of North Texas in Denton. From there, we continued to explore new land-scapes ranging from Stamps, AR to Mangum, OK.

As I began heading south on I-45, making my way to-wards Houston, I recalled all the trips I took north to Fort Worth, Dallas, and other areas. Memories of bypassing in-teresting areas during past excursions played a huge role in becoming a bit more adventurous on this drive. The first area that caught my attention was a frontage road by

Trumbull, which turned out to have pieces of old US 75, the predecessor to I-45.

After discovering portions of the old road and vestiges of a bridge that once carried locomotives from the Southern  Pacific, I decided to head to Ennis where I found a rarity; a thriving drive-in theater. As for Ennis proper, admittedly I was disappointed as the Southern Pacific Railroad museum was closed, but did locate a barber shop where you could almost see Andy, Barney, and Floyd shooting the bull.

My stomach guided me to Dairy Queen for steak burgers. Then I directed Maybelline towards another old US 75 stretch outside Richland. A few minutes after taking some pictures, I reached a crossroad. Should I turn left and head back onto I-45 or down TX 14? I chose the latter and between Wortham and Mexia (Mu-hey-ah) was a slab of history quietly chatting with the ghosts of the Southern Pacific. I wasn't sure how much was paved so I pulled over, waited until traffic cleared and U-turned so I didn't have to be a punch line to "Why did the chicken cross the road?"

Doors opened and footsteps chopped through blades of grass until a concrete bridge and torn chunks of asphalt and concrete greeted me. Goosebumps ran through my body almost as if I was Clyde Barrow attempting to find a hideaway.

With spirit awakened, I continued on TX 14 for a few more miles until I saw a sign that required just the facts. a diner with a plethora of pick-ups and SUVs decorating its exterior, was open and promising. However, time was running short, so I headed east onto US 84 for 30 miles until I got to Fairfield and jumped on I-45.

As I pushed down I-45, things became familiar. The pine trees and the state prison in Huntsville signified the drive was getting shorter. However, the heart was bent on going back to my stomping grounds. After a brief (only 30 minutes) traffic jam outside The Woodlands, I made it to  downtown where I took a few shots of the skyscrapers as I drove. Several minutes later, I reached Texas and remembered the years of sitting on the porch at City Park Central Lane looking at vehicles traveling down 288. I was the visitor being looked upon this time around. After reaching TX 6, a road I traveled on during my formative years behind the wheel, I knew "home" was getting close.

I parked the truck in front of the red brick house decorated with Christmas decorations and a Houston Texans sign and rang the bell. After hugs and handshakes we just talked the rest of the night.

Christmas was spent visiting my Godparents. From listening to Tony Bennett crooning a few old Christmas carols to relatives issuing the hottest gossip, the evening was pleasant. At 9:45 the next morning, after breakfast, it was time to get back on the road. However, there was one more stop to make.

Maybelline began to run low on gas, so I veered into Pearland, a former hangout, and stopped at Raceway. However, it felt different on this stop. I was no longer the local that came here every weekend. As I leered at the automobiles rolling along Farm Road 518, I felt as invisible as if I died and made it a brief stop. The eerie feeling crept inside as I drove into downtown Houston.

I wondered if people would recognize me. After parking the truck at a $12 an hour parking lot, I got out and walked into Two Houston Center. The clicking of my Ariat boots provided the security guard with a steady cadence to help alleviate the loud silence that decked the halls.

At the 29th floor, the doors opened and the boots were silenced by beige carpeting. I was greeted by the receptionist. "Good morning. May I see Lea?"

"Head on to the back. You know where to go," she replied. While I was standing and soaking in the nostalgia from six years of dedicated service, my friend came out and greeted me like a long lost brother. After chatting with former co-workers for an hour or so, it was time for me and Maybelline to get back on the road.

After escaping the dreary mist and Houston traffic, I approached a in Huntsville. As I approached the monument, a line from a Waylon Jennings song crept into my head... "This time will be the last time."

Perhaps this was my last or soon to be last trip down to the area. I pulled Maybelline over on I-45 and walked over to the statue. One could stare, marvel, and get lost in its intimidating pose. After a six minute photo shoot, his stare pointed me back to the truck where I drove up a few exits and attempted to visit the Texas Prison museum, but they were closed.

Fortunately, I decided to get onto TX 75 (between Conroe and Streetman, south of Dallas, formerly US 75) and saw mysterious naked tree branches decorating the asphalt paved winding roads, cool motels signs, and a vintage Humble station that while it was well preserved, appeared stuck in time.

A few miles down, I reached a crossroads and had to decide whether to stay on TX 75 and explore some more or head west on the TX OSR. The Old San Antonio Road is sometimes called "El Camino Real" or "King's Highway". I decided to veer onto the OSR and as soon as the turn was complete, I noticed a concrete marker with faded letters. I stopped the truck before it could introduce itself to  barbed wire. Maybelline, while skidding and angry, was kind enough to let me out. I crossed the road and discovered an old stone monument that displayed the following:

King's Highway
Camino Real
Old San Antonio Road
Marked by the
Daughters of the
American Revolution
and the State of Texas
A.D. 1918

As the excitement wore off, I traveled down some of the road and found two more markers before deciding to make one more stop before heading home. I got back onto I-45 and exited off US 84 in Fairfield where I retraced the route on Christmas Eve until I reached Mexia and Joe Friday's. There, I parked and decided to have a burger well done with sweet potato fries and a Dr. Pepper. It was one of the best burgers I've ever had.

As I washed it down with soda pop, I got back in the truck and found an Exxon station from the 1950s a few miles down the road in Wortham before heading back onto I-45 into Dallas before taking I-35E into the sunset.

It had been a fun trip and I pledged to do it more often. As a result, I now do these short jaunts as often as possible, eager to see new places and soak in their scents and flavors, absorbing as much of the history and the present as I can. I will always love the road and listen for its call, eager to respond whenever I can.

What a Ride!

by Dave Mock

The day started as any other. That is until the mail came. In the mail there was a letter from Lowell, Oregon from Clyde Blakely asking if I might still be interested in buying his 1950 Mercury 2 door coupe. I was very excited, because I had watched and wanted his Mercury since I was in high school. I graduated in 1958 and many years had passed, but I had never forgotten the car.

Clyde had taken the original flathead engine out and replaced it with a 1956 312 CI Thunderbird Special with 225 HP. I had coveted that Mercury since I first saw it and Clyde was finally offering it to me. He said he would like to get $300 for the car, as that was what he had already been offered. Needless to say, I got on the phone immediately and told him "Yes, I said I want the car. A check is already in the mail and you should have it within a week."

There wasn't any rush, he said, because he wasn't going sell it to anyone else. However, I knew that once the word got out that the Mercury was for sale Clyde would be surrounded with all sorts of people begging  to buy it. He was insistent that no one else would get the car, but I knew how persuasive people could be. I told him I would be in Oregon in June, as I was scheduled to attend training for the Army National Guard at Fort Knox, Kentucky. This was in May 1975.

My plan was to pick up the Mercury and drive it, with my wife Sue and our daughters Lisa and Carilynn, to Kentucky for training. We took a flight from Anchorage, Alaska to Portland, Oregon in the first week of June. My sister picked us up at the airport and we headed to Lowell to get the Mercury.

Upon arrival, I discovered the Mercury had changed, and not for the better, in the 15 plus years since I had last seen it. Clyde had not been using the car on a regular basis and it had sat so much that rust had started taking its toll.

 However, it was still the '50 Merc that I had wanted forever and was now mine!

When I told Clyde about my plans to drive the car to Kentucky, he was skeptical. He reminded me that when he had put the car together he did not have room for a fan, so it might run a little warm. I told him that shouldn't be a problem. I would figure out a way to get a fan on it. So, Clyde handed me the keys, signed the title, and after a few hours more of talking I took my prize and headed to my parents' house. My dad laughed when he saw the Mercury, although he wasn't surprised because he knew how much I loved that car.

The next morning everyone loaded into the car and we headed into Eugene, Oregon. The purpose of the trip was to buy some tools, tires, and a fan that I could put on the car. It needed tires, too, and I decided that a set of recaps would work just fine, so I saved a few dollars by buying those. I found a fan that would work perfectly and after I got back to my folks house the fan was installed a few hours later.

We spent about a week in Oregon before we headed out to Kentucky. The plan was that we would go first to Kansas and see Sue's sister, Cindy, who lived in Olathe, just outside of Kansas City. The road trip from Eugene to Olathe was pretty much unremarkable. The family enjoyed the Mercury, especially since the windows rolled down and they were able to have the old fashioned 60/4 air conditioning. (Driving at 60 mph with all 4 windows opened).

The only mechanical problems with the car happened about 100 miles outside of Kansas City. Sue told me she thought she smelled gas and when I pulled over to check out the problem, I discovered that the fuel pump was leaking around the diaphragm and the water pump was starting to seep a bit. Luckily, we made it into Olathe and I went to the parts store the next morning. I got the replacement parts and had them back on the old girl in short order.

Lisa, who was 10, and Cari, who was about 18 months, had lots of room to keep occupied in the backseat. Some of us are old enough to remember when it used to be common for children to move around inside the car without being securely fastened into car seats and seat belts. There was also room for a full sized cooler that we kept stocked with drinks and snacks. The cooler sat on the floor behind the front seat. This setup also gave the kids a place for coloring books and a few other small games and toys.

Sue decided to keep busy by crocheting a bedspread. She joked that she might as well crochet since she couldn't see out of the scratched up windshield on her side of the car. The old tube radio worked, after a fashion, once a few tubes were replaced. After I put new windshield wipers on both sides they worked too.

The car drove smooth and Sue even liked to drive it. After we were on the road that morning, we decided we would stop in Klamath Falls to see Sue's grandparents. This turned out to be a nice benefit, because as we were going through the small town of Crescent Lake the Mercury

turned 200,000 miles. It just so happened there was another '50 Mercury there at the same time, so we took pictures of the two of them together.

Back on the road the next day, Sue and I talked about going to the NSRA Street Rod Nationals East in Maryland. We looked at the time schedule and determined that we had enough time before I had report for training. So, off we went.

Quite often, a car will come back to life after sitting for long periods, just needing to be driven, and by now the Mercury was running fantastic with no issues whatsoever; just a good dependable old car. We did run into some nasty weather, but for the most part there weren't any problems. However, one night we were pushing it rather hard and the generator on the Mercury decided to fail. We were in West Virginia, an area we knew nothing about and where we knew no one.

When we arrived in Wheeling, West Virginia, at midnight, it was obvious we were going no farther until we replaced the generator. It was rainy, dark, and depressing. Here I was in a little town after midnight with a dead generator and battery on a 1950 Mercury.

I pulled into the first service station I saw that had an open sign and decided I would fuel up and wait for morning. However, to my surprise, the man that came out not only pumped the gas, but because I had the hood up and was fiddling around under it, asked what was wrong with the car. When I told him that my 6 volt generator had failed, he said it was not really going to be a problem. He knew someone who owned a parts store and would give him a call to get a generator for me. I told him I didn't want him to bother anyone at that hour and he said not to worry about.

About 20 minutes later, his friend showed up with a new generator that was correct for the 6 volt system on the car. Not only did they help me take the old one off by supplying tools, but he helped put the new one on, as well. The new generator was $12 and the labor to remove and replace the generator and charge the battery was another $10. So, for a total of $22 we were better than new again. On top of that, they were rather insulted that we didn't want to come to their house and spend the rest of the night there. We didn't want to slight them, so we ended up napping until morning and spent a little time with them and their families. It was nice to run into some helpful people in such a small town. We gave them our sincere thanks and hit the road, headed for Maryland.

Once in Maryland, we found the traffic and highway system to be quite a challenge. Arriving at the fairgrounds for the NSRA Street Rod Nationals East, it took no time in finding the registration area and we spent the next few days relaxing and enjoying more new friends. We said our goodbyes and headed south to Fort Knox, Kentucky.

I checked in for my training and got a list of acceptable housing for married personnel and we went on a house hunt. As I was driving down the road, I saw two 1940 Ford Coupes parked in front of Frost's Army Navy Surplus. One of them had a For Sale sign on it and, of course, I had to stop and see how much they wanted.

The man we met told me the price was $1800. Then, he told me that he had the original bill of sale from 1940 for the car. I still had a '40 coupe in Alaska and it needed several major parts like inner fender panels and a few other things. I decided to buy the coupe for parts.

It was an opera coupe that had a Chevy 283 V8 motor with a Powerglide transmission. It was in platinum primer, but at one time had been customized to include a red and white interior and a red metal flake paint job. The car ran really well and drove nice, so I cruised it home while Sue drove the Mercury.

One day while I was at training, my oldest daughter got so ill that Sue decided it was imperative that she see a doctor. Since I was gone, Sue, being as resourceful as she is, decided she would simply drive the '40 to the doctor. She put the kids in the two jump seats and headed to the doctor's office.

When I got home that evening, Sue informed me that I'd have to get another '40 for parts. I asked "Why? What's wrong?" She smiled at me and said, "Nothing at all. I drove it and now I'm keeping it. You'll have to either buy the parts elsewhere or find another car for parts because this one is now mine."

I decided not to argue and focused on the fact that I no longer had to worry that she had nothing to drive while I was away from the house. I was also happy because I knew she liked the 5 window Deuce coupe I had and now she also liked '40 Fords, as well. A good woman can be hard to find, but one that likes old cars is a blessing from above.

One weekend, we decided to take the Mercury and head north to Indianapolis for the Street Machine Nationals. So, we loaded the kids in the car Friday evening after work and headed for Indiana. The fairgrounds were already busy when we arrived on Saturday.

The area was full of beautiful cars, but the best part of the entire weekend was the tour of the Indianapolis Speedway Museum. The host club had made arrangements through the museum that those who wanted to take a spin around the speedway could do so. Who wouldn't take them up on an opportunity like that? We jumped for the chance and patiently waited our turn, since they only allow so many cars on the track at the time.

There were strict guidelines, although I don't remember too many of them. Mostly they were safety related issues like no speeding, no cutting people off, no ramming, and keeping it under 50 mph! I drove and Sue took movies of the entire thing. Driving my '50 Mercury with over 200,000 miles around the Indianapolis Speedway track for three entire laps is definitely one of my favorite memories.

When the group of speedway racers rejoined the rest of the participants, a lot of them were extremely disappointed to discover that if they had gone, they too could have driven on the track. For once, I was in the right place at the right time.

Once we got home from Indianapolis, we settled back into our routine. Although Sue had taken over the '40, there were still days and afternoons that she would take the Mercury if she had to run errands. Her reasoning was that it had a bigger trunk for shopping. It also had a working speedometer and gas gauge. The '40 had neither. In fact, the '40 had no working gauges at all. This didn't seem to bother Sue at all, because she had fallen in love. There was no changing her mind, either. It was hers and it would not be used for parts.

The Mercury had its quirks. Quite often, if you shifted just wrong, the linkage would come apart, which required crawling under the car to fix. Thankfully, Sue wasn't afraid to get her hands dirty, because it always happened when she was driving and the kids were in the car.

In July, we went to the Street Rod Nationals in Nashville, Tennessee in the '40 and were given the Long Distance award. Back then, the Nationals were limited to cars prior to 1948, so taking the Mercury and entering it was out and we decided that since we were going anyway, we'd take the '40 instead. It wasn't as comfortable of a trip for the girls in the little opera seats as it was for them in the back seat of the Mercury, but they didn't complain too much.

One of the cool side notes to the trip is that early one morning Lisa, Cari, and I went out for a quick drive and we happened to find ourselves across the street from Graceland just as Elvis walked out to the gates to say hello to his fans. When I told Sue, she was very disappointed that she didn't get to see him. Our little girls, however, couldn't understand why it was such a big deal to see some guy with lots of black hair that lived in a big white house.

While we were living in Vinegrove, Kentucky, during my training, we met some great people including Tommy and Anna Applegate. They lived in Elizabethtown, the next town over, and quickly included us in their group of great friends. We were invited to BBQs, potlucks, and Sunday dinners.

Whenever it was raining, we knew that taking the '40 was out of the question, because the wipers didn't work. The wipers really weren't that big of a problem. What was, however, was the fact that we had no lights on the '40. The group thought it was funny, so they gave me the nickname "Sundown" because everyone knew that if I was there, and if I was driving the '40, we'd have to leave before dusk.

One day Tommy asked me why I didn't just fix the lights. I told him I didn't have the time with my studying and I only had minimal tools with me. Tommy and a friend told me while Sue and the girls were inside with Anna fixing Sunday super, that we were going to try and fix the lights. The previous weekend the wipers had been fixed with a simple repair and connection of a vacuum line.

I told them that I didn't want to inconvenience them and that I could deal without the lights. Well, their southern hospitality won out and we headed to the garage. Viola! In a few minutes the headlights were functional. It turned out that the previous owner simply hadn't connected the electrical.

The wipers and headlights weren't the only cobble problems the '40 had. The previous owner's idea of restoration or repair left a lot to be desired. As an example, to repair a hole in the firewall, he had taken a beer can and slid it in the hole and called it good. But, little by little, force-feeding of the southern refusal to take no for an answer would win out and repairs were properly done.

Tommy and the group kept after me about the platinum primer. I had to agree that it wasn't so much that it was a washed out color, but it would be best to make the car look different from when I purchased it, so it would no longer be called Frost's '40. Of course, I didn't have access to a place where I could paint the car. With what had become normal dialogue, Tommy said that he had the tools and he would be highly insulted if I didn't take him up on his offer to correct the color.

He loaned me his paint gun and I sprayed the '40 with a dark charcoal primer. Sue was as happy with the new color as I was. To complement the change, I then bought a set of wide whites, '50 Ford beauty rings, and baby moons. We were cool now!

Tommy had lived in the area all of his life, so he knew lots of people and had access to things that a visitor wouldn't. He knew that I was planning on taking the '40 back to Alaska when my training was over and that I really wanted to tow it with the Mercury instead of having Sue drive behind me. He talked with a welder friend of his about making a tow bar for the car and the guy was more than happy to help. The total price of the tow bar for the '40 and installing a trailer hitch on the Mercury was a whopping $35. I was shocked at the low price. The tow bar was made totally from scratch and built like a tank.

At the end of my training, it was time for us to leave all of our new friends and it was difficult. Promises were made to keep in touch and we hoped to see each other in the future. We were back on the road again and headed home.

Our planned route took us through Kansas City again for a quick stop to see Sue's sister and then we headed west. The Mercury hummed along with the '40 in tow and we  were getting 21 mpg. I was pleasantly surprised.

Our plan was to go to West Yellowstone, Montana for a rod run in early August. Since Sue enjoyed camping, we had purchased a tent on one of our stops. We could stop at KOAs and other campgrounds instead of looking for hotels or motels and the girls loved the idea of camping out. It gave them a place to burn off their excess energy and Sue and I liked it because we didn't have to tell them to be quiet all the time.

Our route took us through Mount Rushmore and some of the old ghost towns in the area. Unfortunately, our stop at Mount Rushmore was short because we were quickly eating up the time and if we didn't hurry we would miss the Yellowstone run. By the time we got to Montana, the girls were old hands at camping out and knew what was expected of them. They stayed out of the way when we pitched the tent and got the campfire started. They had lots of fun running around and looking for sticks and small branches for the fires. Plus, they were always excited to roast hot dogs and marshmallows for dinner. Sue would usually fix oatmeal for breakfast since it only took boiling water and the kids loved it.

While at Yellowstone, Sue declared that she was tired of eating Kentucky Fried Chicken, my favorite road food, and told me that we were going to have tacos for dinner. I conceded that whatever she wanted to fix was fine with me, so she took the Mercury and headed into the closest tourist town to buy the necessary fixings.

She didn't say anything when she came back, but I noticed when she was cooking the vitals that she wasn't using a frying pan. When I asked what she was using, she told me in a very matter of fact way that it was a cookie sheet because West Yellowstone did not have any frying pans or anything that would even come close to what she needed other than a cookie sheet. So, that was what she was using. The tacos that night were probably some of the best I've ever had.

We noticed that a couple of guys who were camping next to us seemed to be subsisting on peanut butter sandwiches and Sue invited them over to join us for supper. That was the start of another great friendship. Sue's tacos were enough of a hit that Tom, our new friend, requested them by way of supplying all the necessary items the next afternoon. Sue's cookie sheet tacos had become the talk of the West Yellowstone campground.

The rod run itself was fantastic. The temperatures were perfect and the people were amazing. It remains one of our favorite rod runs of all time. But, as usual, all good things must come to an end and it was time for us to begin our return trek to Alaska. I had to get back to the real work-a-day world and Lisa had to be home for school.

Crossing the Canadian Border at Sweetgrass, Montana, we headed north and did the usual Alcan (Alaska Highway) protection for the '40 when we hit Dawson Creek. We put cardboard on the windshield in hopes that oncoming vehicles wouldn't break the glass. Headlights were protected with special bubble like covers that would keep gravel from breaking them. We also filled the tank in the '40 with fuel in the event that the stations that were supposed to be open weren't; a common occurrence in the days prior to the highway being fully modernized.

Once we passed Fort St. John, British Columbia, the gravel began and would continue until the Alaska border, roughly 1200 miles away. Anchorage was another 450 miles beyond that, giving us approximately 1650 miles to home. We had stocked up on our groceries in Dawson Creek. Our standby snacks were cheese and crackers with Polish type summer sausage. Stacking sausage and cheese on a cracker was called an Alcan Special. We also restocked our hot dogs and buns, marshmallows, milk, juice, butter, and syrup and picked up some rum so when we  stopped at night, Sue and I could enjoy a rum and Coke while sitting around the campfire.

Our first night was spent in a nice campground that supplied firewood and other creature comforts. We had wanted to stop at Liard Hot Springs, but it was closed because of aggressive bears in the area, so we had continued on and found this cozy little haven.

Back on the road again, everything was going along great until a remote stretch of extra rough gravel road along Kluane Lake. Sue said she smelled gas. At first, I didn't pay too much attention to it because of how rough the road was, but then both Lisa and Cari started complaining that it was stinky.

I pulled over, opened the hood, and inspected the engine compartment. Nothing. Then I walked around to the back of the Mercury and I could see gas dripping at a steady rate, a puddle already starting to form. I quickly put a pan under the stream of gas and asked Sue if she had any gum.

I knew from experience that gum would work in an emergency to seal a small rock hole in a gas tank. Sue didn't have any gum, not even some bubble gum for the girls. She told me that she did have some English toffee. It was chewy and extra sticky, and since we had nothing else, why shouldn't I try it.

While Sue chewed the toffee into submission, I took a piece of flannel diaper and found a small screw. I crawled under the Merc, put the toffee over the hole in the tank, and quickly took the screw and flannel and screwed it into the hole in the tank.

Lo and behold, the leak stopped. Now, the only problem was that I knew that a lot of gas had leaked out and we were still miles from a gas station. Luckily, we hadn't used any from the '40 and so I got a hose out of the trunk and hooked it to the firewall mounted electric fuel pump, ran a hose, and pumped the Mercury's tank full. I was so glad that I had completely filed the '40 stateside. This was our version of multiple gas cans.

I looked for the gas station as I pulled into Destruction Bay, but all I saw was a burnt building. Again, I was ever so happy that we had taken the time to fill the '40. Granted, I wasn't thrilled that I had already had to use several gallons, but it was certainly better than being stuck in a remote little village, waiting for the next dump of fuel to arrive.

Upon inquiry, I found out that there was another station about 50 miles up the Lake that usually had fuel. I inspected the "repair" to the Mercury's fuel tank and saw that the gas had turned the toffee into a solid plug that was holding tight.

We arrived at the border fairly early, cleared American Customs, and headed to Scotty Creek, a small stream that had a large gravel area that we knew would be perfect for camping. We pitched the tent for us and let the girls snuggle up in the back seat of the Mercury. Even though we had  gone to sleep late, we were up early the next morning. Sue fixed breakfast while I took the girls for a walk around the area.

We broke camp, packed up, and hit the road. After a few miles, I heard a thumping sound and immediately thought it was a flat tire. I pulled over as soon as I could and got out to take a look. The thumping was being caused by a piece of recap coming off the inside of the tire. Other than that, it looked fine. I took my knife and hacked off the piece of rubber, got back into the car, and started off again.

About 50 miles down the road, the noise started again. So, I got out and cut off another piece of tire. This continued the rest of the way into Anchorage. The noise would start, I'd pull over, cut off a chunk of rubber, and continue down the road. The average mileage between "tire repairs" was about 50 miles.

We pulled up to the house in Anchorage at about 6 pm and unloaded the Mercury and the '40. While Sue and the girls went inside, I walked around the back of the '40 and noticed that the right rear axle bearing had failed. The axle and tire were sticking about eight inches outside of the fender! I shuddered to think of all the damage that might have occurred if we had gone any farther.

The next morning when I woke, I went outside to take the Mercury to the grocery store, but the dependable recap had finally given up and now the car sat on a flat. Here I was at home in my driveway in Anchorage, Alaska with the only flat tire of the entire trip.

We had traveled from Oregon to Kentucky to the East Coast, up to Illinois, back to Kentucky, then back across the States via Kansas, the Dakotas, Montana into Oregon; all the way up the Alcan (Alaskan Highway) without a single flat tire. The Mercury had waited until we had reach Alaska, safe and sound, before it let us down.

This trip remains one of our family favorites. As a side note, the gas tank patch is still in place as of 2015 and just as firm as it was in 1975. It just goes to show that sometimes things done in desperation turn out to be long lasting and solid. What a ride!

Despite Any Problems
I May Mention

by Mike Hoffman

In 2010, I joined the Street Rodder tour from Fife, WA to the Hot Rod Reunion in Bakersfield at the Famoso drag strip. It was to be a 10 day trip there and back. In the end, despite any problems I may mention, it is now my favorite car event.

I had my 34 Ford 2 door sedan with a Quad 4 Olds double overhead cam. Again, despite any problems I men-

tion, this is a well-built car that I enjoy driving.

Once we were all gathered, friendships were rekindled, fluid levels checked one last time, and maps, lunch and potty stops planned. As we all fired up to leave Fife, a bolt broke off my alternator bracket. The belt flew off and flopped around making an awful racket. As I lifted my hood, I peered around it to see taillights and exhaust pipes.

So, I took it to a shop there in Fife, hoping to get things handled quickly. By the time it was all over, they had the car from 1pm till 8pm on this special Saturday and to get the broken bolt out of the block cost $500. Once finished, I hit the highway. I spent all night driving to catch the group. While they partied and ate, I drove. While they rested, I gripped my steering wheel. But, I finally made it to the motel and checked into my room, which the manager had kindly held at the insistence of the group that I would get there.

The next day, we were headed to Crater Lake. About 15 miles before Crater Lake, all twenty cars pulled over to take a break. I was the last one in the line of cars because I had no fenders. We all chatted and people expressed how they were sorry that I'd had trouble, but glad that I caught up and was there now. Once it was time to leave, we all jumped into our rides and as everyone is pulling out, my car wouldn't start.

I couldn't figure out what is wrong. So, I called AAA and they sent a flatbed. I had to wait 3 hours for it, but I finally got to my motel at 8pm in evening and was, once again, caught up with the tour. Again, I had missed everything that happened for the rest of that day. The next morning, as everyone was headed out, I was flat bedded to a shop in town. Apparently, when the fellow in Fife fixed the bolt problem, he pulled the alternator out of way to drill the bolt and broke all of the wires. Once I got those fixed, I drove all day until 9:30pm to catch up with the group at the hotel.

The next day went well. That is until a big truck dropped a limb on the front of my car and broke a headlight. I'm a pretty easy going guy and I figured it was no real problem. Besides, despite any problems I may mention, I was determined to have a great morning and afternoon with the group. Just before Bakersfield, however, my new exhaust header tube broke off a piece and sliced my door. I pulled over and thanked my lucky stars that all of the cars in our group had missed the piece that fell off. I had it welded up the next day and headed for the Famoso track, getting there in the early afternoon.

The Hot Rod Reunion and being at Famoso was wonderful, and despite any problems I may mention, I made a lot of new friends and Hot Rod asked to do a shoot of my car for their new "Overkill" magazine, where it was featured in their first issue.

As I started for home, I lost reverse gear in my transmission. I was pretty sure it was just a linkage problem. Then,  the power window quit working. None of this was major and so, off I went.

Right before the trip, I'd had a new gas tank installed inside the car. It worked well when filling except for those stupid modern day nozzles with the big spring. As I was finishing with a fill on the return journey back north that first afternoon, I pulled back the nozzle and the spring snagged. When it popped loose, it coated my paint and pin striping with gas. What a mess! I began gently wiping it up.

The couple behind me, were quite a pair in their old beater truck, looking like the original Beverly Hillbillies. The lady, and I use the term very loosely, must have thought I was taking too long to finish up. They're yelling obscenities and making hand gestures. Pulling around me, "Babs" leans out of the truck and hocked a big "loogey" in my face and then on the side of my car as I watched the gas peel the pin striping off my paint! She and her "Rock of Jello" slithered away before I could get my hands on them.

I slowly meandered my way back home, wondering what might happen next. The rest of the trip was without issue and despite any problems I may have mentioned, I still enjoyed the getaway and hope to do it again in 2015. I'm just proud to be part of the hotrod fraternity and willing to deal with the things we all seem to go through.

The Road Was a Blur

by Clayton Paddison

There are certain things that take us back to a by-gone era locked away in the vault of our own memories. Mostly they stay hidden, tucked away like ancient texts in a museum. Every so often however, there is something that triggers them and pulls them from the depths such as a smell, a sound, or a sight. Is it the sound of the un-restricted exhaust from an early Ford 4-cylinder? The Smell of Castor Oil and race fuel? Or, is it the pack of period perfect hot rods and race cars hashing out grudge matches on the beach just like Grandpa did way back when?

For the last 3 years, "The Race of Gentlemen" and its creators have sought to do just that. Beyond creating a pre-1953 period racing event, they have carefully crafted an atmospheric vintage wonderland. Entry numbers are kept low and cars carefully handpicked by the organizers to ensure only the most unique automotive examples hit the sand. Simply put, this event is the closest anyone will ever get to time travel.

Since the beginning of its creation, I have been pining to take part with my 1927 Model T roadster, but the distance from my home in Vancouver, WA to the shores of New Jersey proved to be a logistic and budgetary challenge. Year after year however, with the coaxing of event creators Mel Stultz and Bobbi Green, it became harder for me to say no. With good timing and the blessings of my wife, I made up my mind to make it for the 3rd annual race.

Since I don't own a trailer myself, I knew the logistics were going to be tricky. I had driven my T to Utah and back, but I knew cross country was going to be out of the question this time. After a few weeks of asking around, I came in contact with Mike Santiago of Mt. Vernon, WA.

Mike is a brilliant engineer and home grown hot rodder who had been to "TROG" the year before and won. Mike and I have known each other for years through various online hot rod forums, such as the HAMB (Hokey Ass Message Board) on the venerable JalopyJournal.com and so I approached him about partnering for the trip. Mike was very gracious and offered a spot on his three car trailer and a coffin sized spot in the back seat to curl up in between driving shifts. I was beyond happy to oblige.

The car I would be taking was my well-traveled 1927 Model T roadster that I have owned for the past 10 years. I built the car in style of a late 1920's era early Hot Rod or "Gow Job" as they were called in the period. These cars are widely regarded as the "Grandfathers of the Hot Rod" and are something that is only now finally coming back to the main stream again.

I had originally had my first run at building my car (or any car for that matter) between 2006 and 2008 and learned a lot about what I liked and what didn't work, and the difference between the two. Between 2011 and 2012, armed with more experience, I tore it apart, redesigned it, and put it back together again in nine months for a memorable trip to Speed Week in Utah.

The new and improved chassis now sports a modified '26 T block, aluminum head, oversized pistons, full race camshaft, cast header, and a Burns 2x2 intake with twin Stromberg 81 carburetors. This is backed up with a Chicago auxiliary overdrive and a T rear axle. Ford 21" rolling stock with Firestone tires, no fenders, and a chopped ragtop finish it off. The improved chassis handled the Bonneville trip with ease at a steady 55-60 mph on the highway and with six forward gears at my disposal. I hoped it would be perfectly suited to an event like "The Race of Gentlemen".

Since the new chassis was tried and true, not much had to be done for preparation save for a few odds and ends and other cosmetic items. Mike however, had his hands full. In the months that preceded our epic road trip, Mike was busily rebuilding a new engine for his winning car from 2013, in the hopes of beating out the competition again for a second year in a row.

The original motor was a freshened up Model A engine with a flat head cam and featured a rare "Record" OHV 8-valve head that Mike had previously built and decided to use in this car. The "Record" head is very similar to a Cragar head, but with larger ports, so it made full use of the excess cam lift and, of course, Mikes heavy right foot. Even with a failing clutch and only one of his two carburetors functioning, Mike came out the underdog, snagging the trophy and the $1,000 purse.

For 2014's event, Mike knew everyone would be gunning for him and his new motor had to be no holds barred. The new engine would be a Model B, built to the hilt with a milled Winfield head that was pushing an estimated 11:1 compression. Distressingly though, within just days of when we were scheduled to hit the road, Mike was still having head gasket issues. We shared many a late night on brainstorming phone calls and just 4 days before we took off, I suggested packing the "Record" OHV head in the truck "Just in case we need to switch it out in the parking lot".

When the big day arrived, I waited up at my shop with suitcase packed and the T ready to roll for Mike and his uncle, Paul Reichlin, to arrive with the truck and trailer. Just after 5:30pm, I got a text from Mike containing a sad photo of his rear axle in pieces. I knew we were in for a long night so I dozed off in the backseat of my friend Chris' 1917 Hupmobile, knowing it would be a long while until I slept again. At 1:00am, Mike and Paul triumphantly arrived at the shop to col- lect the T and me and by 2:30am we were loaded up and on the highway.

Since we had only a few days to make the east coast for the start of the race, there was no sightseeing on this cross country trip. We wasted no time, and the only stops made were for fuel and food. The days and nights became a blur and we lost all sense of both time and date in an endless cycle of sleeping, fuel- ing, and the droning sights and sounds of the road. After a day and a half since leaving Oregon, we had managed to race across the mighty Mississippi River into Illinois. By Wednesday morning, we had completed the 2,967 mile trip in just 57 hours and 11 minutes and rolled into the "Race of the Gentlemen's" new home in Wildwood, NJ.

The following day, we set about unloading the cars and doing some quick tests on Mike's car to see if it was fit to race. Sadly, the last minute fixes Mike had deployed to cor- rect the head issues weren't working and we begrudgingly accepted that we would be switching heads in the parking lot after all.

Since the races didn't start until Saturday, only the first of the die-hard racers were starting to roll into town. Motor homes, trailers, and multi car haulers began streaming in one after another and gathering in the large parking lot where Mike, Paul, and I were already hard at work pull- ing the engine down. First on the scene was Matt Picaro, a spirited hot rodder and enthusiast from Cream Ridge,

NJ with his Model A roadster #667. Brian Cannon from Hackettstown filed in next, and then the boys from Ray's Hot Rods, the Torranodo's Car Club from Boston, the Deluxe Speed Shop crew from Denver, and the Altar Boys Car Club from New England. It quickly turned into a lively party and everybody pitched in with Mike's engine project.

The weekend also made possible the meeting of a lifetime for me. Since 2008, my modern day pen-pal, David Conwill, and I have been very close friends, despite the fact that he dwells in Eastern Michigan and I live on the West coast. When I had made plans to make the trip, I called David and told him I was making the race and would only be 12 hours away. He quickly made plans to drive down  and meet me in Wildwood and spend the weekend with us.

As Friday dawned, over a hundred people and cars rolled into town at a steady pace. By evening, everyone had arrived and the party was in full swing. It stretched past every hotel room down Atlantic Avenue and filled the surrounding city blocks with the glorious soundtrack of engines barking through uncorked exhaust pipes, laughter, great stories, and clanging beer bottles. This all culminated into the wonderfully wild Motorcycle show dubbed "The Night of the Troglodytes" which was hosted in the courtyard of my hotel until 2:30am. When exhaustion sent most to bed, others wheeled their bikes into their rooms and ripped and roared their engines until daylight.

6:00am Saturday came far too early for David, Mike, and I as we all drug ourselves out of bed and warmed up the cars in the chilly morning air. Our eyes widened and brains perked up however, as we paraded down Ocean Avenue towards the boardwalk entrance. Once our tires hit the sand, it was like stepping back in time. Between the period style clothing and cars, nothing on the beach broke the 1949 illusion. It wasn't hard to get swept up into the magic of it all while peering through period style race goggles at everyone around you.

Last year's race had featured a bracket elimination portion with a $1,000 purse and a free-for-all grudge match day, as well. This year it was decided to forgo the purse prize and the eliminations for straight grudge match races, so that event would stay true to its roots; just some good old racing and gentlemanly sportsmanship. This worked well and really made the event for me. The focus was strictly about racing and having a great time doing it.

From dawn till dusk, we raced up and down the beach, one run after another. The sound of growling exhaust pipes, cheers from the massive crowds, and the waves crashing against the beach made for a magical atmosphere that left us grown men and women feeling like kids living out our favorite stories.

By 8:30am, the pits were full and final preparations were being made for the races to start. As I was attaching my Go-Pro cameras to the T to capture a few laps, I was approached by two members of the race sponsor's club, The Oilers.

"We need five or six cars to do a few quick runs for the media before the races start and we want your car. Grab your helmet and bring your car up to the line," they beckoned me.

I quickly grabbed my gear, gave the T a good hearty pull on the hand crank, and anxiously flew down the return road to the start. A swell of spectators were already along the fence, so the pressure was on! As we waited for the media personnel to get ready, I started running racing techniques through my mind. The big moment was coming, so I ran up the RPMs and when flag girl, Sara Francello dropped the flag, I dropped the clutch and promptly killed the engine. The other car took off roaring, while I bailed out and hand cranked the engine for the now cheering crowd.

 I took off running after my competitor, but never did catch up.

For the next two days, I both won and lost races, making at least 30 runs while fighting the changing tides. Often, like kids at a water park, we would jump back in the race lines with big grins on our faces after having just completed a run. The biggest surprise of the trip for me was how much I learned. Not just about myself, but about my car. As it turns out, I really don't have to baby her as much as I thought before. Although not the fastest, it proved to be one of the more reliable cars at the event. Sand also takes quite a bit of feel and practice to race on, so notes were taken.

With the last of the parties winding down, many of the racers had already pulled out of town and by the next morning, Mike, Paul, myself, and the boys from Denver were the only ones left. We lingered for a while in the afterglow before loading up, shaking hands, and heading for home.

On our way through Philadelphia, we decided to make a last minute detour up north, about 45 minutes to a little town near Harrisburg known as Hershey. Aside from its obvious claim to fame, for the last 60 years Hershey, PA has been the home of the largest pre-war swap meet in the world. Lucky for us, it just so happened to be happening the following day. I have heard plenty of stories about the Hershey Swap Meet and have always wanted to attend. We met up with some buddies from back home that had flown in for the race and the swap meet and we all went in as a pack.

I was blown away by the Swap Meet's sheer size. It was 70 acres from end to end, covering all of the famous Hershey Park parking lots. As far as the eye could see, the meet was stuffed full of top notch car parts, cars, and goodies. After walking the show for two days and collectively buying enough stuff to pack all three of our cars full, as well as the bed of the truck, we said goodbye to the Eastern Seaboard and pointed the front of Mike's truck toward home.

We pressed ahead just as before, nonstop marathon driving with only fuel and food stops along the way. I watched the blurry sea of corn fields in the mid-west fly by my window, then the great flat plains of Wyoming and wide Montana skies. Finally, we had crawled back to our breath taking Columbia River Gorge.

Round trip, we had covered nearly 6,000 miles in less than 10 days. The road was a blur. Even if I had only gotten to run just one lap down the Jersey shore, the comradery of my racing brothers was worth every mile.

About David Dickinson
Creator and Editor

The Old Car Nut Book Series

A s a child, I would lay around the living room, playing with my Lincoln logs, designing homes and landscape designs that would include lots of parking spaces for all of the cars I planned to own. As a teenager, I bought my first '56 Chevrolet Bel Air with the money I had saved from working on farms, in restaurants, delivering newspapers... anything that would pay me so I could get a car when I turned 16. From then on, it was all about keeping the car running to its peak performance and cruising around showing the world my great little ride!

Like everyone else, I had to grow up. Well, kind of. I guess I never got away from cars. As the years roll by, like the odometer on an old car, I keep checking off the miles... and the cars in my past. I always seem to be looking for my next pride and joy. I've had countless cars and there are stories for every one of them. I still change cars often, but wish I could keep every one of them.

I started out by writing my own stories, a few of which appeared in book one. More of them are included in the second book in The Old Car Nut Book series, but I had more stories to share and so do the rest of the old car nuts in America.

The Old Car Nut Book series is my way of sharing the dream with other Old Car Nuts. It is also my way of reaching out to younger car nuts beginning their journeys and fulfilling their dreams. I think it's important to know where the pioneers of the car enthusiast world came from.

As these first three books gain popularity, stories will continue to be gathered and more editions put into print. The response from current contributors, potential contributors and others, anxious to read these stories, has been tremendous.

I plan to compile at least five volumes of The Old Car Nut Book. Book Four will be all about "Racing" and Book Five will include stories from our "Greatest Generations"; those born before 1946. You can be in one of these upcoming books by sending your story in now.

Have a great story, but concerned that you don't write well enough? That's OK. Send it in and let me do what I do. Together, we'll collaborate and turn your story into one you can be proud to share! Go to www.OldCarNutBook.com and click "How To Submit" in the menu for details. You can also contact me directly at Contact@OldCarNutBook. com or 206-354-8347.

I hope you have enjoyed this book and look forward to seeing your nose buried in another volume of The Old Car Nut Book series. In the meantime... tell others, please!

Made in the USA
Lexington, KY
10 January 2016